ST. AUGUSTINE:
ON EDUCATION

ST. AUGUSTINE: ON EDUCATION

Edited and Translated
with an Introduction and Notes

By George Howie, M.A., M.Ed., Ph.D.
Department of Education
University of Sydney, Australia

HENRY REGNERY COMPANY
Chicago

Library of Congress Catalog Card No. 70-88847

MANUFACTURED IN THE
UNITED STATES OF AMERICA

Contents

Socrates death – 399 BC

CHRONOLOGICAL TABLE

The principal sources of St. Augustine's educational theory in relation to the main events of his life

354 A.D. Birth at Tagaste in North Africa — 430 Died at Hippo

374-386 Teacher of rhetoric successively at Carthage, Rome and Milan

386 Conversion to Christianity at Milan

386-387 At Cassiciacum

The Cassiciacum dialogues:

Against the Academics (Contra Academicos)
The Happy Life (De Beata Vita)
The Principle of Order (De Ordine)
Soliloquies (Soliloquia)

387-388 At Milan and Rome

On Music (a dialogue) (*De Musica*)
The Greatness of the Soul (a dialogue) *(De Quantitate Animae)*
The Practices of the Catholic Church (De Moribus Ecclesiae Catholicae

388 Returned to North Africa

388-395 *Free Will* (a dialogue) *(De Libero Arbitrio)*
388-396 *83 Various Questions (De Diversis Quaestionibus LXXXIII)*
c.389 *The Teacher* (a dialogue) *(De Magistro)*
c.390 *True Religion (De Vera Religione)*

391 Ordained Priest at Hippo

396 Consecrated Bishop of Hippo

nearly 800 years after Socrates' death

e.g. as 1973 is to 1173

and, ca. as 396 is to 1196

397 *In Reply to the Letter of the Manichaean (Contra Epistulam Manichaei)*
Christian Education (De Doctrina Christiana) (first two books and part of third book)
397-401 *Confessions (Confessiones)*
399 *The Instruction of the Uninstructed (De Catechizandis Rudibus)*
399-416 *The Trinity (De Trinitate)*
401-414 *The Literal Interpretation of Genesis (De Genesi ad Litteram)*
405-406 *Against Cresconius the Donatist (Contra Cresconium Donatum)*
413-427 *The City of God (De Civitate Dei)*
416-417 *Tracts on St. John's Gospel (In Joannis Evangelium Tractatus)*
419 *The Soul and Its Origin (De Anima et eius Origine)*
422 *The Eight Questions of Dulcitius (De Octo Dulcitii Quaestionibus)*
426-427 *Christian Education (De Doctrina Christiana)* (four books completed)
Reviews (Retractationes)

430 Died at Hippo

Other sources are (a) the correspondence of St. Augustine arranged in three books of *Letters (Epistulae),* covering the years from his conversion in 386 to the year of his death, and (b) *The Sermons of St. Augustine (Sermones)* from the year of his ordination (391) to the year of his death.

Introduction

The Significance of St. Augustine

Aurelius Augustine, Bishop of the North African see of Hippo from 396 to 430 A.D., has been a formative influence of very great strength in the history of Christian thought and letters, and his extensive theological writings have been continually studied and interpreted throughout the centuries that have passed since his death. However, while the doctrinal content of his writings is the province of theology rather than educational theory, the student of education has much to interest him in the philosophical and psychological analysis to which Augustine subjects the lessons of his own spiritual development. Many think of Augustine as a figure of awesome proportions, remote from the ordinary preoccupations of life, and associated with a body of intimidating and seemingly inflexible doctrines such as original sin and predestination. These were, however, the product of his later years, when the liberality of his earlier thought was in some degree constricted under the pressure of the ecclesiastical heresies and schisms with which, as Bishop of Hippo, he became increasingly preoccupied.

In this book we are concerned not so much with the Christian propagandist and defender of the faith as with the cultured, humane Augustine, of whom his friend Possidius wrote that he made the greatest impact on those "who were able to hear and see him face to face and, above all, who had experienced conversation with him."[1] This is the Augustine

[1] Possidius, *Life of Bishop Augustine,* chapter 31 in Migne, *Patrilogia Latina,* vol. 32.

who, as student, teacher and friend, brought to his friend Nebridius "the echo of Christ, Plato and Plotinus."[2] To illustrate Augustine's educational opinions, we shall be drawing largely from his earlier writings, the product of the reflections of the period which began in 386 A.D., the year of his conversion to Christianity. He was then thirty-two years of age, and up to that point had written nothing of any significance to his spiritual growth. In his *Confessions* he refers to only one work which he had written before that period; when he was teaching rhetoric at Carthage, he had composed a treatise, *Concerning the Beautiful and the Fitting (De Pulchro et Apto),* which he had dedicated to a Roman orator, Hiereus, whom he admired.[3] Of its quality he sardonically observes, "With no one to admire it, I admired it for myself." Thus, we are not surprised to learn that he had lost it somewhere; certainly it was of no consequence. St. Augustine's own catalogue of his writings, published with critical comment under the title of the *Reviews (Retractationes)* three years before his death, begins with the dialogue *Against the Academics,* his earliest extant work, written in the year of his conversion, and the first of the "Cassiciacum" dialogues. In fact, Augustine wrote virtually nothing while he was living in a state of uncertainty and spiritual turmoil; but, from his conversion until the very last year of his life, he poured out his thoughts with an unfailing and remarkable strength and continuity of purpose.

St. Augustine was born at Tagaste in the Roman province of North Africa into a divided home, his mother being a devoted and intelligent Christian and his father an unrepentant pagan. After completing the three stages of Roman education – elementary school, grammar school and the school of rhetoric – he was, for a short time, a teacher of grammar in Tagaste, and then of rhetoric in Carthage, Rome and Milan, where his appointment to the imperial chair of rhetoric brought him to the peak of his secular career. But within two

[2] Nebridius, *Letter to Augustine* (389 A.D.).

[3] *Confessions,* iv, 13-14.

years of this seeming climax all was changed, for step by step he had been led to the day of his real destiny, when all the years of indecision and doubt culminated in the "*Tolle, lege*" ("Take up and read") of the garden in Milan.[4] As the immediate consequence of his conversion, he had to give up his secular office of public orator and devote himself to preparation for the exercise of the more rewarding eloquence and service of Christ. He tells us that, at the beginning of the ensuing autumn vacation, he withdrew the service of his tongue from the speech market.[5] He must no longer offer eloquence for sale to the highest bidder, but must use it freely in the cause of truth. Accordingly he left Milan with a few friends and stayed for a period of about seven months (August 386 – March 387) at a small country estate at Cassiciacum in a villa loaned by a grammarian friend, Verecundus. The philosophical debates which took place there, and were taken down by a stenographer, have come to us as the Cassiciacum dialogues, the earliest of St. Augustine's writings.

After this period of recreation following the tensions of the previous years of inward strife and torn loyalties, Augustine and his friends returned to Milan for baptism and later in the same year set off for Rome with the intention of embarking at Ostia for North Africa. But at Ostia his mother, Monica, died, and it was not until the autumn of the following year that Augustine made the crossing to Africa, where he made straight for Tagaste and, as Possidius tells us, set up a monastic community devoted to "fastings, discussions and good works."[6] Within three years of his return to his native Africa,

[4] *Confessions,* viii, 12. The repeated cry, "Take up and read," apparently uttered by a child engaged in play, caused Augustine to open the Scriptures and to read the first words which met his eyes: "Not in rioting and drunkenness, not in chambering and wantonness, not in strife and envying. But put you on the Lord Jesus Christ, and make not provision for the flesh to fulfill the lusts thereof." The result was "as though a light of inner peace flooded my heart and all the darkness of uncertainty fled away."

[5] *Confessions,* ix, 2.

[6] Possidius, *op. cit.,* chapter 3.

he was ordained a priest by Bishop Valerius of Hippo, whom he succeeded five years later. In the same year the barbarians under Alaric burst the barrier of the Danube, ravaged Greece, and began the relentless advance which was to culminate in the sack of Rome (410 A.D.) and bring Geneseric and his Vandals to the very gates of Hippo Regius in the year of Augustine's death (430 A.D.).

The experience of conversion was for Augustine the culmination of years of laborious self-education through trial, error and doubt. However, the moment of illumination was not the completion of his learning, but merely the end of the beginning. Whereas before conversion he had been in spiritual torment, he was now able to develop and strengthen his hold on truth in a less distracted mood. The seven-month stay at Cassiciacum was not a withdrawal from the world, but rather a period of recreation in preparation for more complete involvement. The company at Cassiciacum consisted of Augustine and a few of his close friends and pupils, among them his mother Monica, his natural son Adeodatus, and his brother Navigius. The days were spent partly in practical tasks and partly in intellectual ones; the active physical work on Verecundus' estate was combined with philosophical discussions, at once light-hearted and serious, in which the implications of the new-found faith were carefully explored and the union of Platonism and Christianity consolidated by the give-and-take of question and answer. Conducted in the meadows under the blue sky of the Milanese countryside, or in the bath-house when the weather was cold, the dialogues are excellent practical demonstrations of group learning. The problems discussed arise out of the interests of the participants, who explore them by a method which encourages everyone to make his contribution. Even Augustine's mother, whose principal concern was with the household tasks, is occasionally drawn into the debate and makes characteristically shrewd contributions to it. Augustine, the teacher, expresses a spontaneous delight when one of his young pupils reveals some fresh insight to add to the general enlightenment. Under the conditions necessary for effective learning, i.e., a pleasant informality and respect for individual personality, the group learning advances with good will and concentration of purpose.

The Cassiciacum dialogues are demonstrations of the Socratic method of teaching, in which the teacher puts the questions and the students individually respond to them. However, the outward interchange of question and answer is merely the manifestation of an internal questioning carried on within the mind of each participant. The questions asked by the teacher are repeated within the pupil's mind by an act of his own will, and the answer he gives is first called out within himself in response to an inner question. Thus, in the Cassiciacum dialogues Augustine, like Socrates, acts as a "gad-fly," stinging his friends to an activity of thought. He does this by putting questions; but in fact, as he repeatedly shows, his questions are of secondary importance compared with the inner dialogue carried on within each student's mind. Several allusions made in the course of the dialogues show that this inner discussion continued in the participants' private thinking long after the teacher's questioning had ceased and the formal discussions had ended for the day. In the dialogue called *The Principle of Order,* Augustine remarks on his own habit of spending at least half the night meditating on the philosophical problems currently in his mind.[7]

The quality and intensity of these nocturnal self-questionings can be studied at first hand in the two books of Augustine's *Soliloquies,* which are reports of an inner debate between Augustine and Reason. In a preliminary clearing of the ground for these inquiries, we find St. Augustine's definitive statement of the starting point and final aim of education. Learning must begin with an exploration of the self; it culminates in an understanding of the nature of God: "Inquiry has a double objective—God and my soul."[8] In the first place, the learner must come to understand his own

[7] *The Principle of Order,* i, 6.
[8] *The Principle of Order,* ii, 47. Also *Soliloquies,* i, 7.

nature; otherwise, he will not be in a position to concentrate his inner resources on the search for truth and God. The tentative psychological soundings taken in the *Soliloquies* prepare the way for the more sustained psychological analysis of *The Trinity*.

St. Augustine's earlier writings intimately reveal the essential humanity of his nature and the basic virtues of the teacher, namely a love of his fellow man and a great zest for intellectual inquiry. When, in the *Confessions,* written in the first four or five years of his episcopate, he set out to analyze the motives and impulses of his youth, he was to paint an unflattering picture of the associations he had formed in his years as a student at Carthage and of the delinquent activities in which he had engaged. But there is good reason to suppose that he exaggerates, perhaps unconsciously, when he refers to himself as "the vile slave of evil desires"; for another picture creeps in less obtrusively but very persuasively. Of the same period in Carthage we read:

> There were other things associated with my friends, which laid greater hold on my mind: talking and laughing together; exchanging acts of kindness with one another; reading pleasant books together; bantering one another, and at the same time engaging in serious talk; disagreeing at times without bad humor, just as a man may have a difference with himself; and when discord arose, as it did very infrequently, using it to give an additional zest to our more normal state of concord; teaching and learning from one another in turn; impatiently longing for the return of those who were absent and giving them a joyful welcome on their return. With these and other such expressions, proceeding from the hearts of a group of people who gave and received love in return, expressions shown by the face, the voice, the eyes and by a thousand other delightful gestures, our souls were seemingly kindled into flame and, although we were many, we were joined together as one.[9]

[9] *Confessions,* iv, 8.

This is consistent with the uninhibited good fellowship we find portrayed in the earlier dialogues. Indeed, to scratch the surface of self-reproach in the *Confessions* is to see it as an educational document of great sensitivity and therefore as a primary source for the study of Augustine's educational theory. It takes us through the unremitting labor of soul of one who is determined, in spite of every discouragement, to understand the truth about man and his destiny; it is a dramatic demonstration of persistent self-questioning, which, according to St. Augustine, is the only method of true education. The *Confessions* hurry us along from the reminiscences of early childhood, through the years of formal schooling and the restless fever of adolescence, leading us step by step over a long period of intellectual and spiritual labor, until, in the end, when human learning has revealed its essential barrenness and the exhausted learner is plunged into new depths of despair, divine grace intervenes to achieve the illumination which the learning of man had been unable to give. The *Confessions,* therefore, establish two basic principles of education, as St. Augustine realized them in his own experience: first, they show how much the learner must perform by his own unaided effort; at the same time, they emphasize the necessity and significance of divine illumination. In the fifteen years from the age of sixteen, when he first entered the school of rhetoric at Carthage, until his conversion at the age of thirty-two, St. Augustine received only incidental help from teachers, but did much for himself. The formal rhetorical instruction which he gave his students at Carthage, Rome and Milan, was labored and lacking in purpose compared with the inner ferment of learning, which increasingly possessed his soul and drove him to seek commitment to Christ. Thus, the *Confessions* are a demonstration of the principle which Augustine was to argue more systematically in *The Teacher,* that learning is achieved by the personal activity of the learner and in an inner, voluntary movement of the mind, a movement in which external teachers and formal lessons play only a minor part.

The *Confessions* declare that this way of self-education is never easy. For instance, Augustine reports that he surpassed his fellow students in the ease with which he mastered the *Categories* of Aristotle; however, when he wished to understand the mystery of human existence and the immaterial nature of God, he was more completely dependent on his own resources and encountered many obstacles.[10] In its higher reaches, education carries the learner beyond factual, or scientific, information to a search for the reality that is concealed behind the kaleidoscope of the physical world. Absolute truth—"the eternal reasons of things" (*aeternae rationes rerum*)—although veiled from human eyes by the pressures and distractions of life, is for St. Augustine the final goal of all education, the one pathway to human fulfillment. In this ultimate spiritual quest, laboriously pursued in the face of many contrary influences, there is bound to be inner tension and much trial, error and searching of the soul. As his progress is unfolded in the *Confessions,* we see the obstacles in the learner's path gradually cleared away and the advance continuing with gathering momentum through Aristotle, Cicero and Plato, until, with the final desperate out-pouring of the self in the garden at Milan, the vision of "That which really exists" *(Id quod est)* is given in all its richness.

Only three of St. Augustine's works deal specifically with education. The first of these is *The Teacher (De Magistro),* written in the year following his return to North Africa; it is the report of a dialogue with his son Adeodatus, who had recently died, and deals with the problem of communication between teacher and pupil. The second is *Christian Education (De Doctrina Christiana),* the greater part of which was written the year after his consecration as bishop. The third is *The Instruction of the Uninstructed (De Catechizandis Rudibus),* written about three years later. Of the last two, the former deals with the problem of the Christian curriculum, the latter with the principles of teaching to be observed by the Christian teacher when he instructs those who come to seek

[10] *Confessions,* iv, 16.

an understanding of the faith. Apart from these treatises, the reader must roam widely over St. Augustine's writings to receive additional insight into his educational theory. Thus, twenty-four works in all, including St. Augustine's *Letters* and *Sermons*, are drawn on in this book to provide a conspectus of his views on education. Of these, special mention should be made of *The Trinity,* which provides considerable insight into human psychology.

St. Augustine, like Plato, maintains the substantial unity of the soul. Since the soul is made in the image of God, it would therefore be expected to be three-in-one. With painstaking care, St. Augustine explores man's inner spiritual recesses, and his analysis reveals many indications of the soul's tripartite unity. For instance, there is the trinity of memory, will and understanding, through the combined operations of which knowledge is generated and retained in the mind. The function of the will particularly fascinated Augustine and came to assume great importance in his theory of learning. It is the soul's propulsive, inquiring element, the moving principle behind all human behavior. Being free, the will can move toward either higher or lower things; what matters is that a man love what ought to be loved, and this implies that volition must be effectively controlled by reason and memory. Augustine holds with Plato that man cannot live the life of virtue and happiness unless he realizes his essential unity, in which memory, understanding and will work together in the making and executing of judgments. This unity of the soul is consolidated by liberal education and is demonstrated in a whole-hearted devotion to the life of wisdom. Right love, i.e., a sense of values founded on thought, is achieved through the training of the will, through which the will comes to realize and fully exploit its own God-given freedom and power.

Aspects of St. Augustine's Contribution to Education

St. Augustine's most valuable contributions to the understanding of education stem from his Christian Platonism. In this short review we shall consider this dynamic union of philosophy and Christian revelation under three headings: (a) The Motivation of Learning; (b) Communication between Teacher and Pupil; and (c) The Content of the Christian Curriculum.

(a) *The Motivation of Learning*. Plato and the Platonists had seen education as a reaching out of the soul toward some distant, impersonal source of knowledge variously known as "the Good" or "the One"; Augustine places education within the context of a personal relationship between God, who is the Truth, and man, His beloved creation. Thus, Augustinianism provides a more clearly defined and attractive educational objective than did Platonism and, at the same time, a more convincing explanation of the nature of the inner force which carries learning forward. The proper goal of all educational effort is the understanding of the nature of God; the motive power is Christian love or charity (*amor*), which is the clearest manifestation within the human soul of the divine nature. Through the purposeful, creative love of God, man came into being; this love, which was the force which set the universe in motion, is the same love which is expressed in all the movements of creation, including the strivings of the human soul. Therefore, when man reaches out toward a knowledge of his Creator or develops any constructive purpose, it is love which motivates his action. By God's grace man is, of course, free to direct his love toward worthy or unworthy goals, but, whatever a man may desire to possess, desire itself is the most conspicuous and undeniable fact of learning. We succeed in learning only if we want to learn and, furthermore, only if our desire is directed toward the acquisition of something specific. In Augustine's telling metaphor, love is like the weight in physical objects, which propels them to their natural resting places. When stones are released, they move downward, while smoke moves upward; in each case the movement is well-directed and purposeful, but involuntary. Man alone has the freedom to determine his own direction:

"My love is my weight; wherever I go, it is my love which brings me there."[11]

Man's love, the internal motor of the soul, when it is rightly directed, leads him step by step to an understanding of truth—"the intellectual understanding of eternal things," which St. Augustine calls "wisdom" *(sapientia)*. By contrast there is a lower level of knowledge—"the rational knowledge of temporal things" or "science" (*scientia*). Wisdom can be attained only by purely intellectual inquiry, while science, which is concerned with the things that come into being and pass away, is derived from sense perception. Wisdom is concerned with "the eternal reasons of things" (*aeternae rationes rerum*), in which there is no change or imperfection since they are the thoughts of the Creator. While scientific knowledge is not to be neglected by man, who, through his physical part, is necessarily connected to the temporal world, it must not be pursued to the neglect of the higher knowledge of truth, the unchanging reality which lies behind the change of the physical world. In wisdom alone lies the key to the happy life for man, and it is by the measure of his understanding of absolute reality that the worth of a man's life can be accurately determined.

Within this framework St. Augustine develops his views on the motivation of learning. In the first place learning always has a clear purpose in view; it is a movement stimulated by some particular thing which the mind desires to possess. If a thing is to be desired, the learner must first of all believe that it really exists and can be known; this is to say that, before learning can begin, the object of knowledge must already be partly known. In the case of the objects of intellectual knowledge, they are first seen by faith, which is the precondition of understanding:

> The whole love of the desiring mind, that is, of the mind desiring to know what it does not know, is not the love of what it does not know but rather of what it knows; on

[11] *Confessions,* xiii, 9.

account of this existing knowledge it conceives the desire to add to its knowledge.[12]

For the notion that faith is a precondition of understanding, that knowledge is "the reward of faith,"[13] Augustine finds ample scriptural support in Isaiah's recommendation "Unless ye first believe, ye shall not understand" and in Christ's "Seek and ye shall find."[14] Augustine repeatedly stresses the principle in various contexts:

> If you cannot understand, believe in order that you may understand; faith comes first, understanding follows.
>
> Do not seek to understand in order that you may believe, but believe in order that you may understand; for, unless you believe, you will not understand.[15]

It may be argued that this principle is totally in conflict with modern scientific method, although it is by no means certain that the scientist does not work by what may be called faith, intuition or the exercise of imaginative thinking, which illumines his path well ahead of his experimentally isolated and verified conclusions. At any rate Augustine's theory agrees well with the conviction of the best teachers in every age that new learning is built on existing experience, that it is a movement from the known to the unknown, and that it is most productive when founded on interest specifically directed toward some clearly defined goal. Thus, St. Augustine emphasizes the purposeful nature of learning and sheds light on the conditions on which an adequate sense of purpose can be generated. Of these the most important are that the aim of a lesson must be clearly understood by the learner and that this aim should be voluntarily taken up by him. The movement of learning can be sparked off only if the learner desires to master some knowledge. Therefore, the teacher cannot

[12] *The Trinity,* x, 3.
[13] *Expositions of the Psalms (Enarrationes in Psalmos),* 109, 8.
[14] *Against the Academics,* ii, 3, 9.
[15] *Sermon,* 118, 1. *Tracts on St. John's Gospel,* 29, 7, 6.

force his pupils to learn; all he can do is inspire them with his own enthusiasm and sense of purpose by offering them an enticing glimpse of the distant goal and assisting them to overcome the major obstacles in their path.

The desire to learn can be kindled only if the teacher's attitude toward his pupils reflects the love of God for man. Thus, in the writings of St. Augustine we find a sensitive understanding, based on both experience and thought, of the relationship between teacher and pupil. The teacher must meet his pupils "with a brother's, a father's and a mother's love;"[16] they must "have their dwelling in each other." There can be no stimulation unless it is reciprocal, that is, unless there is a close meeting of minds and mutual regard. The teacher must "love" the subject he teaches and his fellow man; to fulfil these conditions he must himself be bound in love to God, who is the Truth and therefore the source of all teaching and learning.

In the context of this interpersonal relationship the teacher acquires new insights into familiar subject matter through the reactions he calls forth from his pupils. In giving he also receives: "Whatever is loved must inevitably communicate something of itself to the lover."[17] To develop inter-communication the teacher must take the trouble to understand his pupils' minds. Since love is, as we have seen, always specifically directed, the teacher's love must be adapted to individual temperaments and needs: "The same medicine is not to be given to all, although to all the same love is due—to some love is gentle, to others severe, an enemy to none, a mother to all."[18]

(b) *Communication between Teacher and Pupil.* St. Augustine carefully analyzes the act of learning and exposes to critical scrutiny the part played by the teacher. In particular he attacks rote learning, consisting in the unthinking, and therefore meaningless, repetition of words, the "hateful chan-

[16] *The Instruction of the Uninstructed,* 17.
[17] *83 Various Questions,* 35, 2.
[18] *The Instruction of the Uninstructed,* 23.

ting," which in the *Confessions* he condemns as a distressing feature of his own elementary education. He repeatedly dwells on the distinction between words and ideas, i.e., the realities which words conventionally symbolize. Words and their meanings have no organic connection; the association is established by agreement and must therefore be learned. In themselves words are empty of meaning and are capable only of reminding the learner of what he has already experienced at first hand. To the extent that the teacher confines his activity to uttering words, he is ineffectual. Under the promise of reward or the threat of punishment, his pupils may commit his words to memory, but at best they know only the sounds of the words and do not necessarily gain any clear idea of their meaning; rote memorizing is a mere mockery of education, which must be vitally concerned with the development of understanding. This argument is most thoroughly explored in *The Teacher,* although Augustine's impatience with words for the sake of words breaks through in many other places. Several times he interrupts the discussions at Cassiciacum to remind the others that they should stop arguing about words, for learning means the comprehension and clarification of ideas; it must concentrate on "things" (*res*) and not "signs" *(signa)*. Words serve only to recall to mind what is already known; the thoughts themselves, i.e., what is signified by words, cannot be directly transmitted from one mind to another. A speaker's words are conventional representations of his thoughts; when he speaks, it is therefore merely his words and not his thoughts which are transmitted to his class. Thus, the teacher's words can do no more than stimulate other people to follow a course of thinking similar to his own. Therefore, we return to the point that learning is achieved only by a method of self-instruction and inner questioning.

Accordingly, Augustine rejects the view that the teacher is in any real sense the cause of learning, which reaches its goal in the immediate contact of the learner with the thing to be known and which is set in motion by the effort of the learner's free-will. Of the three elements usually considered necessary to every act of learning, viz., teacher, pupil and subject matter, the teacher is commonly regarded as the most important and indispensable. But for Augustine the teacher is not essential, although he can be very helpful. Provided there is a close involvement of the learner with the subject matter, learning will occur irrespective of the teacher's presence or absence; in fact, the learner is his own teacher. The teacher in the classroom, whom Augustine calls "the external teacher," may ask questions or display objects to stimulate the learner's interest, but in the last resort the learner must question himself and seek his own answers.

St. Augustine's views on learning derive from his basic beliefs about the nature of reality. Corresponding to the two realms of existence, material and spiritual, there are two apparently different methods of learning and teaching. The objects of the material world are understood by the voluntary application of the learner's mind to sense data. The teacher exposes to his pupils' senses the objects he wants them to understand. Nevertheless, he cannot convey a knowledge of material things to the minds of his pupils unless they choose to apply their minds to these things; without this personal effort, the learner may look but will not see. On the higher level of learning, where the objects of knowledge are spiritual truths, understanding is achieved only when the learner has involved himself in a prolonged course of internal searching and sustained reflection. But on this level the teacher cannot "show" the objects of knowledge to his pupils; he can merely talk about what he himself thinks in the hope that his pupils will be stimulated to do their own thinking. However, the difference between the two levels of learning and teaching is not as great as might appear; the conception of the teacher who "shows" the things themselves *(res ipsas)* to his pupils, and in this way encourages them to learn, is valid on both levels. In *The Teacher* the distinction is made between the "external teacher" *(magister exterior)* and the "internal teacher" *(magister interior);* the former is the teacher in the classroom, the latter is the Word of God, which in the moment of illumination "shows" the immaterial realities, i.e., the eternal truths, to the learner who is seeking to understand them. Thus, there is less difference between teaching on the levels of sense knowledge and spiritual knowledge than might first appear: both the "external" and the "internal" teachers show the objects of knowledge to their pupils, although by an act of his own will the learner must focus his attention on what is displayed. As the "external" teacher must have light, if what he shows is to be clearly seen, so the "internal" teacher "shows" His truths "bathed in a sort of immaterial light."[19] In so displaying truth to man, God reveals Himself, since He is the truth. The parallel between the function and methods of the two teachers is traced in considerable detail. For example, as the teacher in the classroom cannot coerce, but merely stimulate, his pupils to learn, since they are divinely endowed with free will, so also God, the internal teacher, chooses to wait until the learner has shown the will to learn and developed sustained and serious effort. Then by an act of grace and with all the clarity of spiritual illumination the truth is revealed.

In this account of the way in which man can come to understand absolute truth, St. Augustine was of course replacing Plato's impersonal doctrine of learning as "remembering" with the notion of "divine illumination," based on the conception of a personal teacher vitally concerned with the needs of those who seek His instruction. It is to be expected that the work of the human teacher would reflect, although imperfectly, the work of the superhuman, or internal, teacher, since it is the same love which motivates both. St. Augustine's telling phrase, "Instruction is completed by love" *(instructio amore perficitur)*[20] is therefore as true on the lower level of scientific learning as it is on the level of spiritual understanding.

[19] *The Trinity*, xii, 24.
[20] *The Practices of the Catholic Church,* 56.

From this it is evident that on the higher level, on which wisdom is perfected, the external teacher receeds still further into the background, leaving the learner free to be taught "by the realities themselves made manifest to him by God revealing them to his inner self."[21] The immediate cause of learning is the inner consultation by the learner of the "divine oracle" within him, a personal transaction between the individual learner and God's word (the *logos*), inwardly communicated to his soul. By contrast with the words of the external teacher, which are material and symbolic, the word of the internal teacher is immaterial and direct. It is not a symbol of something other than itself; the teacher and the word he speaks are one and the same, and he makes a direct communication of reality to the mind of the learner. Accordingly the internal teacher is the only teacher "who presides over the minds of men with no physical object coming between."[22] This is the critical point at which the analogy between the two teachers breaks down. The human teacher can merely show signs of the things he is thinking about, whereas the divine teacher shows his thoughts directly to the mind of the learner as the reward of the latter's persistent intellectual endeavor.

Thus, the whole argument in *The Teacher* is designed to encourage a critical appraisal of the nature and function of teaching as it is generally understood. There is much that teachers cannot directly communicate, and they must be careful not to confuse rote memorization with real understanding. "Who is so absurdly foolish," St. Augustine asks, "as to send his son to school to learn what the teacher thinks?"[23] The purpose of schooling is to encourage the learner to think for himself, and this can be achieved only if the teacher deliberately challenges the learner's powers of thought. But, although the teacher cannot inject knowledge into the learner, his own attitudes and habits of mind are necessarily communicated to the learner in a direct and unambiguous fashion.

[21] *The Teacher,* 38 and 40.
[22] *On Music,* vi, 1.
[23] *The Teacher,* 45.

Therefore, there are lessons which the teacher cannot avoid teaching, as St. Augustine recognizes when he says that "teachers offer themselves for imitation, and this is the essence of what people call teaching."[24] With this influence in mind, teachers will recognize that, while their task is a less obtrusive one than they may have assumed, it is nevertheless a demanding and responsible duty.

St. Augustine demands a high standard of professional competence in teachers. He asks for scholarship, a sense of fitness and a persistent love of learning, because it is on this condition alone that they can kindle a similar love in their students' minds. Therefore, teachers should not only recommend to their students, but should also display in their attitudes, St. Augustine's well-known precept: "*Intellectum valde ama*" (Be passionately in love with understanding).[25]

(c) *The Content of the Christian Curriculum.* To his duties as a Christian pastor St. Augustine brought the generous culture of the classical liberal arts curriculum, the "encyclopedia" or "full circle of studies," in which he had been reared both as student and teacher. He realized the important role played by the arts in personal culture, and helped to establish their number as seven with Scriptural support: "Wisdom hath builded her house; she has hewn out her seven pillars" (Proverbs, ix, 1). But more significantly he incorporated the liberal arts in a Christian theory of knowledge. In the first place, he regarded them as the indispensable bases of all knowledge, the proper nutriment of the soul, as food is that of the body:

> The souls of those who have not drunk from the fountains of the liberal arts are, as it were, hungry and famished; this is a condition of sterility, what we may call a spiritual famine; the minds of such people are full of diseases, which betray their malnutrition.[26]

[24] *On Music*, i, 6.
[25] *Letters*, 120, 13.
[26] *The Happy Life*, 8.

The liberal arts are fundamental disciplines, because the principles on which they are founded are absolutely true and are essential elements in the "eternal reasons of things," which are the thoughts of God. Thus, the first principles of the three arts of communication – Grammar, Rhetoric and Dialectic (Logic) – must be understood, not only so that man may enter into more effective communication with his fellow man, but so that he may be more fully able to understand the purposes of God, i.e., eternal truth. Similarly, the sciences of Geometry, Arithmetic, Music and Astronomy, are founded on the truths of number, which God established in the beginning to control the movements of His universe. If man does not understand these, he cannot hope to comprehend the divine plan; he will remain preoccupied with temporal enjoyments and distresses and fail to achieve wisdom, the key to the happy life for man. The educational function of the liberal arts is, therefore, to lead the learner step by step away from preoccupation with the things of change to an understanding of real existence. St. Augustine expresses this most succinctly at the beginning of the 6th book of his treatise *On Music*. His purpose in writing the treatise is:

> that young people, or people of any age whom God has endowed with good ability, should be drawn away under the guidance of reason and by a series of steps from the senses of the body and from physical letters, in which it is easy to become entangled. My desire is that, with the love of unchanging truth, they should attach themselves to the one God and Lord of all, who presides over the minds of men with no material object coming between.[27]

When St. Augustine returned from Italy to North Africa, he had at once realized the need to raise the educational level of Christian education both for those in the priesthood and for the laity in the province. Thus, his experience and natural interest in the field of education, gathered from his practice as a teacher in the secular schools, were brought to bear on his responsibilities as a Christian bishop and remained a life-long

[27] *On Music*, vi, 1.

preoccupation. A recognition of the importance of teaching frequently confronts us in his correspondence with friends who, depressed by the apparent ineffectiveness of their religious teaching, ask for his advice. His student and friend, Possidius, a Christian bishop, tells us in his biography of Augustine that, in the period following his return to North Africa, he was constantly engaged in "teaching and preaching both publicly and privately in his house as well as in his church."[28] Writing of the monastery which St. Augustine established at Hippo, V. J. Bourke makes the following accurate assessment:

> The monastery at Hippo was much more than a quiet home for a few self-effacing men. It was really one of the first theological seminaries. It produced men who made the African section of the Catholic Church flourish in the fifth century as it never has at any other time.[29]

From its earliest beginnings Christianity had grown in an atmosphere of controversy and conflict with the secular culture. Some of the suspicion between the two cultures had been aroused by the lack of formal education in the first disciples and others who had come after them. Fiery Christian apologists, such as Tertullian, had increased the mutual suspicion, a fact exemplified by Tertullian's challenging question, "What has Athens to do with Jerusalem?"—suggesting that Christianity must necessarily be tainted if the Christian permitted himself to enjoy, and draw upon, the secular or pagan culture. Thus, the culture of paganism, founded on the thought of Greece and Rome, and Christianity, resting on the Scriptures, developed a high degree of mutual incompatibility. Of course, the secular culture could not be completely rejected by the Christian who had been reared in the Roman world, and the attempt to shed the intimate associations of his environment imposed an intolerable psychological strain. The internal conflict is most dramatically represented in the dream

[28] Possidius, *op. cit.*, 7.
[29] Bourke, V. J., *Augustine's Quest for Wisdom*, p. 126.

of St. Jerome, a contemporary of St. Augustine, who, on being asked by the heavenly judge, "What art thou?" replied, "I am a Christian"; whereupon he received the devastating retort, "Thou liest. Thou art no Christian but a Ciceronian. Where thy treasure is, there is thy heart also."[30] In spite of this warning Jerome was never quite able to divest himself of his secular library.

The attitude of acceptance toward those elements in the classical culture which were obviously true was typified by Clement of Alexandria (160–215 A.D.). His image of the "one river of truth, into which flow many streams on this side and that,"[31] suggested that men such as Plato and Cicero could have their own degree of insight into truth. If this is conceded, the Christian must use these insights if, as Clement put it, he is "to guard the faith against assault."

St. Augustine himself betrays this inner conflict in the *Confessions,* where he laments his youthful preoccupation with "those idle vanities of Vergil," such as the love story of Dido and Aeneas.[32] Nevertheless, he was sure that Plato was "almost a Christian" (*paene Christianus*). In the Cassiciacum dialogues we find no rejection of secular literature, even on its more worldly and romantic level. For example, in the dialogue, *The Principle of Order,* there is light-hearted banter relating to the young Licentius' preoccupation with verse composition on the subject of Pyramus and Thisbe; St. Augustine urges Licentius to descend from Mount Helicon and start thinking seriously about philosophy, and accompanies his admonition with a quotation from Vergil, in which Apollo is invoked to aid the progress of the battle of wits which is to follow. It is all, of course, a piece of light-hearted skirmishing, serving as a prelude to the serious concentration on the philosophical problem with which the ensuing discussion is concerned. But it does reveal the complete absence of any feelings of guilt with regard to secular literature. In the same

[30] Jerome, *Epistles,* 2, 13.
[31] Clement, *Stromata,* i, 5, 29.
[32] *Confessions,* i, 13.

dialogue, St. Augustine tells us that, when the day's discussions had ended, it was customary to have a member of the group read aloud half a book of Vergil as a means of relaxing their minds after the labor of the day.[33]

The more liberal attitude toward Graeco-Roman culture continued to influence St. Augustine's thinking when, in the early years of his episcopate, he became aware of the need for a more enlightened Christian clergy and laity. In *Christian Education,* and again in the *Confessions,*[34] he notes that, at the express command of God, the Israelites "spoiled the Egyptians,"[35] taking out of Egypt what was most precious to the Egyptians and turning it to their own use. The Christian must follow this example: his duty is to win adherents to the faith, including the cultured pagan, but he is likely to fail unless he himself is liberally educated. The Christian can demolish neither his own doubts nor those of anyone else, whether educated or not, unless he himself is well-educated in secular as well as sacred literature and thought. The Christian teacher, like any other teacher, can communicate with his students only if he stands on common ground with them.

Apart from this argument from expediency, St. Augustine makes it clear that the interpretation of the Scriptures requires the knowledge which is contained in the liberal arts of the secular curriculum. Music and geometry, for example, provide the key to scriptural references. Grammar enables the Christian student to read his own literature with greater perception. Rhetoric and dialectic are indispensable tools for the communication of Christian truth. Thus, we find, in *Christian Education* and elsewhere in St. Augustine's writings, demonstrations of the Christian grammarian, rhetorician and dialectician in action. In replying to the accusations lodged against him by the Donatist Cresconius, St. Augustine cheerfully admits and defends his use of rhetoric and dialectic, which are the proper means of convincing doubters and

[33] *The Principle of Order,* i, 26.
[34] *Christian Education,* ii, 60; *Confessions,* vii, 9.
[35] *Exodus* 3:22 and 12:35-36.

rebutting sophistical arguments against the true faith. The Apostle Paul, and even Christ himself, used these arts in the service of truth in opposition to those who used them in perverted ways for the promotion of falsehood. In themselves, the liberal arts are morally neutral; whether they are beneficial or not is dependent on the intentions of the teacher who uses them.

St. Augustine's attitude toward the problem of the Christian curriculum reveals his confidence in the value judgments of the young. He did not, for instance, forbid Licentius to continue his interest in poetry; the atmosphere at Cassiciacum was permissive, and Licentius' enthusiasm was allowed to work itself out. The result justified the tolerant approach, for Licentius soon wearied of his superficial interests and arrived at the conclusion that philosophy was a more worthwhile endeavor. The study of philosophy was not forced on the Cassiciacum students, but was allowed to begin only when a spontaneous desire to learn had been generated.

In this regard, St. Augustine's message to our age of confusion and crisis is that the educator must not close his eyes or those of his pupils to those aspects of the culture which may not entirely agree with what he seeks to teach. Provided that the teacher, and the school in which he teaches, reflect a stable system of values, the cause of education is advanced by exposing the growing mind to all aspects of the cultural environment. The central thesis of *The City of God* supports this: man is a citizen of two societies, the temporal and the eternal, and must be aware of this double allegiance; when he understands and accepts his position, he finds that the two responsibilities are not wholly incompatible. During this life man is necessarily involved in a double loyalty, but by the manner of his life he can help his fellow man to realize the higher and ultimate loyalty to the eternal city. If the Christian is to have this influence, he must share in the secular culture and not repudiate it. For this reason, in *Christian Education,* St. Augustine outlined a Christian curriculum, in which sacred and secular elements are pooled to assist man's growth in the understanding of his ultimate destiny as well as in the love of his fellow man.

It was important that this liberal attitude should have been proclaimed at a time when the secular culture, already ripe for destruction, was reeling on the brink of immeasurable disaster. It was twenty years before Augustine's death that Alaric sacked the "eternal" city of Rome – "that awful catastrophe," as Gibbon described it, "which filled the astonished Empire with grief and terror." Humanity was to need the Augustinian synthesis of the old culture with the new revelation to rescue it from the long darkness into which the world was to fall. St. Augustine's exposition of the Christian curriculum guided the course of medieval education forward toward the renewal of genuine insight and feeling in the Renaissance. From Cassiodorus (sixth century) through Isidore of Seville and the Venerable Bede to Alcuin and St. Anselm (eleventh century), the debt to St. Augustine's ideas is consistently acknowledged. His treatise, *Christian Education,* was particularly influential in determining the content of the medieval curriculum in the monastic schools. For example, Alcuin, a leading figure in the Carolingian reform of education, quotes with approval St. Augustine's support for the conception of the seven liberal arts; furthermore, he follows St. Augustine's psychological analysis as expressed in the trinity of memory, will and understanding. St. Anselm takes up St. Augustine's views on the motivation of learning seen in terms of "faith seeking understanding." Even Abelard (twelfth century), whose views carried him some distance from Platonism, adopted St. Augustine's *"Quaerite disputando"* (Enquire by discussion) as a text for his school at Melun near Paris.

The Renaissance also expressed its debt to St. Augustine. Dante, for example, had studied the *City of God* and also *The Greatness of the Soul*; it was from the latter that he drew his picture of the soul's upward progress in a series of stages from preoccupation with sense perception to the contemplation of the unseen and eternal. In the *Convivio* he shows how clearly he understood the educational significance of the *Confessions:*

> In the *Confessions* Augustine begins to talk about himself, so that through the progress of his own life, which is from the good to the better and from the better to the best, he may give an example and a lesson, which cannot receive its true support by itself.[36]

Although the Aristotelian bias of St. Thomas Aquinas was to overwhelm the Platonism of St. Augustine in the Roman Catholic tradition, the latter's influence is repeatedly acknowledged in the thinking of the Reformers. Martin Luther declared his preference for St. Augustine over all others. Calvin, although generally associated with some of St. Augustine's gloomier teachings, shows another kind of debt to him in his *Institutes of Christian Religion,* where he echoes the words of St. Augustine's *The Teacher:*

> It is Christ, the interior teacher, who will teach us. It is He who causes men to give us external signs in order that, turning inwardly to Him, we may receive His lessons.[37]

Thus, through the centuries St. Augustine has maintained a continuing dialogue with each succeeding generation of thinkers. His approach to understanding through the interior depths of the self has its echoes in the thought of the modern Christian existentialists, such as Soren Kierkegaard and Gabriel Marcel, who declare that there is not one way of knowing but two, the objective way of science and the more significant and personalized way of wisdom. St. Augustine sees learning as a progressive relationship between the two primary objects of knowledge, "God and my soul"; similarly, Marcel finds it in the living relationship of persons, having its ground and warranty in the love of God for man. Martin Buber defines the Platonic conception of learning as "a voice-

[36] Dante, *Convivio,* i, 2, 14.
[37] Calvin, *Institutes,* iv., 14.

less colloquy of the soul with itself,"[38] which exactly coincides with the spirit of the *Soliloquies*.

St. Augustine's world shared the doubts and crises, which mark our modern world. Thus, his ideas on education have a particular relevance for today, especially for those who hold that there is an infinitely extended universe of spiritual reality transcending the material world. Therefore, St. Augustine has most to say to those who are persuaded that there is more to existence, and hence to education, than our scientific realists suggest. His distinct separation of intellectual understanding and practical knowledge has incurred the criticism of educational theorists of the pragmatic school, e.g., John Dewey, who see learning as the continual reconstruction of experience, and knowledge as always hypothetical and subject to revision. St. Augustine's attitude, as we have seen, is opposed to relativism and to the extension of the method of science to the study of moral and metaphysical problems. For example, he declares that an art is "not something which is observed by experience but something discovered by reason"[39]; thus, the art of music becomes a purely theoretical study of numerical relationships, having no connection with the playing of music, an activity of a lower order based on imitation and the mechanical repetition of techniques rather than on knowledge. Nevertheless, Augustine was also greatly interested in the principles which govern learning on the practical level. He notes, for example, that we learn to walk and talk, not by listening to teachers' verbal expositions but by observation and imitation. The principle of 'learning by doing' is central to St. Augustine's analysis of the direct method of language teaching in *The Teacher* and to his account in the *Confessions* of the natural method by which, as an infant, he learned his native language:

> without fear or torture, merely by noticing things going on around me amid the flattering words of nurses, the

[38] Martin Buber, *Between Man and Man,* Fontans Library, p. 45.
[39] *True Religion,* 54.

jokes of people who smiled on me and the joyful humors of people who played with me. I learned my own language without the pressure of those who forced me on with punishment; in this way my own heart prompted me to give birth to my ideas.[40]

To summarize, St. Augustine made five principal contributions to the theory of education:

First, he declared that wisdom, by which he meant the understanding of absolute truth, is the ultimate goal of education; wisdom (*sapientia*) is a higher value than science (*scientia*), the former being "the intellectual understanding of eternal things" and the latter "the rational understanding of temporal things." Therefore, as educators we must maintain a sense of proportion:

> We should not suppose that it is necessary to happiness to know the causes of the great physical convulsions, causes which lie hid in the most secret recesses of nature's kingdom. But we ought to know the causes of good and evil, as far as man may know them in this life, so that we may avoid the mistakes and troubles, of which this life is so full.[41]

Second, St. Augustine maintains that at the heart of existence there must always be an area of mystery impenetrable to the understanding of man. Scientific research cannot demonstrate everything; certain things must always be accepted on faith. Therefore, teachers must carefully nourish the precious sense of wonder in their students.

Third, St. Augustine emphasizes the basic importance of intellectual inquiry: in *The Greatness of the Soul* Evodius says to Augustine, "If reason teaches this, I require nothing more"; to this Augustine replies, "You are right to ask for nothing more than reason teaches."[42] Understanding counts

[40] *Confessions,* i, 14.
[41] *Enchiridion,* 16.
[42] *The Greatness of the Soul,* 7.

above all else, and therefore "nothing is lost which we earnestly seek for."[43]

Fourth, St. Augustine shows that education is founded on a personal relationship of teacher and pupil and is, therefore, as subtle and inexplicable as personality. In fact, teaching is itself a mystery, as Thomas Carlyle was to understand when he spoke of teaching as "mysterious contact of spirit; thought kindling itself at the fire of living thought."[44]

Fifth, St. Augustine asserts the professional standing of the teacher in a world which has always been inclined to undervalue his contribution. Education is always a good thing; its opposite, ignorance, is therefore evil: "To do evil is nothing other than to stray away from education." Therefore, he advises, "Do not look for an evil teacher. If a man is evil, then he is not a teacher. If he is a teacher, then he is not evil."[45] Like Quintilian's orator ("the good man skilled in speaking"), St. Augustine's teacher carries great responsibilities, for which he can be equipped only if he possesses superior personal qualities. If he falls short in wisdom, he merely leads his pupils away from education to a false and superficial view of life. It is, therefore, dangerous for society to underestimate the importance of teaching, as it is inclined to do, and to minimize the need for the more careful selection and preparation of those who are to enter a vocation requiring the supremely human qualities which St. Augustine himself displayed in outstanding measure.

[43] *On Music,* vi, 23.
[44] *Sartor Resartus,* ii, 3.
[45] *Free Will,* i, 3.

Annotation in Footnotes

All but the shorter works of St. Augustine are divided into books, the books into chapters, and in most cases the chapters into paragraphs. Both chapters and paragraphs are numbered consecutively from the beginning of the book of which they are the sub-divisions.

The references given throughout this volume are to the book and paragraph of the relevant work of St. Augustine. For example, "*The Principle of Order,* ii, 38" signifies the 38th paragraph of the 2nd book of *The Principle of Order.* Exceptions to this are the references to *The City of God* and the *Confessions*, which are by book and chapter only. In the case of *The City of God*, only the chapters are consecutively numbered throughout the books in the original text as printed in Migne's *Patrilogia Latina.* In the case of the *Confessions*, the available translations are marked in books and chapters only. Since the reader may well wish to refer to one or another of these translations, it has been thought advisable to refer to the *Confessions* by book and chapter. Therefore, *Confessions*, viii, 12" signifies the 12th chapter of the 8th book of the *Confessions*.

Scriptural references to the *Psalms* follow the numbering of the *Psalms* in the Vulgate version. From the 10th to the 146th Psalm inclusive, the numbering of later versions is one in advance of the numbering in the Vulgate version.

Chapter One

The Labor of the Soul

"Thou hast made us for Thyself and our hearts are restless until they find their rest in Thee."

(Confessions, i, 1.)

The following passages, drawn primarily from the *Confessions,* outline St. Augustine's personal experience as teacher and student throughout the formative years from infancy to Christian commitment.

It is a cumulative record of sustained and often painful self-examination which effectively demonstrates one of St. Augustine's basic educational principles, namely, that every man who learns must be his own teacher. Truth can be won only at the cost of arduous and prolonged personal effort aided by divine grace. It cannot be communicated by any human teacher.

The *Confessions* are in the form of a prayer to God, who is therefore addressed throughout in the second person.

Infancy and Boyhood

check later text. "sucking" not a learned behavior?

[1]As a baby I learned how to suck, to lie peacefully when happy, to weep when I suffered physical distress. This was all there was.

Later I began to smile, at first while sleeping and later when awake. This has been reported to me, and I believe it

[1] *Confessions,* i, 6.

because I see other babies doing the same thing. I cannot, of course, remember it for myself. Little by little, I began to know where I was, and I had the inclination to express my needs to those who had the means of satisfying them. But I failed because my needs were inside me whereas the people concerned were outside and were unable to enter into my mind by any of their faculties. So I would throw my limbs around and utter sounds, making the gestures of which I was capable, few in number and poor in quality as they were—for they were by no means accurate indications of my needs. And when people did not do what I wanted, either because they did not understand or because it might be bad for me to get what I wanted, I used to fly into tantrums with my elders because they were not my slaves, that is, because they were free people who would not do what I wanted. I avenged myself on them by screaming. That babies act like this I have understood from observing other babies. These others have unwittingly informed me of what I myself was like more accurately than the nurses who knew me.

[2] I advanced from babyhood to boyhood—or rather boyhood advanced upon me, taking the place of babyhood. Yet babyhood did not depart from me. For where did it go? It was simply no longer there. Now I was not a baby unable to speak but a boy speaking. I remember this, and in later years I discovered how I learned to speak. Adults did not teach me by any well-defined sequence of instruction like the way in which I was taught letters at a later stage. The truth is that, striving with cries and various sounds and with the movements of my limbs to express the feelings of my heart and to get what I wanted to have, I did not always succeed in expressing what I wanted to say to the people to whom I wanted to say it. So, using the mind which You gave me, O

[2] *Confessions*, i, 8–9.

God, I recalled the sounds I had heard. I saw and understood that, when grown-up people made reference to something and, in accordance with the sound they made, turned their bodies towards it, the thing was called by the sound they made to draw my attention to it. That this was what they meant was apparent from the movements of their bodies, which are a sort of natural language common to all peoples and made up of facial expressions, glances of the eye, gestures of the limbs, and tones of the voice. All these indicate the feelings of the mind as it seeks things out, possesses them, throws them away, or avoids them. As I repeatedly heard the same words properly used in various sentences, I gradually understood what they signified. Accordingly I brought my mouth to utter the same sounds and began to use them to express my own wishes. In this way I expressed my intentions to whomever I was with at the time through the medium of signs. I thus entered more deeply into the stormy fellowship of human life while I was still under the authority of my parents and at the beck and call of adults.

O God, my God, what miseries and mockeries I now experienced! For it was suggested to me that the right and proper conduct for a boy was to obey my teachers so that I might do well in the world and excel in the skills of speech, thus to gain honor and deceitful riches among men. Miserable wretch that I was, I was sent to school to learn my letters but was unable to see any use for what I was learning. Yet, if I was slow to learn, I was beaten. This procedure was approved by our ancestors, and many who had passed the same way in former days had laid down paths of sorrow along which we too were compelled to go, multiplying grief and toil for the sons of Adam.

Yet, Lord, we found men praying to You. And we learned from these and thought of You, as best we could, as some great being who, although hidden, could hear us and help us. As a boy I started to pray to You, my help and my refuge. When I called upon You, I broke the bonds of my tongue. Small as I was, I prayed to You, with no small feeling, that I should not be whipped at school. When You did not hear me, my stripes, which were then a heavy and serious torture to me, were laughed at by grown-ups, even by my parents, who certainly wished me no harm.

Is there anyone, Lord, whose spirit is so exalted, who cleaves to You with such a strong affection, who is so insensitive (for that can have the same result), who by clinging dutifully to You is so greatly moved, that he lightly dismisses racks, hooks, and such various instruments of torture, from which men everywhere pray in great fear to be spared? Is there a person who can laugh at those who live in such bitter fear of torture, as our parents laughed at the tortures we boys suffered at the hands of our teachers? We were no less in fear of these tortures and prayed no less that we should be spared them. But we nevertheless did wrong by writing or reading or thinking less than was demanded of us. It was not, Lord, that we were deficient in memory or talent, for You had endowed us with these in proper measure for our age. But we found delight in play, and for this we were punished by those who were themselves similarly employed. The trifling pursuits of grown-ups are called business, while those of boys, which are of the same quality, are punished by them. And nobody feels pity either for the boys or for the grown-ups. But someone who possesses good judgment may approve of my being whipped for playing ball as a boy since this game prevented me from learning my letters quickly so that at a later age I might play games of a more detestable sort. Did the man who beat me behave any differently when, on being defeated in some argument with a colleague, he was more tormented by anger and envy than I was when I was beaten by a playfellow in a ball game?

[3] In my boyhood, for which lesser fears were entertained than for my youth, I did not love learning and hated being

[3] *Confessions*, i, 12.

forced to learn. Since I was forced, good was done to me, although I myself did not do well. I would not learn unless I was compelled. But nobody does well against his will, even if what he does is good. Nor did the people do well who forced me. The good came from You, O God. The others could not see how I should employ all that they forced me to learn, except that I should satisfy the insatiable desires for a sort of wealth which is in fact poverty and for a glory which is ignominy. But You, Lord, by whom the very hairs of our head are numbered, used the mistakes of those who urged me to study for my advantage. But my own error, consisting in my unwillingness to learn, You used for my punishment. This was a punishment well deserved by one who was so small a boy but so great a sinner. Thus, You brought me good from those who were not doing good, and You rightly punished my own sinning self. This is how you ordered it and this is how it is: every disordered soul is its own punishment.

Even to this day I have not sufficiently understood why I hated Greek literature, in which I was instructed as a small boy. For I was very fond of Latin literature, not however the teaching I got from my first teachers, but the teaching of those we call grammarians.* For I found my elementary education—in which I was taught to read, to write and to count—as burdensome and as much of a punishment as the whole of Greek grammar. Now this too could spring only from sin and from vanity of life, because I was flesh and "a wind that passeth and cometh not again" (*Psalm* 77, 39). Certainly those first lessons were better, since their effects were surer. Through them I acquired the power to read what I find written and to write what I want to write; and this power remains with me to this day. By contrast, in my later studies I was forced to commit to memory the wanderings of some Aeneas or other, while I simultaneously forgot my own

* The "first teacher" (*primus magister)* was the elementary school teacher, also called *ludi magister* or *litterator,* the "teacher of letters." The "grammarian" *(grammaticus)* was the teacher at the second stage of education, as the "rhetorician". *(rhetor)* was at the third or tertiary stage.

wanderings. I learned to weep for Dido, who killed herself for love, while—wretch that I was!—I endured with dry eyes my own condition, in which I was dying separated from Thee, O God my life . . . .

[4] I made a mistake when, as a boy, I gave my love to those empty studies rather than to the other more profitable ones. Truly, I hated the latter and loved the former. Indeed one and one make two, and two and two make four, was a hateful chant to me. At the same time the wooden horse filled with armed men, Troy consumed with flames and the ghost of Creusa—these were most pleasurable sights to me.

Why then did I hate Greek literature, which has similar stories to tell? For Homer also has great skill in weaving such tales and is endowed with the same charming unreality. Yet to me he was hateful. I imagine that Vergil arouses the same response in the minds of Greek boys that Homer did in me. The hard labor of completely mastering a foreign language mingled all the charming quality of the Greek tales with poison. For I knew none of the Greek words and I was unrelentingly driven to learn by savage threats and punishments. But at one period of my life, when I was a young child, I knew no Latin. Yet I learned it without fear or torture, merely by noticing what went on around me amid the flattering words of nurses, the jokes of people who smiled on me, and the joyful humors of people who played with me. I learned my own language, without the pressure of those who compelled me with punishment, because my own heart prompted me to give birth to my ideas. This would not have been possible for me unless I had learned some words, and I learned these not from teachers but simply from people talking. In their ears I also brought into being the feelings of my mind. All of this clearly demonstrates that a free curiosity is a greater encouragement to learning than a frightening com-

[4] *Confessions,* i, 13–14.

pulsion. Nevertheless, by the dictates of your laws, O God, compulsion acts to restrain the free flow of curiosity. These laws are imposed by torments, which range from the canes of teachers to the sufferings of the martyrs and have the effect of mingling in us a health-giving bitterness, which summons us back to You from the soul-destroying pleasure which first influenced us to turn our backs on You.

[5] I used to steal from my parents' cellar and table, either at the imperious command of gluttony or to have something to give to other boys, who sold me their playthings, although they found as much pleasure in them as I did. Even in play I pursued victory by cheating, being overcome by the empty desire to win. But there was nothing I liked to experience less and nothing I used to denounce more violently, when I caught anyone in the act, than this very cheating which I practiced on others. Yet when I myself was found out, it pleased me to fly into a rage rather than to give in.

Is this the innocence of boyhood? No, Lord, it is not! I ask for Thy mercy, O God. For as one age of our lives is succeeded by another and the canes of schoolmasters give place to more severe punishments, likewise all of this behavior is directed away from pedagogues and schoolmasters to prefects and kings, away from nuts and balls and sparrows to preoccupation with gold, estates and slaves. Therefore, it was surely in the small stature of a child that You, O Lord our King, saw the symbol of humility, when You said with approval, "Of such is the Kingdom of Heaven" (*Matthew,* 19, 14).

Yet, O Lord, my thanks would have been due to You, most excellent and most good Founder and Ruler of the Universe and our God, even if You had willed that I should not survive

[5] *Confessions,* 1, 19–20.

beyond boyhood. For even at that age I existed, I lived, I experienced sensation. As early as this I took thought for my safety, and this was a trace of that most secret unity from which my being was derived. With my interior sense I watched over the integrity of my senses, and even in the midst of my petty preoccupations and my thoughts on matters of no importance, I took delight in truth. I disliked being misled, had an active memory, had learned how to speak, found satisfaction in friendship, and avoided pain, meanness and ignorance.

The Adolescent and the Peer Group

[6] In the time of adolescence I burned with the desire to get my fill of hell, and with heedless folly I luxuriated in a variety of murky lusts. My "beauty consumed away" (*Psalm* 38, 12) and I became rotten in Your eyes. Yet all the time I was pleasing to myself and was anxious to be pleasing in the eyes of my fellow man.

All that mattered to me was to love and to be loved. But I knew no moderation in the meeting of mind with mind at the point where the bright-shining boundary of friendship is placed. From the muddy desire of the flesh and from the hot, bubbling passions of adolescence, mists rose up to cloud over and darken my heart, so that the serene illumination of love could not be seen apart from the dark fog of lust. Both love and lust seethed within me and hurried me, in the weakness of my youth, over the craggy places of lust and plunged me into a whirlpool of infamous sins. Your wrath had grown strong against me, and I did not know it. I was deafened by the clanging chain of my mortal nature, the punishment for the pride of my soul. I was moving further and further away from You, and You allowed me to go. I was tossed around,

[6] *Confessions,* ii, 1–2.

poured wastefully away and dissipated through my fornications. And yet You said not a word – You, my Joy, who have come to me so late. At that time you were silent and I, in proud dejection and restless weariness, wandered far from You to sow more and more of the seeds which bear no fruit except griefs.

[7] Where was I, and how far had I gone in exile from the delights of Your house in that sixteenth year of my life of the flesh, when the madness of lust, licensed by human shamelessness but not licensed by Your laws, brought me under its sway and I gave myself wholly to it? My family had no thought of saving me by marriage from my headlong flight to destruction. Their only thought was that I should learn to turn as fine a speech as possible and that my tongue should be trained in the art of persuasion.

In that year my studies were interrupted. I had gone to live in the nearby city of Madaura* to study grammar and rhetoric, but I was brought back from there while money was being accumulated to provide for the longer journey to Carthage. It was my father's determination rather than his means which sent me there, for he was a citizen of Tagaste, possessing only slender resources. To whom am I telling all this? Not to You, O my God, but rather I am telling it in Your presence to my own kind, to the human race, or to whatever small part of it may come upon my writings. Why am I telling it? Indeed, it is so that I, and anyone else who reads this, may realize in thought the depths out of which our cry must go up to You. For what comes closer to Your hearing than a heart that confesses You and a life that is built on faith?

At that time my father was praised by everyone, because

* Madaura, the birthplace of the orator Apuleius (flor. 158 A.D.), was 20 miles south of Tagaste.

[7] *Confessions,* ii, 2–3.

he strained his resources to give his son what he needed to travel abroad to study when many far wealthier citizens had no such thought for their children. Yet this father showed no concern about the way in which I was growing toward You or about the purity of my life, as long as I developed in eloquence, or rather was cut off from Your cultivation, O God, who are the one, true and good Lord of Your field, which is my heart.

Now in that sixteenth year of my life when a period of idleness was imposed upon me by my family's necessitous circumstances, I began to live in my parents' home, enjoying a complete holiday from school. In that period the thorny briers of my lusts flourished and grew up over my head, and no one's hand was there to root them out.

[8] There is nothing which so thoroughly deserves to be condemned as vice. Yet, in a desire to avoid having fault found with me, I gave myself more completely to vice, and, when the opportunity was lacking to commit a crime and so to become the equal of my abandoned companions, I claimed to have done things I had not actually done. I felt that, the greater my innocence, the more contemptible I would seem, and that, the purer I was, the more worthless I would be held. Such were the companions with whom I roamed the streets of Babylon* and wallowed in its dirt, as if I were rolling amid cinnamons and precious ointments. The unseen enemy was treading me down, leading me to involve myself more closely in that city's very center. He was seducing one who was open to seduction.

* Babylon metaphorically represents the temporal city as opposed to the eternal city of God.

[8] *Confessions,* ii, 3.

[9] Certainly Your law, O Lord, punishes theft, and this law is written in the hearts of men, where not even evil-doing rubs it out. No thief is content to have another thief steal from him, not even if the one thief is rich and the other steals from him through poverty. Yet I deliberately chose to steal. I was not driven to it by any degree of want, unless perhaps by a want of and aversion from justice and an excess of iniquity. For I stole what I did not lack; indeed, what I already possessed was of much better quality. I did not resort to theft because I wanted to enjoy the article I stole. I enjoyed the act of stealing itself and the sin. There was a pear tree close to our vineyard, a tree heavily laden with fruit that was not very attractive either in appearance or in taste. Some of us young criminals, who according to our wicked habit had continued our play in the streets until dead of night, proceeded to carry away a huge load of pears from the tree, not to eat them – for we did little more than taste them – but to throw them to the pigs. This gave us all greater pleasure because it was forbidden. This, O God, was my heart; this was my heart, on which You had pity even in the depths of the abyss. Now let this heart of mine tell you my motives when I was evil for no reason and when there was no reason for wickedness, except the wickedness itself. The wickedness was despicable, and yet I loved it. But it was my own destruction that I loved and my own falling away rather than the thing toward which I fell. My soul was depraved and was casting itself down into destruction from the security which rests with You, seeking nothing at all from the shame except the shame itself.

[10] What was it that, in my miserable state, I loved in you, O my theft, a deed carried out in the course of that night in

[9] *Confessions,* ii, 4.
[10] *Confessions,* ii, 6.

the sixteenth year of my life? Because you were a theft, you were not lovely. Are you then anything at all that I should talk to you? The pears we stole were beautiful, because they were made by You, who are the most beautiful of all, the Creator of all, the good God, my supreme and true good. The pears were beautiful, but they were not what my wretched soul desired, for I had all the better ones I wanted and I plucked the others only that I might steal. As soon as I had gathered them, I threw them away and feasted on only my own iniquity, in which I rejoiced with great delight. If any part of those pears entered my mouth, it was the sin which gave the deed its seasoning. Now, O Lord my God, I ask what gave me pleasure in the theft, which indeed possessed no beauty in itself. The theft had not the beauty which exists in justice and prudence, nor the beauty which is found in the mind and memory of man, in his senses or in his animal life. Nor did it have the beauty which makes the stars lovely and glorious in their courses, nor the beauty of the heavens, the earth or the sea, which teems with developing life coming to replace with new birth the life which passes away. It had not even that imperfect and counterfeit beauty associated with those vices which lead man astray.

[11] What advantage did I then gain—wretch that I was!—from those deeds which I now blush to remember, and especially from that theft in which I loved nothing except the act of thieving itself. Even the very act was nothing, and its effect was to make me still more miserable. But, as I recall my state of mind at that time, I would not have stolen the pears alone. No, I would certainly not have done it alone. Therefore, in this situation I was in love with something more, namely, the companionship of the friends with whom I did it. Then there was something apart from the theft which I loved. No, there was nothing else, because the companion-

[11] *Confessions,* ii, 8–9.

ship was also nothing. What is the true explanation? Who is there who can tell me the answer, except He who illumines my heart and seeks out its dark, shadowy places? What is it that my mind is seeking to ask, to discuss and to ponder over? If at the time I had liked the pears which I stole and wanted to enjoy them, I could have committed the deed alone, if that would have been enough to bring me the pleasure. I would not have inflamed the itching of my desire by consorting with accomplices. But since the pleasure I experienced was not in the pears, it was in the evil deed itself and was brought into being by my association with those who were committing the same sin.

What was the state of my mind? Clearly it was too shameful. Woe is me that I experienced it! But what was it that I felt in my mind? Who is there who can understand evil-doing? There was laughter among us, as if our hearts were tickled because we were deceiving those who had no idea what was being done to them and who were strongly against it. But why was my delight such that I did not carry out the deed alone? Is it that nobody finds it easy to laugh when he is alone? Indeed, nobody finds this easy, and yet laughter does sometimes overcome men individually and in solitude. This is when something particularly ludicrous is presented to their senses or to their minds. But I would not have done this deed by myself. Certainly this would have been altogether impossible.

Here then in Your presence, O God, is the vivid remembering of my soul. I could not commit that theft alone. My pleasure lay, not in what I stole, but in the mere fact that I did steal. Certainly I would not have liked to do it alone; nor would I have done it alone. Alas for this friendship that is most unfriendly, this incomprehensible enticement of the mind, this greedy desire to hurt another merely in sport and for the fun of it, this desire to inflict loss on another without any accompanying gain to oneself or any motive of vengeance! Let someone call out, "Come, let us go to it," and we are not ashamed to appear shameless.

[12] I came to Carthage, and on every side a cauldron of shameful loves seethed and clamored around me. I was not yet in love. Yet I loved to love, and, because of the need that was hidden away within me, I hated myself because I lacked the need. I was searching for something to love, because I was in love with loving and I hated a path of life that was secure and free from snares. For deep within me I was hungry for want of that inner food, which is You, my God, and yet I did not feel any hunger for that food. I was without the desire for the food that does not pass away. I did not have this hunger in full measure, but, the emptier I was, the more distasteful it was to me. With all this my soul, sick and in misery, was projecting itself, covered in sores and greedily desirous of scratching itself by rubbing against the things of sense. Yet, if these things had no soul, they would not, in fact, inspire love. To love and to be loved was pure sweetness to me, and all the more sweet if I enjoyed the body of a person who also loved me.

So I polluted the fountain of friendship with the foulness of lust and clouded over its clear waters from the hell of lawless desire. And yet, shameful and unseemly as I was, my vanity was so excessive that I longed to be polished and urbane. Also, I ran headlong into the love by which I longed to be entrapped. O God, my mercy, with how much bitter gall did You in your goodness sprinkle all that sweetness! I was loved, and I came to the binding moment of consummation. With joy I was being bound with troublesome chains so that I might be beaten with the burning iron rods of jealousy, suspicions, fears, tempers and quarrels.

I was carried away by stage plays filled with representations of my own miseries and charged with fuel to fires. Why is it that a man wants to be made sad by griefs and tragic events which he himself would not want to suffer? Yet the spectator wishes to experience the grief derived from such events, and that very grief brings him pleasure. This is indeed

[12] *Confessions,* iii, 1–2.

a wretched form of madness, for the more a man has such feelings in himself, the more he is moved by them. When a man suffers in his own person, it is called misery, but, when he suffers in sympathy with others, it is called pity. What sort of pity is this which springs from fictitious events portrayed on the stage? The spectator is not called upon to give help, but merely to display grief. And the person who acts out these representations is appreciated to the extent that he causes grief to arise in the spectator. If the tragic events which affect the characters, whether these events happened long ago or are purely fictitious, are so poorly played that the spectator is not moved to sorrow, he goes away from the theatre disgusted and critical. On the other hand, if he is moved to tears, he stays where he is, intent upon the scene and thoroughly enjoying it. Thus, tears and sorrows are things to be loved, although all men undoubtedly want to be joyful. Or is there pleasure in feeling pity, although nobody likes to be miserable? Such a feeling of pity cannot exist apart from grief, and this is the only reason why sorrows are loved.

[13] At that time I loved to feel sorrow and I continued to search for what would make me sad, for in regard to the misery of others, even if it was merely being acted out and portrayed in mime, the more the actor's skill drew forth my tears, the more it pleased and enthralled me. How was that surprising in an unhappy sheep like me, who, straying from Your flock and impatient of Your watchfulness over me, was rendered ugly by a foul disease? That was the source of my love of sorrows. It was not that I wanted to be too deeply pierced by them, but rather that I would receive, as it were, a scratch on the surface when I listened to them and watched them portrayed on the stage; for I had no desire to suffer the things that I was watching. Yet, this scratching was followed

[13] *Confessions,* iii, 2.

by angry swelling with a poisonous infection and flowing pus, just as when one is scratched by nails. Such was my life—if one can call it a life, O my God.

[14] Those of my interests which were regarded as reputable were directed toward the law courts, in which I would gain a reputation for excellence in proportion to my capacity to practice deception on others. So great is the blindness of men that they glory even in their blindness! And now I was Head of the school of rhetoric, a position in which I boastfully revelled and which puffed me up with vanity. But You know, O Lord, that I was much more restrained than the "Wreckers"* and entirely removed from their destructive behavior. "Wreckers" was the stupid and diabolical name which in their eyes was like a badge of sophistication. Yet I associated with them with a shameless sense of shame, caused by the fact that I was different from them. I was in their company and at times enjoyed their friendship. But I always hated the deeds they carried out, that is, their "wreckings," as when they insolently attacked the modesty of perfect strangers, disturbing it by uncalled-for jeering and drawing sustenance from it for their malicious mirth. Their behavior bore a striking resemblance to the behavior of devils. They could have had no more appropriate name than "wreckers," because it was clear that they had been first "wrecked" and overturned in their own persons, being themselves secretly mocked and led astray by deceiving spirits in those very acts in which they themselves loved to mock and deceive others.

In the company of such as these, I passed this period of weakness in my life. I was studying the textbooks of elo-

*"Eversores," literally "Overturners," a name which appears to have been given to a delinquent element among the student body at Carthage.

[14] *Confessions,* iii, 3–6.

quence, for it was in eloquence that I had the desire to excel, a desire springing from a damnable and vainglorious purpose associated with the delights of human vanity. Following the usual curriculum, I had arrived at a book written by a certain Cicero, whose tongue almost everyone admires, if not his heart. That book of his contains an exhortation to philosophy and is called *Hortensius*.* It changed the whole feeling of my mind, giving a new direction to the prayers I offered to You, O God, and providing me with new purposes and ambitions. Suddenly I realized the worthlessness of all my empty hopes, and with an incredible upsurging of the heart I began to yearn for the immortality of wisdom. Thus, I began the progress of ascent which would bring me back to You. It was now my nineteenth year, my father had died two years before, and it was with my mother's remittances that I appeared to be buying my instruction in eloquence. But in fact I was not using Cicero's book to sharpen my tongue, for it was not so much the qualities of its style which won me over as what it said.

How I burned, O my God, how I burned to take wings and fly upward from earthly things to You! And yet I was quite ignorant of Your purpose for me, for it is with You that wisdom rests. Now love of wisdom is called by the Greek word "philosophy," and it was an enthusiasm for philosophy that this book kindled within me. There are people who lead men astray by philosophy, coloring and covering up their errors with its great, fine-sounding and honorable name. Almost everyone of this kind who lived in Cicero's time or in earlier times is noted and pointed out in that book. It also illustrates that wholesome advice given by Your Spirit through Your good and saintly servant: "Beware lest any man spoil you through philosophy and vain deceit, after the tradition of men, after the rudiments of this world, and not

* The *Hortensius*, a lost work of Cicero, in which Cicero maintained the superiority of philosophy over rhetoric, which was supported by his friend Hortensius.

after Christ. For in Him dwelleth all the fullness of the Godhead bodily." (*Colossians* 2: 8-9.) But as You know, O light of my heart, these writings of the Apostle were not yet known to me at that time. Yet the one thing which delighted me in the advice given by Cicero was that I should love, seek out, follow after, hold and cling to, not this or that school of philosophy, but wisdom itself whatever it might be. His exposition excited and inflamed me and I burned with enthusiasm, although one thing checked the ardor of my zeal. This was that the name of Christ was not there, for this was the name which, according to Your mercy, O Lord, my tender young heart had dutifully sucked into myself even with my mother's milk, and which I held deep within me. Whatever made no mention of that name failed to win me completely, however learned it was or however well-polished or true.

Hence, I decided to direct my mind to the Holy Scriptures to see what sort of books they were. And lo! what I found was something not revealed to the proud and not yet disclosed to children, something which is lowly when it is approached, but high, exalted, and veiled in mysteries to one who advances through it. But I was not the sort of person who could enter therein or bend my neck to follow its steps. When I first directed my attention to the Scriptures, I did not have the feelings which I have just described. To me they seemed unworthy of comparison with the dignity of Cicero. My puffed-up pride rejected the restraint which was theirs, and my gaze could not penetrate into their interior depths, although these were of the kind which could grow up in small children. But I disdained the thought of being a little child. Swollen with arrogance, I was a big man in my own esteem.

I fell in with some people who indulged in high-sounding ravings,* who were very carnal and talkative, and in whose mouths were the snares of the devil and bird-lime com-

* The sect of the Manichaeans, i.e., followers of the Persian Mani of Ecbatana, who had founded a new religion in the 3rd century, A.D.

pounded of a mixture of the syllables of Your name, the name of our Lord Jesus Christ, and the name of the Paraclete, the Holy Ghost, the Comforter. These names were never off their lips, but they were only sounds and noises of the tongue, for their hearts were empty of truth. They would call out "Truth, truth," and they talked to me about it continually. Yet truth was nowhere within them, and they spoke falsehood not only about You, who are truly the Truth, but also about the elements of this world, the things which have been created by You. For the love of You, my supreme and good Father, who are the beauty of all beautiful things, I should have passed beyond even those philosophers who spoke the truth about these elements. O truth, truth, how deeply within me even then did the marrow of my soul pant after You, when repeatedly and in various ways I heard those men sounding Your name, even if it was only with the voice and from many large books. Those were the dishes in which I, who was longing for You, was served with the sun and the moon, beautiful works of Yours, but still only Your works and not You yourself, nor even Your first works. For Your spiritual works precede those material things, although the latter shine brightly in their celestial places.

Yet my hunger and thirst were not even for those first works, but for Yourself, the Truth, "with whom there is no change nor shadow of alteration" (*James* 1: 17). And still the Manichaeans continued to set splendid phantasies before me in those same dishes. It would have been better for me to love the sun, which is at least real to the sight, than to love those illusions, which deceive the mind through the eyes. However, I devoured the illusions because I thought they were Yourself, but not greedily, because You did not taste in my mouth as You actually are. Indeed, those empty falsehoods were not You, and I was not nourished by them, but only more thoroughly exhausted. Food has the same appearance in dreams as it has to people when awake. Yet what people eat in dreams does not nourish them, for they are asleep. Their phantasies were not in any way like You, as You have now spoken to me, for they were material images and counterfeit objects. The true objects, which we see with our physical vision, whether in the heavens or on the earth, are more real than these phantasies are. We share the vision of those objects with beasts and birds, and the objects are more real than when we call them up in the mind's eye. And those mental images, in turn, are more real than the larger and infinitely extended objects which we form from them and which themselves have no real existence at all. Such were the empty vanities on which I nourished myself at that time; and yet I was not nourished.

[15] I was entirely ignorant of that other true reality, and I was influenced in a subtle sort of way to give my support to those foolish men who were deceiving me when they posed such questions as these: "Where does evil come from?" "Is God limited by a physical shape?" "Does God have hair and nails?" "Are we to class as good men those who had many wives at the same time, who killed men and offered sacrifices of living creatures?" In my state of ignorance I was troubled by all this and, although I was moving away from truth, I imagined that in fact I was advancing toward it. I did not know that evil was merely a deprivation of good proceeding up to the point where it ceases to have any existence* But how was it possible that I could see this, when my eyes could see only as far as physical objects and my mind could see only imaginary forms. I was not even aware that God was a

* The view of evil in negative terms as a falling away from excellence was derived from neo-Platonism. It is to be contrasted with the Manichaean conception of evil (personified as the Prince of Darkness) as a positive, dynamic force engaged in continual warfare with goodness (personified as the Prince of Light).

[15] *Confessions,* iii, 7.

spirit, having no limbs which could be measured in length and breadth and having no bulk at all. For the part of a bulk is less than its whole, and, if it is infinite, then a part of it, which is contained within a fixed space, is smaller than its infinite expanse. A bulk cannot exist everywhere in its entirety as a spirit can and as God can. Furthermore, I did not know what the principle is within us in virtue of which we are like God or in what sense the Scriptures can speak of us as being made "in the image of God" (*Genesis* 1: 27).

The Young Teacher

[16] Throughout the period of nine years from my nineteenth to my twenty-eight year, we went on being led astray and leading others astray, being ourselves deceived and deceiving others, in the pursuit of various forms of lust. We did this publicly, through teaching the subjects which are referred to as "the liberal arts," and privately, under the false name of religion. Here we were proud, there superstitious, and everywhere empty. On the one hand, we pursued the vanity of popular fame, even to courting applause in the theatre, indulging in poetic competitions, fighting over grass garlands, and engaging in the idle vanities of stage spectacles and the unrestrained practice of lusts. On the other hand, we were seeking to be purged of all this filth when we carried food to those who were called "the Elect" and "the Holy Ones,"* who, in the laboratory of their stomachs, were to turn it into angels and deities, through whose agency we were to be set free. These were my preoccupations, which I carried out with my friends, who were deceived by my help and in my company.

* The reference is still to the Manichaeans.

[16] *Confessions,* iv, 1.

[17]In those years I taught the art of rhetoric and, overcome by greed for gain. I was offering for sale the power of all-conquering speech. But, as You know, O Lord, I was more pleased to have students who were good according to the accepted standard of goodness. Without deceit I instructed them in the instruments of deceit, not so that they would use these instruments against the life of an innocent man, although they were sometimes employed to save the life of a guilty one. And You, O God, saw me from afar as I stumbled along that slippery way. In the midst of so much smoke, you saw me giving off some sparks of faithfulness, which in the task of instruction I showed to those who shared with me a love of empty vanity and a quest for deceit. In those years I possessed only one woman, and she was not joined to me in what is properly called marriage. She was one whom a wandering passion, barren of forethought, had tracked down for me. Yet it was only one woman I had, and I was faithful even to her bed. Indeed, in this experience with her I showed by my own example what a difference there is between the bond of the marriage covenant, entered into for the sake of bringing forth offspring, and the bargain of a licentious love, where a child may be born unwanted, although, when he is born, he compels us to love him.

[18]There were other things associated with my friends which laid greater hold on my mind: talking and laughing together; exchanging acts of kindness with one another; reading pleasant books together; bantering one another and at the same time engaging in serious talk; disagreeing at times without bad humor, just as a man may have a difference with himself; when discord arose, as it did very infrequently, using it to give additional zest to our more normal state of concord;

[17] *Confessions,* iv, 2.
[18] *Confessions,* iv, 8.

teaching and learning from one another in turn; impatiently longing for the return of those who were absent and giving them a joyful welcome on their return. With these and other such expressions, proceeding from the hearts of a group of people who gave and received love in return—expressions shown by the face, the voice, the eyes and by a thousand other delightful gestures—our souls were, so to speak, kindled into flame and, although we were many, we were joined together as one.

[19] I used to say to my friends: "Surely it is only the beautiful that we love. But what is beautiful? What is beauty? What is it which allures and attracts us to the things we love? Surely, unless there were grace and beauty in these things, there would be no way in which they could draw us to them." So I looked, and I observed that in physical objects there was one kind of beauty which derives from their forms as a whole, but another sort which owes its seemliness to an appropriate relationship with something else; for example, the relationship of a part of the body to the whole body, of a shoe to the foot, and so on. This thought took possession of my mind from the depths of my heart, and I wrote some books called *About the Beautiful and the Fitting*.* There were, I think, two or three of them, but You know, O God, for I have forgotten. They are no longer in my possession; somehow or other they have strayed away from me.

But why was it, O Lord my God, that I was prompted to dedicate these books to Hierius, a Roman orator, whom I did not know by sight but whom I had admired because of his bright reputation for learning and because of some words of his which I had heard with pleasure? He pleased me the more because he was pleasing to others and because they used to

* *De Pulchro et Apto,* written about 380 A.D.; non-extant.
[19] *Confessions,* iv, 13-14.

lavish praises on him, being amazed that a man from Syria, who had received his first training in Greek eloquence, had later emerged as a wonderful orator in Latin, and that he was so learned in everything related to the study of philosophy.

[20] But I did not yet see that this great question [i.e., the nature of the Beautiful and the Fitting] hinged upon Your wisdom, O all-powerful One, who is the author of all wonderful things. My mind took account only of physical forms. I defined and distinguished "the Beautiful" in terms of what is so "in itself," and "the Fitting" as that which derives its seemliness from an appropriate relation with something else; and I founded my argument on physical examples. Also, I looked at the nature of the soul, but the erroneous view I had of spiritual things did not allow me to see the truth. Yet all the time the very force of truth was pressing itself on my gaze, and I was turning my throbbing mind away from the immaterial to lines, colors, and swelling bulks. But I could not see these things in my mind, and therefore I decided that I could not see my mind either. Also, when I loved the peace I found in virtue and hated the discord in vice, I took note of the unity of the former and the divided nature of the latter. Thus, it appeared to me that the rational mind and the nature of truth and of the supreme good were to be found in that unity. On the other hand, in my wretched folly I thought that I could find the substance of the irrational life, whatever that substance might be, and the nature of the chief evil in the divided nature of vice. This nature would be not only a substance but a real living thing, and yet it would not derive from You, O my God, from whom everything comes. I called the unity a "monad," as though it were a sexless soul, and the divided nature I called a "duad," for example, the anger displayed in deeds of violence and the lust associated with

[20] *Confessions,* iv. 15.

deeds of passion. But I did not know what I was talking about, for I had not yet grasped and learned that evil was no substance and that our mind is not the supreme and unchanging good.

Just as wrong-doing arises when that movement of the mind in which the stimulus to action lies, is vicious and thrusts itself forward insolently and aggressively, and just as disgraceful conduct results when that disposition of the soul by virtue of which the desires of the flesh are encouraged, is unrestrained, so false opinions contaminate life if the rational mind is itself vicious. So it was at that time with me, who did not know that it was by another light that my soul must be illumined in order to be a partaker in truth, for the soul is not in itself the essence of truth; for "Thou wilt light my lamp, O Lord; Thou wilt enlighten my darkness, O my God" (*Psalm* 17:29), and "Of Thy fulness we have all received" (*John* 1: 16). For "Thou are the true light which enlighteneth every man that cometh into this world" (*John* 1: 9), because "In Thee there is no change nor shadow of alteration" (*James* 1:17).

But I was pressing on toward You, and at the same time being pushed back from You, so that I experienced the taste of death, for You resist the proud. What could be a better example of pride than that, with incredible folly, I should declare that my nature was the same as Yours?* But, because I was changeable – a fact which was clear to me from my desire to be wise, the aim being to change from a worse to a better condition – I preferred to hold that You also were changeable rather than to hold that I was not exactly what you were. It was in this way that I was pushed back. You resisted my windy obstinacy, and I continued to think of imaginary forms of a physical sort. Although I was myself flesh, I went on accusing the flesh, and, being a wandering spirit, I did not turn back to you. In my wandering I moved

* The Manichaean doctrine that the good soul was of the same substance as God.

toward those things which have no real existence, either in You or in me or in the body, and which were not created for me by Your truth, but which were formed out of matter by my vain conceit. I spoke to your faithful little ones, that is, my fellow-citizens, from whom I was unwittingly moving into exile, saying to them in my prattling and foolish way, "Why does the soul go astray, when God created it?" But I would not have anyone say to me, "Why then does God go astray?" I preferred to maintain that Your unchangeable substance was forced to go astray rather than to recognize that my own changeable substance had strayed from the path of its own volition and had fallen into error by way of punishment.

[21] What advantage was it to me that, when I was hardly twenty years of age, there came into my hands some writings of Aristotle called the "Ten Categories"? I hung on the name of this work as on something great and divine, and longed for it at the time when my rhetoric teacher at Carthage, along with others who were held to be wise, mentioned it with cheeks swelling with pride. I read this work and understood it unaided. I compared my impressions of it with others, who spoke of their difficulty in understanding the book, even under the most learned masters, who not only lectured on it but also drew many diagrams in the dust. These people could not tell me anything about it which I had not already understood when I read it by myself. What the book had to say about substances—for example, man—seemed perfectly clear to me. So it was also with the qualities which are in substances, such as a man's shape, which may be of this kind or of that; or his stature, meaning how many feet tall he is; or his relationship to other people, such as whose brother he is; where he is placed or when he was born; whether he is

[21] *Confessions,* iv, 16.

standing or sitting, or has his shoes on, or is armed, or is doing or suffering this thing or that; and all the countless things which are to be placed in these nine categories, of which I have given some examples, or in the chief category of substance.

What advantage did I derive from all this? I actually put obstacles in my way, when I tried to understand You, my God, who are marvellous in Your simple and unchanging nature, on the assumption that anything that existed was entirely contained within the ten categories. It was as if You also were subjected to Your own greatness or beauty, so that these qualities were in You as their subject, as is the case with physical objects. The truth is that Your greatness and Your beauty are Your very Self. Now a physical object is not large and beautiful merely by virtue of its being a physical object, for it would still be an object even if it were less large and less beautiful. Indeed, the thoughts I had of You were false and far from the truth, the fictions of my own wretchedness and not the supports of Your blessedness. You had given the command, and so it came about in me that "the earth should bring forth briars and thorns to me" and that "in the sweat of my brow I should eat my bread" (*Genesis* 3: 18-19).

Moreover, what advantage did I get from being able to read and to understand without help all the books I could find on the subjects which are called the liberal arts, at a time when I was still the most abject slave of my evil desires? I enjoyed the books, and yet I remained ignorant of the source of whatever was true and certain in them. The fact is that my back was turned to the light and my face toward all that was illumined by the light. The result was that my face was not itself illumined. Whatever was related to the art of rhetoric or of logic, to the dimensions of shapes [i.e., geometry], to music or to number, I understood without much difficulty and with no need of a teacher. You know this, O Lord, my God, because speed of understanding and acute perception are Your gift.

[22] Let me now, in the sight of my God, speak out about the twenty-ninth year of my life. A certain Manichaean bishop called Faustus had come to Carthage. He was a great snare of the devil, and many people were caught in the snare through the charm of his persuasive speech. As for myself, although I admired it, I was nevertheless able to distinguish between the charm of his style and the truth about the matters which I was so eager to probe. I was looking, not so much to the quality of the vessel in which his talk was served up, as to the actual knowledge which that Faustus, who was so highly esteemed among his people, would set before me for my consumption. For before his arrival, rumor had spoken of his great learning in all reputable studies and of his outstanding scholarship in the liberal arts.

[23] For nearly the whole of that period of nine years, when I listened to the Manichaeans with an unsettled mind, I was looking forward to the arrival of this Faustus with a yearning that was not sufficiently controlled. The others, to whom chance had introduced me, promised me Faustus when they themselves were unable to answer the questions I posed about the matters which concerned me. They said that, on his arrival and in discussion with him, these questions, and any more difficult ones I might care to pose, would be most lucidly disentangled. When he came, therefore, I found him agreeable and pleasant in speech, and yet his chatter was on the same lines as what all the others indulged in, although he employed a good deal more charm.

But where my thirst was concerned, what use was the most elegant bearer of the most precious cups? Already my ears had had more than enough of such chatter. I did not consider it one whit better because it was better expressed or truer

[22] *Confessions,* v, 3.
[23] *Confessions,* v, 6–8.

because it was eloquent. I did not infer that Faustus' soul was wise because his face was comely and his speech attractive. Clearly those who promised him to me were not good judges of content; they looked on him as prudent and wise just because they enjoyed hearing him speak.

But I have realized that there is another kind of person who is suspicious even of truth and who is unwilling to accept it if it is spoken in language which is polished and eloquent. Now You had already taught me, O my God, in marvellous and secret ways, and it is because I know the truth that I believe that You are my teacher. There is no teacher of truth except You, wherever or from whatever source truth shines upon me. It was therefore from You that I had learned that the truth of what is said should not be judged by the eloquence of the diction any more than something should be judged untrue just because the signs uttered by the lips have a disordered sound. Again, a statement is not true just because it is spoken in an uneducated manner or is not false merely because the style of speech is elegant. Now wisdom and foolishness are like good and bad food in the following respect. Just as each kind of food can be served in elegant or in homely dishes, so wisdom or folly can be dished up in language which is either ornate or plain.

Therefore the eagerness with which I had waited so long for Faustus was certainly satisfied by his actions and attitudes in debate and by his language, which was appropriate and which he matched with great ease to the expression of his views. I was thus pleased and joined with many others in praising and extolling him, and I was even among the most vocal of them. But I was annoyed that, because of the pressure of his congregation around him, I was not permitted to bring him the anxious questions in my mind, and to share them with him in informal discussion in a situation allowing for an exchange of ideas. When this opportunity did occur and, along with my friends, I was able to address myself to him at a time which was suitable for mutual conversation, I brought out certain problems which were troubling me. At once I found him ignorant of all the liberal disciplines except grammar, and even there he was only moderately well-informed. He had read some of Cicero's speeches, a very few books of Seneca, and such writings of his own sect as had been written coherently in Latin. With this and the daily practice he had in speaking, he was equipped with an eloquence which was more acceptable and attractive since his abilities were well-controlled and he possessed a kind of natural grace.

Is this not so just as I remember it, O my God, Judge of my conscience? My heart and my memory are open to You, who were dealing with me at that time according to the secret mystery of Your providence, and who were already setting my shameful errors before my face so that I should see and hate them.

For when I was convinced that Faustus was ignorant of those arts in which I had thought that he excelled, I began to despair of his being able to clear up and resolve the problems which were troubling me. Yet, of course, he could have been ignorant in regard to these, while still having a grasp of the truth of piety. But this would have been possible only if he had not been a Manichaean, for the Manichaean books are filled with long drawn-out stories about the sky, the stars, the sun and the moon. In regard to all this, I no longer felt that Faustus could give me what I was really desiring, which was an adequate explanation of these matters, based on a consideration of the numerical calculations which I had read elsewhere.* From such a study I could have discovered whether the explanations were really as the Manichaean books said they were, or at least whether equally good explanations could be got from these books. But when I brought out these questions for consideration and discussion, then with his great modesty he would not venture to take up the challenge. For he knew that he did not know these things, and he was not ashamed to admit it. He was not the sort of garrulous

* That is, in the books of writers on astronomy.

person, many of whom I had endured, who would make the attempt to teach me and yet would say nothing at all. He had a heart which was not rightly disposed toward You but which, in spite of that, showed a proper degree of caution with respect to himself. He was not altogether ignorant of his own ignorance, and he had no desire to become rashly involved in a discussion of matters from which he could not extricate himself or easily retire. And this quality of his also pleased me, for the modesty of a mind which admits its weakness is better than a knowledge of the things which I desired to know. At any rate, this is how I found Faustus to be with regard to all the more difficult and subtle questions.

This was how the enthusiasm with which I had applied myself to the writings of Mani* was dulled, and I was the more despairing of their other teachers, since, for all his reputation, Faustus had been so ineffectual with regard to the many problems which troubled me. Yet I began to spend time in his company because of the enthusiasm which we shared for the subject of literature, which I was teaching young men at that time as a professor of rhetoric at Carthage. We began to read together books which he had heard of and had wanted to read or books which I thought were suitable to his intelligence. But all the effort I had decided to put out on advancing myself in the sect was completely destroyed through my acquaintance with that man. I did not completely break with the Manichaeans, but I had simply found nothing better than the path on which I had somehow or other stumbled. Therefore, I decided to content myself for the time being, unless by some chance something more desirable was shown to me. Hence, that Faustus, who had been a deadly snare to many people, began to loosen the snare in which I had been trapped, although he had no intention of doing this and had no idea that he was doing it. For Your hands, O my God, in the secret place of Your providence did not abandon

* Mani, the Persian founder of the Manichaean sect; born at Ecbatana about 215 A.D.

my soul, and from the blood of my mother's heart sacrifice was offered to You day and night in my behalf through her tears. And You dealt with me in marvelous ways. It was You, my God, who did it, for "the steps of a man are directed by the Lord" and "he shall well like his way" (*Psalm* 36: 23). How then shall we come to salvation unless through the work of Your hand, making anew what it has already made?

And so You brought it about that I was persuaded to travel to Rome and preferred to teach in that city what I was already teaching at Carthage. I shall not fail to admit to You the reasons which induced me to do this, because in this turn of events, as well as in others, Your most secret depths and Your ever-present mercy toward us must be pondered and declared. I did not decide to go to Rome for the higher financial rewards and the greater reputation promised to me by the friends who advised me, although at that time these considerations also influenced my mind. My chief, and practically my only, motive was that I had heard that in Rome young men applied themselves to their studies more quietly and were restrained by a better-regulated rule of discipline. They were prevented from rushing in a headlong and insolent manner into the classroom of a teacher other than their own; in fact, they were completely excluded from it except with the permission of the teacher. By contrast, the students at Carthage enjoy a degree of license which is shameless and beyond all proper limit. They burst in impudently and, with expressions of mad fury, disturb the order which a teacher has established for the benefit of his students. The intruders commit many wanton acts with extraordinary stupidity, acts which ought to be punished by the laws. But the perpetrators are protected by custom, which shows up their more wretched condition since they are now doing what is in a sense allowed but what, nonetheless, will never be permitted by Your eternal law. They think they are escaping unpunished, when in fact their own blind behavior is their punishment, and they are suffering incomparably worse things than they are inflicting on others. So it was that, as a teacher, I had to put up with habits in others which I had rejected for myself when I was a student. Therefore, I decided to go to a place where, according to the information I had from those who knew, such behavior was unknown.

Approach to Commitment

[24] During the time I spent at Rome I was again linked with those deceived and deceiving "saints," not only with the "Auditors," among whose number was the man in whose home I had fallen sick and convalesced, but also with those whom they call the "Elect."* For I was still of the opinion that it is not we who sin, but some other nature within us which sins. It pleased my pride to be exempt from blame and, when I committed some crime, not to admit that I had done it, that thus You would heal my soul because it was sinning against You. I was delighted to excuse myself and to accuse something which was with me but which was not myself. Yet certainly I was entirely myself, and it was my wickedness which had divided me against myself. My sin was the more incurable because I was not thinking of myself as a sinner, and my wickedness was execrable, O all-mighty God, in that I preferred to have You vanquished within me for my destruction rather than to have myself vanquished by You for my salvation. You had not yet "set a watch before my mouth and a door about my lips, so that my heart might not incline to evil words to make excuses in sins with men that work inquity" (*Psalm* 140: 3-4). Therefore, I was still united with the "Elect." Yet, despairing of my ability to go forward in that false teaching, I began to be more slack and careless in

* The reference is to the Manichaeans, among whom there were two grades of "saints," namely the "Auditors" or disciples, and the "Elect," i.e., those who were fully initiated into the deepest mysteries.

[24] *Confessions,* v, 10.

my attention to those principles with which I had decided to rest content as long as I found nothing better.

Now the thought also suggested itself to me that those philosophers called the Academics* were wiser than the others, because they thought that everything should be held in doubt, and that it is impossible for men to discover any particle of truth. Although I did not yet properly understand their meaning, I shared the common view of their opinions when I interpreted them in this way. Thus, I did not neglect to advise my host against the over-confidence which I felt he had in the fabulous stories with which the books of the Manichaeans were packed. Yet I was on terms of more intimate friendship with the Academics than with other men who had not joined in their heresy. I did not, however, spring to its defense with my old enthusiasm. Yet the friendship of those people, of whom Rome sheltered a greater number, made me reluctant to seek anything else, especially since I despaired of finding truth in Your Church, O Lord of heaven and earth, Creator of all things visible and invisible. For the Manichaeans had turned me against Your Church, and it seemed very unseemly to believe that You were endowed with the form of human flesh and were contained within the physical outlines of our limbs. The greatest and practically the only cause of my unavoidable error was that, when I wanted to think of my God, I could not think in any way but in terms of physical masses. The fact was that I could not think of anything as existing unless it was of this kind.

For this reason, I believed that evil was a substance of a similar sort, which had its own foul and misshapen mass, either dense, which the Manichaeans called earth, or fine and subtle, like the material of air. They imagine this substance to be a malignant mind which creeps over the earth. And because my piety, such as it was, led me to believe that the

* The philosophers of the "New" Academy, characterised by their scepticism. The most famous representative of the school was Carneades.

good God did not create any evil nature, I decided that there were two masses opposing each other, both infinite but the evil one more constricted and the good more widely expanded. From this dangerous beginning the rest of my sacrilegious ideas followed. For when my mind attempted to revert to the Catholic faith, it was continually beaten back because the Catholic faith was not what I thought it was. It seemed to me that I was more observant of my duties to You, O my God, to whom I confess Your mercies, when I believed You to be infinite in all Your other parts, even if I was forced to agree that You were finite in this one part where the mass of evil was set against You. I thought this better than to think of You as limited in all Your parts by the form of a human body. Also, it seemed better to me to believe that You had never created any evil than to believe that anything like what I pictured as the nature of evil had come from You. For, in my lack of knowledge, I thought of evil not just as some substance or other, but as a physical substance, because I had not learned to think even of mind except in terms of a subtle material, which was nevertheless diffused throughout space.

[25] Thus, I busily set about the task for which I had come to Rome, the teaching of the art of rhetoric, first gathering together in my home a few students who had begun to know me and who had also made me more widely known. Then I found that in Rome certain things were done which I did not experience in Africa. It was certainly obvious to me that the "wreckings"* carried out by a set of depraved young men did not occur at Rome. On the other hand, I received the following warning: "All of a sudden many of the young men are planning to avoid paying their teacher's fees and to transfer

* See above note on the "Wreckers," p. 46.
[25] *Confessions,* v, 12.

themselves to another teacher. They are people who have no sense of honesty and who have small regard for justice compared with the love of money." My heart also hated them, although not with a perfect hatred. For it is possible that I hated them more for what I was to suffer at their hands than for the mere fact that they were committing unlawful acts.

[26] Thus, when a message came from Milan to the city prefect at Rome, asking him to provide a teacher of rhetoric for Milan, a travel warrant being provided at public expense, I became a candidate for the position with the support of those very ones who were under the influence of the Manichaean vanities. In fact, my reason for applying was to be free of them, although neither they nor I realized this at the time. I wanted Symmachus*, who was prefect at the time, to prescribe a trial speech for me and, when he had approved it, to send me to Milan. Consequently, I did come to Milan and to Ambrose the bishop, well-known as one of the best men of his time, a devout worshipper of You, one whose eloquence was at that time actively serving to Your people the fatness of Your wheat, the joy of Your oil, and the sober intoxication of Your wine. You thus led me to Ambrose without my knowing it so that, in full consciousness of what I was doing, I should be led by him to You. That man of God received me as a father, and in a manner becoming a bishop he welcomed my arrival at Milan. I developed a love for him, not in the first place as a teacher of truth, because I had completely despaired of finding truth in Your Church, but as one who was kind to me. I listened carefully when he preached among his people, although my motive was not right. In fact, I was studying his eloquence to see whether it equalled his reputation or reached a higher or lower water mark than was prom-

* Symmachus, a strong defender of paganism and himself an orator of repute.

[26] *Confessions,* v, 13.

ised. I used to hang intently on his words, having little interest in his subject matter and in fact being contemptuous of it, while I took pleasure in the charm of his talk. Yet, although it was the talk of a more learned man, it was less cheerful and pleasing than Faustus' talk, that is, as far as the manner of speaking was concerned. In regard to the subject matter there was no comparison. Whereas Faustus was wandering about among the Manichaean deceptions, Ambrose was teaching the doctrine of salvation in a most wholesome manner. But salvation is far removed from sinners of the sort that I was at that time, and yet slowly but surely I was coming nearer, even though I did not yet know it.

[27] I was searching for the origin of evil, but my search was being conducted in the wrong way and I could not yet see the wrong inherent in my search. Before the gaze of my mind I used to lay out the whole of creation, including both what we are able to see there—for example, earth, sea, air, stars, trees and mortal living things—and what we cannot see—like the firmament of the Heaven above us and all its angels and spiritual inhabitants—although I saw even the latter as set here and there, each in its own place, according to my imagination. So I made Your Creation into one vast mass, distinguished according to the various kinds of physical things in it, whether they were actually physical objects or merely such things as I imagined spirits to be. The vast size of this mass was not measured by its actual bulk, for I could not know how big that was. I made it as large as pleased my fancy, although it was certainly finite on every side. But I saw You, O Lord, encompassing and penetrating this mass on every side, but everywhere infinite, like a sea spreading across immeasurable distances on this side and that, and yet only a sea. Also, it was as if this sea had within itself some sort of

[27] *Confessions*, vii, 5.

sponge, huge and yet finite, a sponge filled in every part from that immense sea. Thus, when I thought of Your Creation as finite but full of Your infinity, I used to say: Here is God and here is what God has made. And God is good and most mightily and exceedingly superior to all this. Yet it is a good God who has made it good. Look, how He encompasses and fills the whole! Where then is evil? What is its source, and how has it crept in here? What is its root? And its seed? Has it absolutely no existence? But why then are we afraid of and on our guard against what does not exist? On the other hand, if our fear is without foundation, then the fear itself, by which the heart is pricked and tortured for no reason, is evil. It is all the more serious an evil, if what we fear has no existence and yet we are afraid of it. Therefore, either there is something evil which we fear or the fact that we are afraid is itself evil.

Where then does evil come from, when God, who has made all these things, is good? It was the greater and supreme good who made the lesser goods; but both the Creator and what He has created are all good. Where does evil come from? Was there some evil matter from which He made all this, matter which He shaped and ordered but in which he left something which He did not convert into good? Why should this be? Was it possible that He could be impotent to change and alter this material as a whole, so that no evil should remain in it, while He nevertheless remained omnipotent? Finally, why did He want to make anything from it instead of causing it, by the same omnipotence, to cease existing entirely? Was it possible that this material really existed against His will? If it was eternal, why did He permit it to exist so long through the infinite periods of past times and then so long afterward decide to make something from it? Or at the time when He did suddenly wish to act, surely, being omnipotent, He would rather have made it cease to exist, so that He should exist alone as the true, supreme and infinite good. Or if it was a bad thing that He, who was good, should fail to construct and establish something good, could He not have removed and annihilated that evil matter and formed good matter from which to create everything? For He would not be omnipotent if he were unable to establish something good except with the help of matter which He himself had not created.

Such were the thoughts which I turned over within my unhappy breast, oppressed as it was by a gnawing worry that I should die without discovering the truth. But the faith of Your Christ, our Lord and Saviour, as held by the Catholic Church, was firmly fixed in my heart, although in many respects it was still not well formed and still diverged from the rules of doctrine. Yet my mind did not abandon this faith; in fact, as day followed day, it drank more deeply of it.

[28] In the first place, You desired to show me how You "resist the proud but give grace to the humble" *(James* 4: 6) and with what great mercy the way of humility has been shown to men in that "the Word was made flesh and dwelt among men" *(John* 1: 14). Therefore, through the agency of a man who was swollen with very great pride, You procured for me some books of the Platonists* translated from Greek into Latin. In those books I found the following argument, fully supported by many different reasons although not in the same words: "In the beginning was the Word and the Word was with God and the Word was God. The same was in the beginning with God. All things were made by Him and without Him was not anything made that was made. In Him was life and the life was the light of men. And the light shineth in darkness, and the darkness comprehended it not." I also read that, although the soul of man "bears witness of the light," it is nevertheless not itself the light, but that the Word, that is God Himself, is "the true light which lighteth every man that

* Probably the writings of the neo-Platonists. In *The City of God,* viii, 12, Augustine lists the most prominent of these—Plotinus, Iamblichus and Porphyry.

[28] *Confessions,* vii, 9.

cometh into the world"; and also that "He was in the world, and the world was made by Him, and the world knew Him not." But what I did not read in those books was that "He came into His own, and His own received Him not. But as many as received Him, to them gave He power to become the sons of God, even to them that believe on His name." (*John* 1: 1-12).

[29] All of this then suggested to me that I should turn again to myself. So I entered into the depths of my being under Your guidance, and I was able to do it because You helped me. I entered and with the eye of my soul, such as it was, I saw above the eye of my soul and above my mind the unchangeable light. It was not that common sunlight which is open to the eye of the flesh, nor was it, as it were, a greater light of the same kind, as if this sunlight of ours were shining with a much more intense brilliance and were filling everything with its greatness. This other light was different – completely different – from all lights of that kind. It was not above my mind as oil lies above water or as the sky is over and above the earth. Rather it was above me because it made me, and I was beneath it because I was made by it. It is the man who knows truth who knows that light, and he who knows that light knows eternity.

[30] Now that I had read the books of the Platonists, who suggested that I should search for an immaterial truth, I came to see Your "invisible things which are understood by the things that are made" (*Romans* 1:20). And, although I fell

[29] *Confessions,* vii, 10.
[30] *Confessions,* vii, 20.

back, I realized nevertheless what it was that I was not allowed to behold due to the darkness of my mind. I was sure that You are infinite, but not diffused throughout space, whether finite or infinite. I was convinced that You really exist, never different or varying either in any part of You or by any motion, and that all other things derive from You. The fact that these things exist was the surest proof of Your existence. I was completely certain of all this, and yet I was too weak to enjoy You. I certainly chattered on as if I were knowledgeable, but, if I had not searched out Your way in Christ, our Saviour, I would have been, not knowledgeable, but ready for destruction. For now, being overwhelmed with my punishment, I had begun to have the desire to appear wise, and, far from indulging in tears, I was rather inflated with knowledge. Where then was that charity, which builds on the foundation of humility, which is Jesus Christ? When would those books teach me that? Yet I believe it was Your will that I should encounter those books before I made a study of the Scriptures. Your purpose was that the impression made on me by the books of the Platonists should be stamped on my memory. Then when, at a later time, I was tamed through the reading of Your books and my wounds were touched by Your healing fingers, I might clearly see the difference between presumption and confession, between those who see where they must go but do not see the way, and those who do see the way which leads to that blessed country which should be not only seen but also dwelt in. If I had been first formed by Your Holy Scriptures so that You had become sweet to me through my familiarity with them and then at a later stage I had come upon those books of the Platonists, they could possibly have snatched me away from the solid ground of piety. And, even if I had remained firm in that wholesome state of mind which I had drawn from the Scriptures, I might have imagined that that state of mind could be developed by studying the books of the Platonists and no others.

[31]What was there that remained unsaid within myself? With what lashes of rebuke did I not scourge my soul, that it should follow after me as I strove to go after You? Yet my soul recoiled and would not go, although it found no excuses for itself. All arguments had been used up and refuted. There remained only a silent trembling, and my soul experienced a fear as of death lest the flow of habit, which was the very cause of its wasting away, should be broken.

In the midst of this great struggle in my inner dwelling place, a struggle which I had stirred up against my own soul in that chamber of ours which is the heart, I seized upon Alypius and called out to him with a countenance as troubled as was my mind: "What is the matter with us? What is this that you have heard? The uneducated rise up and seize upon heaven by force. Yet here we are with all our learning—look how we wallow in flesh and blood! Because they have gone ahead of us, is there any reason why we should be ashamed of following them? Are we not ashamed that we do not even follow?" These were the sort of words I uttered, and then my seething passion tore me away from Alypius, who stood silent, gazing at me in astonishment. For I did not sound like myself. My brow, cheeks, eyes, color and the manner of my speech gave a clearer indication of my mind than the words I uttered. Attached to our lodging there was a small garden, of which we had the use, as we had of the whole house since its master did not live there. The tumult in my breast had brought me to this place, for here nobody could interrupt that fiery struggle into which I had entered with myself until it should reach its outcome in the way in which You knew that it would, although the issue was hidden from me. I was raving with a health-giving madness and dying so that I might live, knowing what an evil thing I was and yet not knowing what a good thing I was soon to be. I went into the garden with Alypius close after me, for his presence was never an in-

[31] *Confessions*, viii, 7–8.

vasion of my privacy. How indeed could he leave me alone in that state? We sat down as far away from the house as possible. I was groaning in spirit, raging against myself with seething indignation, because I was not going over to Your will and covenant, O my God, where all my bones were calling out that I should go and which they were extolling to the skies. But the journey there was not to be done in ships, in chariots or on foot, like the journey from the house to the place where we were sitting. To make this other journey, and indeed to arrive at the destination, was merely a matter of making an effort of the will, but the will had to be strong and whole. It was not a matter of my soul engaging in a wrestling match with itself, turning and twisting this way and that in its half-wounded condition, with one part of it struggling in conflict with another which was tumbled to the ground.

Finally, amid all this turmoil of indecision, I made many physical movements of the kind that men sometimes want to make and cannot, either because they do not have the limbs or because their limbs are bound by chains, or weakened by infirmity, or prevented by some other cause. If I tore my hair, beat my forehead, locked my fingers together and clasped my knees, I did it all because I willed it. But I could have willed it, and yet not have been able to carry it out, that is, if my limbs' power of motion did not answer the command. So I performed many actions in regard to which the will to do them was not the same thing as the ability to carry them out. Yet I did not do what I wanted to do with an incomparably greater desire, although I would soon be able to do it when my will would support me; for soon, when I did will, my will would be complete. For in that matter the power to act was merely the will to act, and to will was simply to do. Yet the act was not done. My body found it easy to obey my soul's slightest command to move its limbs at its pleasure. It was otherwise with my soul itself, which did not find it as easy to carry out its own great resolution with an action of the mere will alone.

The Climax of Faith

[32]Thus, I was sick and in torture, accusing myself far more bitterly than I had been accustomed to do, twisting and turning myself in my chain until it should be completely broken, that chain by which I was now so slightly held. Yet it was still holding me, and You stood over me in my secret depths, O Lord, and in the severity of Your mercy You redoubled the lashes of fear and shame, lest I should slacken my efforts again and that slender tie which remained might not be broken, but should become strong again and bind me more tightly. For I went on saying within myself, "Come, let it be done now; let it be done now," and with the very words I was already moving toward a resolve. Now I almost made it, but not quite; yet I was not slipping back into my former state, but was standing hard-by and drawing my breath. And now I was trying again and was still a little nearer and yet still a little nearer. And now, now I was all but touching and grasping it; and yet I was not there, nor was I actually touching and grasping it, still hesitating, as I was, to become dead to death and to become alive to life. The lower state, to which I had become accustomed, was stronger within me than the better state, which was quite untried by me. Thus, the more closely the point of time approached in which I was to become different, the greater was the horror it inspired in me. Yet it did not force me back; it did not turn me away, but merely held me in suspense.

Those trifles of trifles and vanities of vanities, my mistresses of former times, kept me back, and, softly plucking at the garment of my flesh, murmured softly, "Are you sending us away?" and "Shall we not be with you now or forever more from this time on? From this moment, shall this thing or that be forbidden to you forever?" What were they suggesting by saying "this thing or that," as I have written it? What were they suggesting, my God? Let Your mercy keep it away from

[32] *Confessions,* viii, 11–12.

the soul of Your servant! What uncleanness, what infamies they were suggesting! But now I was hearing them much less than half as loudly. They no longer came to meet me and, as it were, openly contradicted me. But they went on muttering, as it were, behind my back and, as I was taking my departure, they continued to pluck furtively at me, so that I should look back. Yet even this kept me back, as I hesitated to snatch myself away and to shake myself free of them and to leap over to the road to which I was being summoned. For unruly habit said to me, "Do you think you will be able to get along without these?"

But now the voice of habit was becoming very faint, for in the direction toward which I had set my face, and where I was trembling to go, there was being opened up to me the pure dignity of Continence, serene and not wantonly merry, honorably wooing me to come to her and not to linger, stretching out to me loving hands to receive and embrace me, holy hands full of a host of good examples.—Yet I was still too much ashamed, because I still had in my ears the murmurings of those vanities and I was still suspended in doubt. But again Continence seemed to speak to me: "Make yourself deaf against those unclean bodily members of yours, so that they may be destroyed. They speak to you of delights, but not of such delights as the law of the Lord, your God, knows." This was the argument which went on in my heart, an argument concerning myself and at the same time against myself. In the meantime Alypius kept by my side and silently waited for the outcome of this unusual excitement within me.

But when deep reflection had drawn out all my wretchedness from my secret depths and piled it up in the full sight of my heart, a great tempest broke out, bringing a heavy rain of tears. So that I might pour them forth without restraint and with all their proper expressions I withdrew from Alypius, feeling that solitude was more appropriate to the business of weeping. I went far enough away from him that his presence should not be an additional burden to me. This was my state at the time and he was aware of it, for I suppose I had said something which made it apparent that my voice was now choked with tears. Thus, I had risen to my feet, but he remained where we had been sitting, filled with amazement. I stretched myself out – I know not how – under a certain fig tree, giving full reign to my tears, and they poured forth from my eyes, an acceptable sacrifice unto Thee. And I uttered many things, indeed not in these exact words, but this was my drift: "How long, Lord? How long? Wilt Thou be angry forever? O remember not our former iniquities." (*Psalm* 78:5, 8). For I felt that those iniquities still held me back, and I continued to utter these cries of misery: "How long? Is it to be 'tomorrow and tomorrow'? Why not now? Why should not this very hour make an end to my uncleanness?"

As I was saying all this and weeping with the most bitter grief in my heart, suddenly I heard a voice from a neighboring house – a boy's or a girl's, I am not sure – chanting over and over again, "Take up and read; take up and read." Immediately the expression on my face was altered, and I began to ask myself most searchingly whether children had the habit of chanting a phrase such as that in some kind of game, but I could not remember that I had ever heard anything of the sort. So, holding back my flood of tears, I rose to my feet, convinced that I was receiving a command from God that I should open the book and read the first passage I came upon. For I had heard about Anthony* that, while he was reading the Gospel at a place he had come upon by chance, he received the following advice, as if what he was reading was actually being spoken to him: "Go and sell all that thou hast and give to the poor and thou shalt have treasure in heaven; and come and follow me" (*Matthew* 19:21). It was said that, on hearing this oracle, he had been instantly converted to You. Stirred by this, I went back to the place where Alypius was sitting, for I had left the Apostle's book there when I had

*Anthony, the Egyptian monk and the founder of Eastern monasticism. In *Confessions,* viii, 6, Augustine tells of the impression made on him by an account of the life of Anthony given him by another African, Pontitianus.

risen from the place. I seized on the book, opened it, and in silence read the passage which first caught my eyes: "Not in rioting and drunkenness, not in chambering and wantonness, not in strife and envying. But put ye on the Lord Jesus Christ and make not provision for the flesh to fulfil the lusts thereof" (*Romans* 13:13). I had no wish to read beyond that, nor was there any need, for in that very instance, just as the sentence came to an end, it was as though a light of inner peace flooded my head and all the darkness of uncertainty fled away. Then, holding the place with my finger or with some other mark, I closed the book and, with a face which now radiated peace, I told Alypius all about it. In the same way he told me what was happening within himself, of which I was quite ignorant, and asked to see what I had read. I showed it to him, and he went on reading even beyond where I had stopped. I did not know what followed, but this was it: "Now him that is weak in the faith, receive ye" (*Romans* 14:1). Alypius applied these words to himself, and made this clear to me. So he was strengthened by the suggestion, and with a good determination and purpose he joined himself with me. This determination was very much in harmony with his character, which in former times had been very different from and much superior to mine.

Then we went in to my mother and gave her the news, which brought her great joy. We told her how it had come about, and she rejoiced with a triumphant joy, blessing You who are "able to do exceeding abundantly above all that we ask or think" (*Ephesians* 3:20), because she knew that You had given her much more in regard to me than she had been accustomed to ask for with all her pitiful tears and groans. For You had turned me around to Yourself, so that I desired neither a wife nor any of the hopes of this world, standing in that rule of faith in which You had shown me to her in a vision so many years before. You turned her grief into a far richer joy than she had asked for, a joy much dearer and purer than she had anticipated at the prospect of having grandchildren from my body.

[33]In Your sight I thought it best not to snatch the service of my tongue from the speech market too suddenly, but rather to withdraw it gently, being anxious that young men, who give no thought to Your law or Your peace but only to lying follies and to battles in the law courts, should not purchase from my mouth the arms to serve their madness. But fortunately only a very few days remained before the vintage vacation, and I decided to endure them, so that I might give up my post in a regular manner and thereafter not put myself up for sale again, now that I had been redeemed by You. So our purpose was known to You, but not to anyone other than our friends. It had been agreed among us that the news should not be spread abroad to anyone, although, as we had made our way up from the valley of tears and as we sang the song of degrees,* You had given us sharp arrows and destroying coals as a defense against the deceitful tongue, which offers opposition under the guise of looking after one's interests and which consumes as it loves, just as it also does with its food.

You had sped the arrow of Your love through our hearts, and we were bearing Your words fixed deep in our vitals. Also the examples of Your servants, whom You had brought from darkness to shining light and from death to life, were stored up in the inner places of our thought, where they were burning and consuming our heavy slothfulness, so that we should not fall into the depths. These examples kindled our flame so brightly that a blast of contradiction from a deceitful tongue could not extinguish it, but only cause it to burn more brightly. But because our vow and our purpose would find people who would commend it for the sake of Your name, which You have sanctified through all the earth, I thought that it would be taken as a sign of boastfulness if, instead of waiting for the vacation time which was so near at hand, I brought forward my departure from a public profession which was practiced in full view of everybody. The eyes of every-

*The reference is to Psalms 119-133, known as the "Songs of degrees" *(cantica graduum)*.

[33] *Confessions*, ix, 2-4.

one would be turned on my action; they would observe how near at hand was the vintage time, which I wished to anticipate, and there would be a good deal of talk about my wishing to seem important. What purpose would have been served if discussion and argument raged around my motives and if our good was badly spoken of?

Furthermore, that very summer, under the strain of too much reading and writing, my lungs had begun to give way. I was having difficulty in breathing, and pains in my chest betrayed the weakened condition of my lungs, which prevented my achieving a moderately clear tone or indulging in too prolonged an exertion of the voice. At first this had worried me, because it was now almost making it necessary for me to lay down the burden of my teaching, or at least to interrupt my career for a time, if I was to be cured and restored to health. But when the full desire for leisure to know that You are the Lord rose up and became strong within me—You know about this, O my God—I even began to take pleasure in the fact that this perfectly truthful excuse was also available to me, with which I could curb the annoyance of people who, for the sake of their sons, would be opposed to setting me free. Such then was the joy with which I was filled, and I continued to endure the remaining period of time until it should come to an end—it was about twenty days. I bore it, but it took courage, because the desire for gain, which used to help me to carry the heavy burden of my work, had left me. I would have been crushed if patience had not taken its place. One of Your servants, who are my brethren, may say that I sinned in this regard, because I had entered Your service with a full heart and yet was able to go on sitting, even for one hour, in the chair of untruthfulness. I do not dispute it. But surely, O most merciful Lord, You have pardoned and remitted this sin in company with all my other sins, horrible and destructive as they were.

Verecundus* was fretting with anxiety on account of the

*A teacher of grammar at Milan and a friend of Augustine.

blessing we had received, for he saw that because of his own chains, by which he was very strongly bound, he was losing our fellowship. He was not yet a Christian, although his wife was one of the faithful. Yet she was the tightest chain of all, keeping him from the path on which we had set off. He declared that he would be a Christian in no other way than that, and for him it was impossible. But he kindly offered us his country house to stay in as long as we wanted. . . .

This then is what engaged us – consoling Verecundus in his unhappy state, since our friendship was unimpaired in consequence of our conversion; exhorting him to fidelity in his condition, that is, the married state; and waiting for Nebridius to follow after us. He was so near to us that it was quite possible that this would happen, and in fact he was just at the point of taking the step when the days of waiting rolled by at last. They seemed so long and so many, because of my longing for the leisure of freedom, in which I should sing from the bottom of my heart: "My heart said unto Thee, 'I have sought Thy face; Thy face, O Lord, I will seek' " *(Psalms* 26:8).

So the day arrived when I was to be actually released from the profession of rhetoric, as I had already been released in my mind. And so it was done. You rescued my tongue as you had already rescued my heart, and, setting off for the country house with all my friends, I joyfully blessed You. As to what I achieved there in writing – writing which was now indeed designed to serve You, although during this period of pause it was still tainted by the school of pride; this is attested by the books recording the discussions I held there either with my friends who were present or with myself alone in Your presence.* Other evidence is found in the letters which I wrote to

* The reference is to the "Cassiciacum dialogues," the records of discussions which actually took place at Verecundus' country house at Cassiciacum, near Milan. The books recording 'discussions with

Nebridius, who was not with us. But when will there be enough time to tell of all Your great benefits toward us at that time, especially since I must hurry on to other more important matters?

O God, what words did I address to You when I was reading the psalms of David, those songs of faithfulness and sounds of devotion, which shut out the spirit of swelling pride! I was uninstructed in that love which is Yours alone, being one who was on holiday in a country house and receiving his early instruction along with Alypius, who was in the same condition. My mother was there too, keeping close to us, a woman in appearance but with a virile faith, having the serenity of age combined with a mother's love and a Christian's devotion. What words did I continue to speak to You in those psalms! How I was set on fire with the desire to recite them throughout the whole world, if I could, in answer to the pride of man! And yet they are being sung throughout the whole world, and "there is no one who can hide himself from Thy heat" (*Psalms* 18:7). How strongly and yet with what keen sorrow did I express my displeasure with the Manichaeans, because they had no knowledge of those sacraments and those healing medicines of Yours, and because they were insanely opposed to the antidote by which they might have been made sound in mind! I wished that they could be somewhere nearby at that time, and yet without my knowing that they were there, so that they could look on my face and hear my words and see what effect was wrought in me when, in that time of leisure, I read the fourth Psalm: "When I called

myself alone in your Presence" were the 2 books of *Soliloquies*. Nebridius, one of Augustine's most advanced students, with whom he exchanged letters on some of the deepest problems of philosophy, had stayed in Milan to assist Verecundus in his teaching of grammar. The friends present with Augustine at Cassiciacum were his mother, Monica; his son, Adeodatus; his brother, Navigius; two cousins, Lastidianus and Rusticus; two pupils, Licentius and Trygetius; Alypius, one of Augustine's closest friends, who had been a student of his at Carthage.

upon Thee, O God of my justice, Thou didst hear me; when I was in distress, Thou hast enlarged me. Have mercy upon me, O Lord, and hear my prayer" (*Psalms* 4:1). Would that they could have heard me without my knowing that they were listening. Then they could not have said that it was on their account that I was saying all the things I said as I read those words. If I had known, then I would not have said them; or I would have said them in some other way if I had realized that they were hearing and seeing me. Even if I had said them, the Manichaeans would not have received them in the way in which I was speaking them, that is, with myself and to myself in Your presence and out of the intimate feelings of my soul.

The Voyage in Retrospect

[34]As far back as my nineteenth year, after I had made the acquaintance of that book of Cicero called *Hortensius* in the school of the orator, I was kindled with such a great love of philosophy that I began to think about going over to it without delay. But there was no lack of clouds to confuse my course, and I admit that, for a long time, I looked up to the stars which were sinking into the ocean and leading me into error. For a sort of childish superstition frightened me away from enquiry. But when I became more resolute, I dispelled that gloom and persuaded myself that I ought to believe those who teach rather than those who give orders. I fell in with men* who held the view that the light which is seen with the eyes must be among the highest and most divine objects of worship. I gave no assent to this but thought that they must be covering up in those wrappings something big, which they would at some time or another be disclosing to me. But when I had routed them and got out of their way, the Academics

* The Manichaeans.
[34] *The Happy Life,* 4.

for a long time after the crossing of that sea held the tiller, which put up a resistance to all the winds in mid-ocean. Then I came to that country where now I live. It was here that I learned to which wind I should trust myself. For I have observed many times in conversation with our bishop [Ambrose] and with yourself [Theodorus] that, when God is being considered, there must be no thought of anything material. And so it is when the soul is being considered, for it is of all things the nearest to God. But I admit that the allurements of a woman and of my office (of public orator) held me in check, preventing my flying into the bosom of philosophy, for I intended, after I had achieved all this, at last to fly with full sails and with the force of all my oars into the haven of philosophy—a thing which is granted to only a few very fortunate men—and to rest there. When I had read a very few books of Plato, for whom you, I believe, have a great admiration, and had compared with them the authority of those who have handed down the sacred mysteries, I was so fired with enthusiasm that I wanted to cut all my cables, except that I was influenced by the opinion of certain men. What else remained for me then but that a tempest, which was accounted a misfortune to me, should come to my aid, as I lingered among things that were unnecessary? Accordingly I was aflicted with such a great pain in my chest that, being unable to sustain the burden of my profession, by which I was perhaps being wafted to the land of the Sirens, I cast it all away and brought my battered and leaking ship through to the calm waters I had longed for.

Chapter Two

Basic Principles of Education

In this chapter the basic elements most relevant to St. Augustine's view of education are set out. If man's life is to bring him abiding satisfaction, it must be consistently inspired by the desire to understand the eternal reasons of things. In rational activity directed to the progressive expansion of knowledge man finds the truly happy life. Happiness is, therefore, a condition of purposeful, intelligent activity, a labor of the soul, in which the generating power is Christian love. A man's love may be directed to higher or lower ends, but it is always something specifically directed, which is satisfied only by the achievement of the goal which he sets before himself. Thus, faith, which is the love of what ought to be loved, is the prerequisite of understanding. Without faith there is no direction to human life but only the pursuit of shadows.

The selections below show the vital connection between intellectual effort and human happiness. This is a theme which runs through the first two of St. Augustine's writings *(Against the Academics and The Happy Life),* and which never ceased to inspire his thinking in all its aspects. To educators it suggests that education must be a joyous activity directed by love of what is intellectually satisfying. Education is not an irksome preparation for the happy life. It *is* the happy life.

The Love of God and the Supreme Good for Man

[1]Take the discussions or the writings of any philosophers you like or the laws of any state. Not one of them is in any way comparable with the two precepts on which, as Christ says, all the Law and all the Prophets depend: "Thou shalt love the Lord thy God with all thy heart and with all thy soul and with all thy mind, and thou shalt love thy neighbor as thyself." (*Matt.* 22:37-39.) Here is the whole of physics, because in God, the Creator, are all the causes of all natural things. Here is the whole of ethics, because a good and honorable life is not formed in any other way than by loving the things which ought to be loved in the way they should be loved, that is, God and our neighbor. Here is the whole of logic, because God and God alone is the truth and light of the rational soul. In this, too, is the proper safety of a state. For no state is well founded and guarded except on the foundation and in the bond of faith and of firm concord. This is so when the highest and truest common good is loved, that is, God, and when men love one another most sincerely in Him, and love one another for the sake of Him, from whom they cannot conceal their real motive in loving.

[2]All philosophers in common have sought to grasp the happy life by studying, by inquiring, by engaging in discussion and by living. This has been the one and only reason for philosophizing. Now I consider that philosophers are no different from us in this respect. For, if I ask you why you have believed in Christ and why you have become Christians, every man gives this true answer: "To achieve the happy life." Therefore, the appetite for the happy life is common to

[1] *Letters,* 137, 17.
[2] *Sermons,* 150, 3.

philosophers and Christians alike. But the question and the difference of opinion relate to where this prize, about which there is no dispute, can be found. It seems to me that it is characteristic of all men to seek the happy life, to want the happy life, to desire, long for and pursue the happy life. I see, then, that I have underestimated the matter when I said that the appetite for the happy life is common to philosophers and Christians alike. I ought to have said that it is the desire of all men, both good and bad. For the good man is good so that he may be happy. So too the bad man would not be bad if he did not hope that as a result he might be happy. In regard to good men, the matter at issue is easy; they are good because they are seeking the happy life. However, there may be some doubt as to whether evildoers also are in search of the happy life. But if I could separately interrogate evildoers apart from good men and say, "Do you wish to be happy" nobody would say, "No." For example, take a thief. I ask him, "Why do you indulge in theft?" He replies, "So that I may have what I did not have." "Why do you wish to have what you did not have?" "Because it makes me unhappy not to have it." If it therefore makes him unhappy not to have it, he imagines that its possession would make him happy. But in this he is ignorant and goes astray, since he wishes to be happy as a consequence of evil. Now being happy is a good thing for everyone. Where then has he gone astray? Because he seeks what is good and does what is bad. What then does he seek? Why does the greed of bad men reach out after that which is the reward of good men? The happy life is the reward of good men. Goodness is their work, their happiness, their reward. God commands the work; it is He who puts down the reward. He says, "Do this and you will receive this." But the evildoer replies to us, "Unless I do evil, I shall not be happy." It is as if someone were saying, "I cannot come to what is good unless I am bad." Do you not see that good and evil are opposites? Do you seek the good and do the evil? You are running in opposite directions. When do you reach your goal?

Socrates
To know
the good
is to do it

[3]Because love is a movement [of the soul] and every movement is always toward something, when we ask what ought to be loved, we are therefore asking what it is that we ought to be moving toward. So, if love is to be loved, this certainly does not apply to the love of anything, for there is also a base love in virtue of which the mind pursues lower things. This is more properly called desire and is indeed the root of all evils. Therefore, we should not love something which can be taken away while we are still enjoying it. What, then, is the thing, the love of which we ought to cherish? Only what cannot fade away while it is being loved. It is the thing in regard to which possession and knowing are one and the same. Take, for example, gold and silver, or any physical object. To possess them and to know them are not one and the same thing. Therefore, they should not be the objects of our love. There are things which can be loved and yet not possessed. Among these are things which ought not to be loved—for example, a beautiful body—as well as things which ought to be loved—for example, the happy life. There are also things which we may possess but not love—for example, fetters. It is therefore proper to ask whether, in regard to an object which is possessed intellectually, a man may fail to love it when he possesses it, that is, when he knows it. We see some people, for example, who learn mathematics simply so that they may become wealthy or may please other people. When they have learned it, they direct it to the same objective which they had set before themselves when they were learning it. However, to possess any subject of study is to know it. It may then be possible that a man may possess such a thing, that is, a thing which is possessed by the understanding, and yet may not love it. But however good a thing is, if it is not loved, it cannot be perfectly possessed, that is, known. For

[3] *83 Various Questions*, 35.

who can know how good a thing is if he does not enjoy it? There is no enjoyment where there is no love. Thus, a man does not possess what ought to be loved if he does not love it. No one, therefore, knows the happy life and is unhappy. The reason is that, if it ought to be loved, as is certainly the case, knowing it and possessing it are one and the same thing.

Since this is so, the happy life consists simply in the possession with understanding of what is eternal. The eternal, in which alone we can properly put our trust, is what cannot be taken away from the person who loves it. To possess it is to know it. The eternal is the most valuable of all things. Therefore, we cannot possess it except with that part of us by which we excel the rest of creation, that is, with the mind. Whatever is possessed by the mind is possessed by knowing it. And no good thing is perfectly known which is not perfectly loved. Yet, although the mind has a monopoly of knowing, it has no monopoly of loving. Love is a sort of appetite, and we see that appetite exists in the other parts of the soul. If this appetite lives in harmony with the mind and the reason, the mind is left to contemplate the eternal in peace and tranquillity. So the soul ought to love with all its other parts this supremely important matter which must be grasped by the mind. Whatever is loved must necessarily communicate something of itself to the lover. Thus, it happens that, when the eternal is loved, it communicates to the soul something of its own eternity. Therefore, in a word, the happy life is the life of eternity. What then is the eternal which affects the mind with its eternity but God? The love of what ought to be loved is called charity. Therefore, every thinking man should keep before his mind the precept "Thou shalt love the Lord thy God with all thy heart and with all thy soul and with all thy mind" (*Matt.* 22:37). And also the following words of the Lord Jesus, "This is life eternal that they might know Thee, the only true God, and Jesus Christ whom Thou hast sent" (*John* 17:3).

[4]As far as can be seen, philosophers have aimed at a threefold division of knowledge; or rather they were enabled to see that there was a threefold division—they did not determine that it should be so but only discovered it. The first part is called "physical," the second "logical" and the third "ethical." The Latin equivalents of these names are now commonly used in the writings of many authors, so that the parts are called "natural," "rational" and "moral." I have touched lightly on this in my eighth book (*City of God,* viii, 4 ff.). I would not argue that these philosophers, when they formulated this threefold division, had any thought of God in terms of a Trinity, although Plato is said to have been the first to discover and commend this distribution. He realized that God alone could be the author of all natural things, the bestower of intelligence, and the kindler of love, by which the good and happy life becomes possible. Philosophers have different opinions about the nature of things, about the method of investigating truth, and about the good to which we ought to refer all our actions. Nevertheless, it is certain that all their energies are devoted to these three important general questions. Although there is a confusing diversity of opinion and although every man strives to establish his own opinion in regard to each of these questions, not one of them doubts that nature has some cause, knowledge some method, and life some aim. Also there are three things which every craftsman must possess if he is to accomplish anything—nature, education and practice. Nature is to be judged by natural capacity, education by knowledge, and practice by its fruit. I am aware that, properly speaking, fruit is concerned with enjoyment, practice with use. The difference would seem to be that we are said to enjoy what, in itself and without regard to other ends, delights us, and to use what we seek for the sake of something else beyond it. Thus, temporal things are to be used rather than enjoyed in order that we may be worthy to enjoy the things of eternity. We should not be like those

[4] *The City of God,* xi, 25.

perverse people who want to enjoy money but to use God, since they do not spend money for God's sake but rather worship God for money's sake. According to the generally accepted way of speaking, we use fruits and we enjoy uses. We correctly speak of the "fruits of the field," which we certainly all use in this temporal life. It was in accordance with this usage that I said that there were three things to be observed in a man: nature, education and practice. Out of these, as I said, a threefold division of knowledge, which is aimed at the attainment of the happy life, has been discovered by philosophers. There is natural philosophy with reference to nature, rational philosophy with reference to education, and moral philosophy with reference to practice. Now if we had been the authors of our own nature, we would have generated our own wisdom and would not require education to get it, that is, we would not need to learn it from others. Our love, proceeding from ourselves and returning to us, would be enough to enable us to enjoy the happy life, and there would be no need of anything else to enjoy. But now, because our nature has God as the author of its being, there is no doubt that we must have Him for our teacher if we are to know truth. We also need Him to bestow on us an inner sweetness if we are to be happy.

[5]The man who asks how he can enjoy the happy life is indeed asking just this: "Where is the highest good?" that is, "Where is the highest good established, not according to the perverted and rash opinions of men, but according to certain and unchanging truth?" Now it is generally agreed that man's supreme good is located either in the body, in the mind, in God, in two of these, or in all three combined. If you have found that neither the supreme good nor any part of it whatsoever is in the body, the remaining alternatives are that it is

[5] *Letters,* 118, 13–20.

Hierarchy God Mind Body

in the mind, in God, or in both combined. But if you have also discovered that what is true of the body in this respect is equally true of the mind, where, except in God, will you now place man's supreme good? It is not that there are no other goods, but the good which is called the supreme good is that good to which all others are referred. Every man is happy in the enjoyment of that for the sake of which he wants to have everything else. This is because it is loved for its own sake and not on account of something else. We call it the supreme good, because at this point we can find nothing toward which it can advance or to which it can be referred. In it is the resting place of desire; in it the security of fruition; in it is the most tranquil satisfaction of a perfect will.

Give me a man who sees at once that the body is not the good of the mind, but that the mind is rather the good of the body. We shall not, of course, ask such a man whether the highest good of which we are speaking, or any part of it, is in the body, for that the mind is superior to the body is a truth which it would be very foolish to deny. Similarily it would be foolish to deny that the agent who confers on us the happy life, or any part of it, is superior to the person who receives it. The mind does not, therefore, receive either the supreme good or any part of the supreme good from the body. People who do not see this have been blinded by that sweetness of physical pleasures which they do not see as the consequence of imperfect health. Yet perfect health of the body is the consummation of the immortality of the whole man, for God has endowed the soul with such a powerful nature that, from the overflowing happiness which is promised to the saints when time is completed, something flows over into the lower part of our nature, that is, the body. This is not the happiness which belongs to that part of us which enjoys and understands, but it rather consists in the fullness of health or, in other words, in the vigor of incorruption. As I have said, people who do not see this point engage one another in restless arguments, each maintaining the view which pleases his own fancy. But all of them place the supreme good of man

object of wisdom [= God] is superior to body and mind
God the agent which grants mind the power to grasp forms

in the body. Thus, they stir up crowds of disorderly carnal minds. Of these the Epicureans have enjoyed the greatest authority with the ignorant multitude.

Give me a man who is quick to see that, when the mind is happy, it is not happy in virtue of any good thing which belongs to itself. If this were so, it would never be unhappy. Therefore, we shall not ask such a man whether the highest good, that is, the good which confers happiness, or any part of that good, is in the mind. For when the mind rejoices within itself, as if on account of some good which belongs to itself, it is proud. But when the mind sees that it is subject to change – and this is something understood from the mere fact that the mind may be transformed from foolishness to wisdom – and when it discovers that wisdom is unchangeable, it must at the same time see that wisdom is something superior to its own nature. It must also realize that it finds richer and more certain joy in sharing in wisdom and in being illuminated by wisdom than it does in itself. Thus, the mind gives up boasting and subsides from self-conceit. It strives to cling to God and to be recreated and reformed by Him who is unchangeable. It now sees Him as the author of all the several species of things with which it comes in contact, either through the physical senses or through the intellectual powers of the mind. It also sees Him as the author of the capacity for receiving forms, which exists before any form has actually been received, the formless being defined in terms of what is capable of receiving a form. So it is that the mind experiences a lack of stability, which increases as it loosens its contact with God, whose being is perfect. Therefore, the mind sees that God is perfect, because He is unchanging and so neither grows nor falls away; and that any change by which the mind clings more completely to God is better for itself; and conversely that every change by which it falls away is wrong. Furthermore, it sees that all falling away leads toward destruction. Although it is not clear that anything comes to complete destruction, everyone sees that falling away brings destruction to the extent that an object is no longer what it was. From this the mind infers that the one reason that things fail or are liable to fail is that they were made out of nothing. Thus, their property of being and of enduring, and the arrangement whereby each, according to its imperfections, finds its own place in the complex whole, are all connected to the goodness and omnipotence of Him whose being is perfect and who is the Creator, able to make out of nothing, not merely something, but something great. The mind discovers that the first sin, that is, the first voluntary failure, consists in the mind's rejoicing in its own power, which is rejoicing in something which affords it less pleasure than it would have if it were rejoicing in the power of God, which is indeed greater. Some people, who would be ashamed to place man's supreme good in the body, consider the powers of the human mind and place man's supreme good there. By so doing they assign it to a lower level than that to which the purest exercise of reason would have assigned it. Among Greek philosophers who hold these views, the Stoics have been supreme in regard both to their numbers and to the subtlety of their argument. However, in consequence of their view that everything in nature is material, they succeeded in turning their minds from the flesh rather than from material things.

Among those who say that our supreme and only good is to enjoy God, by whom we ourselves and all things were made, the most outstanding have been the Platonists. Not without reason, they judged it their duty to refute the Stoics and the Epicureans, but the latter particularly and almost exclusively. The Academics and the Platonists are identical, as is shown plainly enough by the succession of their disciples. Ask me who was the predecessor of Arcesilas, the first who, keeping his own views hidden, confined himself to refuting the Stoics and Epicureans, and you will find that it was Polemon. Ask who came before Polemon; it was Xenocrates. But Xenocrates was Plato's disciple and was appointed by Plato to be his successor in the Academy. Thus, if we set aside the representatives of conflicting views and consider the question of the supreme good in itself, you will find at once that two errors come into headlong collision. The one declares that the supreme good for man lies in the body; the other declares that it lies in the mind. You also find that true reason, by which God is seen as our supreme good, is opposed to both of these errors. At the same time, reason does not teach us what is true until it has first made men unlearn what is false. Now consider the question in relation to the advocates of different opinions, and you will find the Epicureans and Stoics engaged with each other in the fiercest struggle. On the other hand, you will find the Platonists trying to resolve the controversy between them, concealing their own views on the truth and devoting themselves only to probing and overthrowing the vain confidence with which the other philosophers cling to error.

The Platonists, however, were not as good at supporting the role of true reason as their opponents were at supporting their errors, for all of them lacked that example of divine humility which, in the fullness of time, was revealed through our Lord Jesus Christ. He is the one example before which, even in the mind of the most fiercely arrogant person, all pride yields, breaks and dies. Therefore, the Platonists could not by their own authority lead the mass of mankind, blinded by the love of earthly things, into faith in invisible things. Yet they saw mankind moved, especially by the arguments of the Epicureans, not only to drink deeply of the pleasures of the body, to which they were naturally inclined, but even to defend physical pleasure as the supreme good. The Platonists also saw that those who were moved by the praise of virtue to abstain from this pleasure found it easier to regard pleasure as having its true seat in the soul, for it is from the soul that good actions proceed and they were able in some measure to form an opinion about these. At the same time, they saw what would be the effect of trying to introduce into the minds of men the notion of something divine and supremely unchangeable, that is, something which cannot be experienced by any one of the physical senses but which is to be understood only by the mind. If they declared that this something excelled the mind itself and that it was in fact God who is set before the human soul to be enjoyed by it when it is purged from all stains of human desires, God in whom every longing for happiness finds rest and in whom alone we ought to find the completion of all good things, men would not understand them and would be much more ready to give the palm of victory to their antagonists, the Epicureans or the Stoics. The result of this would be most destructive to the human race, because the view which is true and profitable would be soiled by the derision of the uneducated masses.

So much for ethical questions. To turn to questions of physics, if the Platonists taught that the original cause of all natural things is immaterial wisdom, and if, on the other hand, other sects of philosophers never got away from material things – some attributing the first principles of things to atoms, others to the four elements, of which fire was particularly powerful in the making of things – who could fail to see which side would be preferred? For the great mass of unthinking men is given over to the body and is unable to conceive of an immaterial power with the ability to structure the universe.

There remains the class of rational questions. For you know that all questions relating to the pursuit of wisdom are classified under three heads: ethical, physical and rational. The Epicureans said that the senses are never deceived, while the Stoics admitted that the senses are sometimes mistaken; both, however, placed the standard by which truth is to be grasped in the senses. Who, then, would listen to the Platonists when both of these other sects opposed them? Who would think the Platonists fit to be classed as men, let alone wise men, if they unhesitatingly declared that there is something which cannot be experienced by touch, smell, taste, hearing or sight, and which cannot be conceived by any image associated with the things with which the senses acquaint us?

Empirical criterion of truth shared by Epicureans and Stoics

What would they think, moreover, if the Platonists went on to say that this alone really exists and is capable of being perceived because this alone is unchangeable and eternal, and that this is perceived only by the intelligence, the one faculty by which truth is found insofar as it can be discovered by us?

Therefore, because the Platonists held opinions such as these, opinions which they could not impart to men given over to the flesh, and because they did not have sufficient authority among the common people to persuade them to accept what they ought to believe until their minds could be brought to a state in which these things could be understood, they chose to hide their own opinions. They contented themselves with arguing against those who boasted that they had found the truth, although, in fact, these people were declaring that truth is discovered through the physical senses. Why should we inquire about the nature of the Platonists' teaching? Certainly it was not divine or endowed with any divine authority. But consider this one point. Cicero clearly showed in many ways that Plato placed the supreme good, the causes of things and the certainty of the processes of reason in wisdom. This is not human wisdom but divine wisdom, from which the light of human wisdom is in some way kindled. It is wisdom which is wholly unchangeable, and truth which is always in agreement with itself. Cicero also tells us that the Platonists attacked those who called themselves Epicureans and Stoics and who attributed the supreme good, the causes of things and the certainty of the processes of reason to the body or the soul. This was the situation after several centuries, so that even at the beginning of the Christian era, when the faith in things invisible and eternal was proclaimed for man's salvation by means of visible miracles to men who were unable to see or imagine anything except material things, we find, in the *Acts of the Apostles,* that these same Epicureans and Stoics opposed the blessed Apostle Paul, who was beginning to plant the seeds of that faith among the Gentiles.

[6]Man, as he sees himself, is a rational soul using a mortal and earthly body. Therefore, a person who loves his neighbor does good partly to his neighbor's body and partly to his soul. What concerns the body is called medicine; what concerns the soul is called education. Medicine includes everything which either preserves or restores the body's health. It includes, therefore, not only what belongs to the art of medical men properly speaking, but also food and drink, clothing and shelter, and every means of covering and protection against injuries and accidents from without as well as from within. For hunger and thirst, cold and heat, and all violence coming from outside the body prevent the continuance of the health to which we are now referring.

Education, which serves to restore mental health and without which physical health is of no help in banishing our troubles, is a subject of great difficulty. We said that, in the case of the body, looking after diseases and wounds—a thing which few people can do properly—is quite a different thing from satisfying the cravings of hunger and thirst and giving help in all the other ways in which one man may at any time render help to another. Thus, in the case of the mind, there are some things in regard to which the high and rare excellence of a teacher is not much in demand, for example, advising and encouraging people to give to the poor the things to which we have already referred, that is, the things which are required for the body. When we actually do this, we give sustenance to the body; but, when we teach that this should be done, we assist in the instruction of the mind. There are, other cases, however, in which mental diseases, which are of many different kinds, are healed in a strange and indescribable way. If God's medicine were not sent to man from heaven, there would be no hope of salvation, because men advance in sin with such immoderate haste. Indeed, even in regard to physical health, if you look to the roots of the matter, you cannot think how it could come to man, except

[6] *The Practices of the Catholic Church,* 52–56.

Person benefited by educator experiences fear and love
Educator (= conferrer of educational benefits) experiences only love

from God, who determines the condition and well-being of all men.

As far as we can understand from the Holy Scriptures, this education we are discussing, which is the medicine of the mind, includes two things: restraint and instruction. Restraint is accomplished by fear; instruction by love. I am here referring to the person who is benefited by education, for, in the person who confers the benefit, there is no fear but only love. In regard to both of these persons, God Himself, by whose goodness and mercy we are anything at all, has given us a rule of education in the Old and New Testaments. For although both fear and love are found in both Testaments, fear predominates in the Old and love in the New. The Apostle calls it "bondage" in the former and "liberty" in the latter. It would take too long to tell of the marvelous order and divine harmony of these Testaments, and many good and learned men have spoken on the subject. It would require many books to set forth the theme and explain it as far as is possible for man. In any event, the person who loves his neighbor tries to the best of his ability to ensure his neighbor's safety in body and soul. The care of the body is, however, always related to the health of the mind, in regard to which he who loves his neighbor proceeds by the following steps: first, that his neighbor should fear God and, then, that he should love Him. This is true excellence of conduct, and it is in this way that the knowledge of truth, which we eagerly pursue, is gained.

Happiness Consists in Knowledge

[7]Nobody is so outrageously stupid as to ask, "How do you know that a life of unchangeable wisdom is preferable to a life of change?" For that very truth, whose source he is asking

[7] *Christian Education,* i, 9.

about, is unchangeably fixed in the minds of all men and presented to their common contemplation. The man who does not see it is like a blind man in the sun, who derives no benefit from the brightness of its light which shines so directly and clearly upon him and pours into his very eyes. On the other hand, the man who sees but shrinks from this truth has a weak mental vision because he is accustomed to the shadowy things of the flesh. Thus, men are driven back from their native land by the contrary winds of evil habits. They pursue lower and less valuable ends in preference to those they admit to be better and more excellent.

[8]How do I seek You, O Lord? For when I am seeking you, I am seeking the happy life. I shall seek you in order that my soul may live, for my body derives its life from my soul. How then do I seek out the happy life? I do not possess it until I say in that part of me where I must say it: "It is enough." How do I seek it? Do I seek it by remembering, as if I have forgotten it and nevertheless know that I have forgotten it? Or is it through the desire to learn something unknown to me, whether it is something I have never known or something I have so forgotten that I do not remember having forgotten it? Surely, the happy life is the object of everyone's desire, and there is absolutely no-one who does not desire it. Where did they come to know it that they should so desire it? Where have they seen it that they should love it? Clearly, in some way or other we do possess it. There is indeed a way by which a man is happy in the possession of it. There are even those who are happy in the hope of happiness. Yet such people possess the happy life in an inferior way to those who are happy in the actual possession of it. However, they are in a better situation than those who are happy neither in the hope nor in the actual possession of it. Even these, unless

[8] *Confessions,* x, 20.

Words + Knowledge cf. 297

they possessed some measure of the happy life, would not have the desire to be happy. And it is quite certain that they do have this desire, for they have come to know happiness in some way or other, and they possess it by some knowledge or other. I am anxious to know whether this knowledge is in the memory, because, if it is, we were at some former time happy, either each of us separately or in that man who was the first to sin, the man in whom we all died and from whom we are all begotten in misery. I am not asking this question at present, but I am asking whether the happy life exists in our memory, for we could not love it unless we knew it. We hear the name, and we all declare that we are seeking the thing itself, for it is not a sound which gives us pleasure. When a Greek hears the word "happiness" pronounced in Latin, he is not delighted because he does not know what has been said. On the other hand, we are delighted to hear it, just as he would be if he heard it in Greek. The reason is that the thing itself is neither Greek nor Latin, although Greeks, Latins and men speaking every other tongue are eagerly in pursuit of it. It is therefore known to everyone. On being questioned as to whether they want to be happy, all would say with one voice and with no hesitation that this is exactly what they want. This could not be unless the thing itself, of which this is the name, were held in memory.

[9]AUGUSTINE: I am asking you what view you think we should take of wisdom itself. Do you think that each man has his own private wisdom? Or is there one wisdom commonly available to all men so that, the more a man has of it, the wiser he is?

EVODIUS: I do not yet know what you mean by wisdom. I note that people express different views as to

[9] *Free Will*, ii, 25–27.

what actions or words are wise. Even soldiers think that they are acting wisely. On the other hand, so do those who despise military service and give their energies and their labor to the cultivation of a farm. This is the work they prefer, and they connect it with wisdom. Those who are smart at thinking of ways and means of making money see themselves as wise. Those who neglect or cast away all this and all temporal things of the same kind, and who devote themselves completely to inquiring into truth that they might gain knowledge of themselves and of God, consider this the great task of wisdom. And those who do not wish to abandon themselves to the leisurely existence necessary for seeking and contemplating truth, but who would rather, with a view to improving the welfare of their fellows, take up laborious responsibilities and duties and engage in the activity of regulating and governing human affairs with justice, also think themselves wise. People who do both of these things, living partly in the contemplation of truth and partly in dutiful labors which they think they owe to their fellow men, think that they hold the palm for wisdom. I pass by the innumerable sects, each one of which sets its own members above all others and imagines that they alone are wise. Thus, because we are concerned in our present discussion with stating in our answers not what we believe but rather what we clearly understand, I shall not be able to reply to your question about the nature of wisdom until I establish what I believe on a sure foundation of contemplation and reason.

AUGUSTINE: Surely you do not think that there can be another form of wisdom besides the truth in which the supreme good is perceived and grasped. All of those people whom you have mentioned, who are pursuing different ideals, are seeking the good and avoiding evil. They are pursuing different ideals because different things seem to them to be good. Therefore, whoever seeks what he ought not to pursue is making a mistake, even if he is pursuing it because he thinks it good. The man who seeks nothing at all cannot make a mistake; nor can the man who seeks what he ought to seek. To the extent that all men seek the happy life, they do not go astray. But to the extent that a person does not adhere to the way of life which leads to happiness, he goes astray, even if he professes and declares that his only aim is to attain happiness. We go wrong when we follow something which does not lead to our objective. The more a person goes astray on the road of life, the less wisdom he has, for he is the further from the truth in which the supreme good is perceived and grasped. Everyone becomes happy in virtue of his pursuit and possession of the supreme good, and there is never the smallest argument that that is what we want. Since it is agreed that we all want to be happy, it is also, therefore, agreed that we want to be wise, for nobody is happy without wisdom. This is because nobody is happy except by virtue of the supreme good, which is perceived and grasped in that truth which we call wisdom.

Thus, before we become happy, the idea of happiness has nevertheless been impressed on our minds our minds. It is through this that we know and say confidently and without hesitation that we want to be happy. Likewise, before we are wise, we have the idea of wisdom stamped on our minds. Because of this connection, each one of us, if he is asked whether he wants to be wise, would reply without hesitation that he does.

Perhaps we are now agreed about what wisdom is. You may not be able to define it verbally, but, if you had no notion of it in your mind, you would never know either that you wanted, or that you ought to want, to be wise. I am sure that you will agree to this. Now I want you to tell me whether you think that wisdom, like the principle of number and like truth itself, shows itself in common to all who reason. Or do you still think that there are as many different wisdoms as there are wise men, on the grounds that I cannot see anything which is in your mind or you anything in my mind?

EVODIUS: If the supreme good is one and the same for all men, then the truth in which it is perceived and grasped, i.e., wisdom, must be common to all men.

AUGUSTINE: Do you doubt that the supreme good, whatever it is, is the same for all men?

EVODIUS: Indeed I do, for I see different people taking pleasure in different things which they regard as the supreme good.

AUGUSTINE: I would indeed wish that the certainty of people regarding the nature of the supreme good equaled their certainty that, whatever it is, it is the necessary condition of human happiness. But since this is a complex question which perhaps necessitates a prolonged discussion, let us consider, generally speaking, that there are as many supreme goods as there are things which different people seek as the supreme good. Surely it does not follow that wisdom itself is not the same thing for everyone because these goods, which men see in it and choose, are many and varied. If you think this, you can even doubt that the light of the sun is one thing since there are many different things which we see in that light; from these each man chooses according to his will what he enjoys through the sense of sight. One man willingly looks upon the towering height of a mountain and rejoices in that sight; another looks at the level expanse of a plain; still another delights in hollow valleys; another in green woodlands; another in the restless level expanse of the sea; and someone else loves to look at all of these or combines some of their beauties to add to the enjoyment of looking. Thus, although there are many things which men see in the light of the sun and which they select for their enjoyment, nevertheless the light itself, in which every man who looks sees and grasps what he enjoys, is one thing. Thus, although many and varied are those good things from which a man may choose what he wants, and may rightly and truly set it up as his supreme good, seeing and grasping it for his enjoyment, it is nevertheless possible that that very light of wisdom, in which these things can be seen and grasped, is one and the same for all wise men.

[10]When we had all gathered together in one place at my request with a view to discussing this, and when the time seemed right, I said, "Surely you have no doubt that we ought to know what truth is." "Certainly not," said Trygetius, and the others indicated by their expression that they agreed. Then I said, "What if we can be happy, even with no understanding of truth? Do you think that an understanding of truth is necessary?" Then Alypius said, "I think that in this discussion it is safer that I should be the arbitrator. For a journey to the city has been arranged for me, and I must therefore be relieved of the burden of taking a part in the discussion. At the same time I could more easily pass the part of arbitrator to someone else than the part of advocate on either side. So henceforth you should not expect anything from me in favor of either side." When everyone agreed to this, and I had repeated my question, Trygetius said, "Certainly we wish to be happy, and if we can become happy without truth, then there is no necessity for us to seek truth." "What do you say to this?" I said. "Do you think that we can be happy if we have not discovered truth?" Then Licentius said, "We can, on condition that we are searching after truth." Then, nodding my head, I requested the opinion of the others. So Navigius said, "What Licentius has said moves me, for this very thing may be the secret of the happy life, namely, spending one's time in the search for truth." "Then give us a definition of the happy life," said Trygetius, "so that I may frame a suitable answer on that basis." "What do you think the happy life can be," I said, "other than living in accordance with what is best in man?" "I shall not be too rash in giving an answer to this," he said, "for I think you must clarify for me what exactly is the best in man." I said, "Who will doubt that the best part of man is simply that part of the soul which all the other parts of him must obey when it commands? Now to prevent your asking for another definition, this part can be called "mind" or "reason." If you do not

formal rather than substantive definition

[10] *Against the Academics,* i, 5–6.

Happy life = life lived in accord with reason

agree with this, ask yourself how you would define the happy life or the best in man." "I do agree with it," he said.

"Then let us return to the question," I said. "Does it seem to you that the happy life is possible without the discovery of truth, provided only that truth is actually being sought?" "I repeat my opinion," he said, "I reject this." "What do the rest of you think?" I asked. Then Licentius said, "I absolutely agree with the proposition. Our ancestors, who are said to have been wise and happy, lived well and happily for this reason alone: they sought after truth." "I thank you," I said, "because you have made me arbitrator along with Alypius. I admit that I was beginning to envy him. One of you, therefore, is of the opinion that the happy life is found simply in the pursuit of truth, whereas the other thinks it impossible unless truth is discovered. Then Navigius indicated a little while ago that he wanted to come over to your side, Licentius. So I am looking forward very much to seeing how you will each support your opinions. For the matter at issue is a great one and is worth careful discussion." "If the matter is great," said Licentius, "then the discussion of it requires great men." I said, "Do not look for what is hard to find everywhere in the world, particularly in this country house. But rather explain why and on what grounds you think as you do, since I feel that the opinion which was drawn from you was not thoughtlessly delivered. Indeed, it is by application to great problems that small men are frequently turned into great men.

[11]Philosophy is concerned with a double question: first it poses questions about the soul and then about God. The former lead us to a knowledge of ourselves, the latter to a knowlege of our origin; the former is more attractive to us, the latter is more valuable; the former makes us fit for the

[11] *The Principle of Order,* ii, 47.

happy life, the latter actually makes us happy. The first questions are for learners, the second for the learned. This is the sequence of studies in wisdom by which a man becomes equipped to understand the order of things, that is, to distinguish between the two realms of existence and to recognize the very parent of the universe, of whom the soul has no knowledge except the knowledge of its own ignorance of Him.

The Motivation of Learning

[12]Because no one can love something which is completely unknown to him, we must carefully examine the nature of the love demonstrated by those who are eager for knowledge. This is the love of those who do not already know, but want to understand, some branch of knowledge. Now concerning those matters with reference to which we do not commonly speak of study, love often arises from heresay when the mind is kindled with the desire to see and enjoy something which is said to be beautiful. This is because the mind is generally acquainted with the qualities of beauty possessed by physical objects from having seen them very often and because the mind has the means of inwardly approving what it outwardly longs for. Under these circumstances the love which is stirred up is not the love of a thing which is completely unknown, for it is known in a general way. Thus, when we love a good man whose face we have never seen, we love him because of the knowledge we have of his virtues, which we certainly understand. Then again, when we apply ourselves to learning, it is rather the authority of the people who praise and teach the subjects concerned which kindles our love. But in spite of that, if we did not already have in our minds some knowledge of the subjects, however slightly impressed this

[12] *The Trinity,* x, 1–3.

knowledge may be, we could not burn with the desire to know them. To take an example: who would give any effort or thought to the study of rhetoric, unless he was first aware of the existence of an art of speech? Sometimes we hear and experience with admiration the outcomes of these studies. As a result we long to master the skills for ourselves through study that we might achieve the same results. It is as if someone who knows nothing of letters were told that there is an art by which a man can send words that are unspoken and made by the hand to a person in a distant place, words which the person can understand, not with his ears, but with his eyes. If the person were to see that this was actually being done, would he not long to know how it was possible and spare no effort to find out? This is the way the enthusiasms of learners are aroused. Nobody can in any way love that of which he is totally ignorant.

Thus, if someone hears a sign which is not known to him, like the sound of a word, he does not know what is meant and therefore wants to know what it is. In fact, he wants to know what the thing is which this sign calls to mind. For example, if a man were to hear the word "*temetum*" (wine) and, not knowing it, were to ask what it meant, he must necessarily already know that it is a sign and not an empty sound, that is, that it means something. In some respects the three syllables of the word are already known to him, and his soul has received the impression of its articulate form through the sense of hearing. What else is required so that the word may become better known when he already knows all the letters and syllables? He must at the same time have known that the word was a sign; this aroused the desire to know what it signified. The more a thing is known, but yet not completely known, the more does the mind desire to know what remains. If the person knew it to be only a spoken sound and were not aware that it was a sign of something, he would ask no more about it, because his senses would have already given him all the possible information about the thing sensed. But because he knows it to be, not only a spoken sound, but also a sign, he wants to know it perfectly; and no sign is perfectly known unless what it signifies is known. Thus, the person who seeks with enthusiastic diligence to know this, and perseveres in the search under the impetus of desire, cannot surely be said to be without love. What is it then that he loves? Certainly nothing can be loved unless it is known. He does not love the three syllables which he already knows. If what he loves is that he knows them to be meaningful, this is not the point now in question, for it is not this which he seeks to know. In regard to what he wants to know, we are asking what it is he loves but does not yet know. We are therefore wondering why he loves, because we know most certainly that nothing can be loved unless it is known. What then does he love except that he knows and perceives in the reasons of things the excellence that there is in learning? For in learning the knowledge of all signs is contained. He also realizes what advantage there is in being skilled in signs, because it is through them that men in society mutually communicate their own perceptions. Without these signs, the assemblies of men would be worse than utter solitude, that is, if people did not mingle their thoughts in conversation.

"Known" object of love is the Idea of "excellence in learning"

Thus, the soul becomes aware of this proper and useful idea and knows and loves it. Therefore, the man who searches for the meaning of any vocal sounds of which he is ignorant, studies so that the idea can become perfected in himself to the greatest possible extent. For it is one thing to see the idea in the light of truth and another matter altogether to desire it as being within his own capacity. He sees in the light of truth how great and good it is to understand and speak the languages of all peoples and thus to hear no language as a foreigner and to be heard by nobody as a foreigner. The advantage of this knowledge is then perceived by thought; thus, what he loves is already known to him. The attention of those who learn is so focussed upon the goal, and their enthusiasms are so stimulated that they busy themselves about the subject and yearn to master it throughout all the labor they exert to develop the skill. Their purpose is to be able to practice what they know in advance in thought. Thus, the nearer a person approaches to the goal in hope, the more fervently he burns with love for it. The reason for this is that subjects are studied more eagerly when men do not despair of being able to master them; for, when a man has no hope of attaining his goal, his love is lukewarm, however excellent the goal may seem to him. Accordingly, because knowledge of all languages is almost universally felt to be impossible to attain, everybody studies hardest to learn the language of his own nation. But no one, even one who feels that he cannot grasp his own language perfectly, is so lazy in regard to this knowledge that he does not want, when he hears an unknown word, to know what it is and to find out about it if he can. While a man is searching for information, he is certainly filled with enthusiasm for learning, and it would appear that he is in love with something which he does not know. But the case is really otherwise. In fact, his mind is under the influence of an idea which it already knows and grasps. This idea makes clear the value to be derived from the communication of minds through hearing and speaking well-known words. It lights a flame of enthusiasm in the person who is seeking out what he does not know, while at the same time he is gazing upon and loving the ideal which he already knows and to which his studies refer. Thus—to take the example I used earlier—if someone were to ask, "What is '*temetum*' (wine)?" and if someone else were to respond, "What does it matter to you?", he would answer, "In case I hear someone speaking and do not understand him. Or perhaps I may read the word somewhere and not know what the writer means." Who then would say to him, "Do not worry about not understanding what you hear or not knowing what you read!" For almost every rational soul quickly sees the value of the skill through which the thoughts of men are mutually made known through the utterance of significant sounds. On account of this advantage, which is known and therefore loved, the meaning of an unknown word is eagerly sought out. Thus, when a man hears and learns that wine was called "*temetum*" by our ancesters but that the word has fallen out of current usage, he will perhaps think that he still needs to know the word to help him with books written by people in the past. But if he thinks that such books are superfluous, perhaps he will conclude that the word is not worth committing to memory. This would result from his realization that it has nothing to do with that kind of learning which is known to him and which he gazes upon and loves.

Therefore, without exception, the love of the desiring mind, that is, of the mind which wants to know what it does not know, is not the love of what it does not know. Rather it is the love of what it knows, on account of which it wants to know what it does not know.

[13]It is in Thy gift, O God, that we rest. It is there that we enjoy Thee. Our rest is our proper place. It is to that place that our love lifts us up and Thy good spirit exalts our humility from the portals of death. In goodness of will is found our peace. A physical object moves by its own weight toward its own proper place. Weight tends not only downward but always toward its own proper place. Fire moves upward; a stone downward. All physical substances are moved by their weights and go toward their own proper places. Oil poured under water is carried to the surface of the water. Water poured over oil sinks below the oil. They are all moved by their weights and go toward their own proper places. Things out of their place are disturbed. Restored to order, they are at rest. My love is my weight. It is by this that I am carried wherever I am carried. By this gift of Thine we are set alight and carried upward. We are kindled, and we go on our way.

[13] *Confessions,* xiii, 9.

[14]The mind is carried wherever it is carried by its love as if by a weight.

[15]If we were animals, we would live the life of the flesh and of the senses, and this would be all the good we should need. When all was well with us in this regard, we would seek nothing beyond it. Similarly, if we were trees, we could not indeed love anything with any movement of our senses. Nevertheless, we would appear to be showing a kind of longing for the things we need to make us more abundantly and richly fruitful. If we were stones or waves or wind or flame or anything of that kind, we would indeed have no sensation or life. Yet we would possess a kind of attraction toward our own proper position and natural order. For the movements caused by the weights of physical objects are, as it were, their love, whether they are carried downward by their heaviness or upward by their lightness. For an object is carried in whatever direction it is carried by its weight, just as the soul is carried by its love. We are, however, men, made in the image of our Creator. . . . Thus, since we see in ourselves His image, let us in the manner of the younger son in the Gospel return to ourselves and arise and go back to Him from whom, because of our sin, we have departed. In Him our existence will have no death, our knowledge no error, and our love no vexation.

[16]EVODIUS: I am quite clear on the point that the freedom of the will is to be counted among the good

[14] *Letters,* 157, 9.
[15] *The City of God,* xi, 28.
[16] *Free Will,* iii, 1–3.

things and, indeed, among the chief of these. In consequence we are bound to admit that such freedom has been given to us, and was rightly so given, by God. Therefore, if you think it the proper moment, I want to ask you what is the source of the movement by which the will turns itself away from a good which is unchangeable and the common property of everyone and toward its own private possessions or the possessions of others, or toward the lowest things.

AUGUSTINE: What need is there to know this?

EVODIUS: Because, if free will has been given to us complete with that movement as one of its natural functions, it cannot prevent itself from turning toward these things. Hence, no blame can be attached to the will when it is coerced by nature and necessity.

AUGUSTINE: Do you like this movement or not?

EVODIUS: I do not.

AUGUSTINE: You find fault with it then?

EVODIUS: Yes.

AUGUSTINE: You then find fault with a movement of the soul to which no blame can be attached.

EVODIUS: It is not that I find fault with a movement of the soul to which no blame can be attached, but that I rather think that there is some blame in being turned to changeable goods after abandoning unchangeable goods.

Basic question: are psychological movements free or determined
if determined, then ethics are irrelevant to man

AUGUSTINE: You then find fault with something which you "rather think" is so.

EVODIUS: Do not take me up on a question of phrase. What I said was, "I rather think there is blame." I meant it to be understood beyond doubt that there is clearly some blame. By the expression "I rather think" I was, of course, dismissing as ridiculous the suggestion that there could be any doubt about such an obvious matter.

AUGUSTINE: Consider the nature of this most obvious truth which has thus quickly forced you to forget your previous admission. If this movement is natural or irresistible, then it certainly cannot be blamed. Yet you are so strongly convinced that it is blameworthy that you think it ridiculous that any doubt should be entertained on that score. Why, then, did you think it fitting to state, or at least to say with some hesitation, what you yourself show to be patently false? You said, "If free will has been granted on the condition that this movement should be a natural one, then the will cannot prevent itself from turning toward these things. So no blame can be attached to it when it is coerced by nature and necessity." You ought to have no doubt that it was not so granted since you do not doubt that the movement is blameworthy.

EVODIUS: I said the movement itself is blameworthy, and therefore I do not like it and cannot doubt that it should be censured. But I say that the soul, which is drawn by that movement from unchangeable good to changeable goods, ought not to be blamed if its nature is such that it has no choice in the matter.

AUGUSTINE: Concerning this movement which you grant is blameworthy – whose movement is it?

EVODIUS: I see it in the soul, but I do not know whose it is.

AUGUSTINE: You do not deny, do you, that the soul is moved by that motion?

EVODIUS: I do not.

AUGUSTINE: Do you deny that the movement by which a stone is moved is a movement of the stone? I am not referring to a movement which we impart to the stone, or which is imparted to it by some force outside itself, for example, its being thrown into the sky. I refer to the cases when it turns and falls to the ground by the law of its own nature.

EVODIUS: I admit that the movement by which it is, as you say, turned back and makes for a lower level, is a movement belonging to the stone – but it is a natural movement. If this is the sort of movement which the soul has, then it also has a natural movement. Therefore, it cannot be blamed for a movement which is in accordance with its nature. Even if it moves to its destruction, it is nevertheless moved by the necessity of its nature. Furthermore, since we do not doubt that the movement is blameworthy, we must entirely reject the proposition that it is natural. Therefore, it is not like that movement by which the stone is moved according to the law of its own nature.

AUGUSTINE: Did we get anywhere in our two previous discussions?

EVODIUS: We certainly did.

AUGUSTINE: Then I think you will remember that in the first discussion it was definitely established that the mind can never be the slave of desire except by its own private consent. We said that it cannot be forced to this disgraceful state either by a superior nature or by an equal nature, because that would be wrong. Nor can it be coerced by an inferior nature, because the inferior has no power over it. The conclusion remains that that movement by which the mind turns its desire for enjoyment away from the Creator and toward what is created, is peculiarly its own. If this movement is deemed blameworthy—and you concluded that anyone who doubted this deserved to be laughed at—it is certainly not natural but voluntary. It is like the movement by which the stone is carried down to earth in that, just as the latter is a movement of the stone, so the former is a movement of the soul. Nevertheless, there is this difference: the stone has no power to stop the movement by which it is carried downward; the soul, on the other hand, is not moved in this way unless it so wills, that is, to abandon higher things and choose what is lower. So the stone's movement is natural, while the soul's is voluntary. This is why, if anyone declares that the stone is doing wrong because it heads downward by its own weight, he is, to put it mildly, convicted of being not just denser than the stone but completely mad. We prove the soul guilty of wrongdoing when we show that it has deserted the higher things and preferred to enjoy the baser things. Therefore, why ask where this movement originates by which the will turns away from the good which is unchangeable and toward what is subject to change, since we admit that it is a movement of the soul alone, voluntary, and for that reason blameworthy. All useful instruction on this matter has this aim, namely, to condemn and to restrain this movement, to turn our will to the enjoyment of eternal good, and to prevent it from lapsing into the enjoyment of temporatl things.

EVODIUS: I see, and in a sense I grasp that what you are saying is true. There is nothing which I realize more strongly within myself than that I am moved to enjoy this or that. Now, what could I call mine if the will by which I make my choices is not mine? I can find nothing. Who, then, is to be held responsible except myself if I use my will to do any evil deed? Because God, who is good, has made me, and because I can do nothing right except through the agency of my will, it is clear that the will has been given to me by God for this special purpose. If the movement by which the will is turned in this direction or that were not voluntary and entirely within our power to control, then a man could not be praised when he turns his will to higher things nor blamed when he twists, as it were, the hinge of his will toward lower things. He would then never need to be warned to neglect the latter and to seek after eternal things, to avoid evil living and to choose the life of goodness. Now, whoever thinks that man ought not to be warned about this should certainly be removed from the society of men.

[17]If goodness leads us to the happy life, then I would define goodness solely in terms of the perfect love of God. The generally accepted four-fold definition of the virtues, as I understand it, is derived from the various forms of love. Thus, I would not hesitate to define these four virtues, although I would wish that their influence were as much in the hearts of men as their names are on their lips. Temperance is love giving itself perfectly to what it loves; fortitude is love easily enduring everything for the sake of the thing which is loved; justice is love serving the loved one alone, and for that reason exercising right rule; prudence is love wisely distinguishing between what assists it and what puts obstacles in its path. However, we have said that perfect love is not the love of anybody but only of God, that is, of the supreme good, of perfect wisdom and harmony. Thus, we may phrase our definitions as follows: temperance is love keeping itself pure and complete for God; fortitude is love easily enduring everything for the sake of God; justice is love serving God alone, and for this reason exercizing right rule over all other things which are subject to men; prudence is love correctly distinguishing between what assists it toward God and what puts obstacles in its path.

Faith and Understanding

[18]Faith, by which men come to believe in God, is partic-

[17] *The Practices of the Catholic Church,* 25.
[18] *The Trinity,* xiii, 10.

ularly necessary in this mortal life, which is so full of errors and tribulations.

[19]Faith opens up the approach to understanding; lack of faith closes it. Who would not be moved to belief by the great evidence of order in created things from the beginning of time, by the continuity of time, which enables us to believe in the past from the evidence of the present, and which confirms preceding events by subsequent ones, and events of former times by more recent ones?

[20]Do you wish to understand? Then believe. For God has said through the Prophet, "Unless you believe, you will not understand" (*Isa.* 7:9). It is relevant that our Lord went on to add this: "If any man is willing to do His will, he shall know of the doctrine whether it be of God or whether I speak of myself" (*John* 7:17). What is the meaning of the words "If any man wills to do His will."[2] I had said, "If any man believe," and this is the counsel I had given to you. If you have not understood, then I say, believe. For understanding is the reward of faith. Therefore, do not seek to understand in order that you may believe. Rather believe in order that you may understand, because "Unless you believe, you will not understand." I have then recommended the obedience of believing as the means of making understanding possible and have said that the Lord Jesus Christ added in the very next sentence, "If any man is willing to do His will, he shall know of the doctrine." What, then, is meant by "know"? It means "understand." Then "if any man is willing to do His will" means "if any man believe."

[19] *Letters,* 137, 15.
[20] *Tracts on St. John's Gospel,* 29, 6.

[21]For the purpose of learning we are inevitably guided in two ways, that is, by authority and by reason. Authority takes precedence in order of time, but in actual reality reason is first. What takes precedence in the course of action is one thing, but what we set higher on the scale of our desires is another. Thus, although to the ignorant multitude the authority of good men seems safer, reason is nevertheless better suited to the educated. Nobody becomes learned except by moving from an uneducated state, and no uneducated man knows in what guise he ought to appear before his teachers or by what sort of life he can become a ready pupil. This is why it is authority alone which opens the doorway to all who desire to acquire the advantages of a knowledge of the most important and difficult matters. The man who enters by this door unhesitatingly follows the precepts of the good life, and this makes him a ready pupil. Then at last he will learn how these principles, which he has up to this point followed without the aid of reason, are permeated by reason. He will also learn what is the nature of reason itself, which, after the careful nursing of authority, he will now steadfastly and capably follow and understand. He will also know what is meant by intellect, which comprehends everything, or rather which is the sum total of everything. Finally, he will come to know what is the first principle of all things, which lies beyond all things. But few reach this knowledge in the present life. Even after this life, there is nobody who can pass beyond it.

There are people who are satisfied with authority alone and who give themselves steadfastly to good habits and right desires, and yet either despise or do not have the capacity for receiving instruction in the liberal arts, the supreme studies. In some sense I would indeed call these people happy while they are alive among men. Yet I firmly believe that, when they have left the body, their liberation will be achieved with more or less ease according to the quality of their lives.

[21] *The Principle of Order,* ii, 26–27.

Now authority is partly divine and partly human. But the true, firm and supreme authority is that which is called divine. . . . We must call that authority divine which not only transcends all human powers in regard to the signs whereby it reveals itself through sense perception, but which also, while it leads man forward, shows him to what an extent it has lowered itself for his sake and warns him not to be enchained by the senses, to which all these signs seem wonderful. It bids him mount upward to the intellect, showing him simultaneously what great things the intellect can do, why it does them, and how little it esteems them. This divine authority must necessarily show its power by its acts as it must show its clemency by its humility and its nature by the precepts it conveys. All of this is transmitted to us secretly and powerfully in the sacred mysteries into which we are initiated. It is by these that the lives of good man are most easily purified, that is, by the authority of the mysteries and not by the devious winding ways of discussion.

Nevertheless, human authority is very often deceptive. But quite appropriately it seems to be most outstandingly effective in those who set forth many proofs of what they teach, to the extent that the perceptions of the uneducated are able to grasp it, and who live in accordance with their teachings. If such teachers were to enjoy some of the rewards of fortune, they would reveal their greatness in the use they make of them and, even more so, in the small value they put on them. In such cases it is very difficult to blame anyone who puts his trust in these teachers when they teach the rules for the conduct of the good life.

[22] AUGUSTINE: Putting one's trust in authority is a different matter from trusting in reason. Relying on authority, however, reduces the distance to be covered and involves no labor. If this satisfies you,

[22] *The Greatness of the Soul,* 12.

then there are many things on this matter you can read which have been written by famous and inspired men who have said what appeared to them to be essential. They have given these things as helpful suggestions to the less well educated and have expressed the wish that these things should be taken on trust by those for whose minds there is no other help, either because they are too dull or because they are too busy with other things. When such people – and there is certainly a great number of them – want to get a rational understanding of truth, they are only too likely to be deceived by arguments which bear only a superficial resemblance to reason. Thus, these people slip into various harmful opinions in such a way that they can never, or at least seldom, escape and be set free from them. For such people it is most useful to put their trust in a most reliable authority and regulate their lives in accordance with it. If you think this the safer procedure, far from making an objection, I heartily approve. If, however, you cannot keep in check that desire by which you persuaded yourself to come to truth by way of reason, you must take many devious routes to ensure that you are guided, not just by reason, but only by that reason which alone is worth the name, that is, right reason; and not only by right reason, but by reason so well-established and distinct from all resemblance to falsehood – if indeed this can be established by man – that no arguments, whether true or false, can lead you astray from it.

EVODIUS: From this moment I shall not seek for anything too hastily. Let reason guide and direct me where it will, provided only that it remain my guide.

CHAPTER THREE

The Psychology of the Learner

A contemporary Augustinian scholar has said that Augustine was "the first thinker who brought into prominence and undertook any analysis of the philosophical and psychological concepts of persons and personality."* Earlier thinkers had looked to the cosmos to unfold the ultimate secrets of reality and of the divine nature, but for Augustine they are all within man himself. Therefore, the whole of knowledge can be summed up in terms of "God and my soul." Augustine's analysis of the functions of the soul in *The Trinity* reveals a long succession of analogies of the Three-in-One. To ponder the vast resources of the human understanding, memory and will is to gain a real insight into the nature of infinite existence, which is the characteristic of God.

St. Augustine's first concern was to establish the immaterial nature of the soul and then to argue against the view that what is immaterial is in fact "nothing." A bag filled with air is not empty, although the air is invisible. Therefore, how much more substantial is the soul, which cannot be perceived by the senses but which nevertheless is the living agent which initiates and directs all the behavior of man. It is the soul and not the body which lives, and therefore it is the soul which controls the body and not the body which controls the soul. Thus,

* Paul Henry, S.J., *St. Augustine on Personality* (New York: Macmillan, 1960), p.1.

Augustine interprets all human experience in terms of the soul's action on the body. For example, sense perception is the soul's taking note by its own volition of the physical effects of environmental stimuli. According to Augustine's hierarchical principle, the inferior can never affect the superior in any way.

The following selections show St. Augustine's acute insight into human psychology. They end with the famous description of memory from the *Confessions,* in which Augustine explores the richly endowed storehouse of the mind. In so doing he suggests the great possibilities of education, which must start from the command "Know thyself" and must move to a knowledge of the nature of the divine.

The Origin and Nature of the Soul

[1]REASON: What do you wish to know?

AUGUSTINE: Everything which I have prayed for.

REASON: Sum this up in brief.

AUGUSTINE: I wish to know God and my soul.

REASON: Nothing more?

AUGUSTINE: Absolutely nothing.

[2]God made man in His own image in that He created for man a soul, in virtue of which he should be superior in reason and understanding to all the creatures of the earth, the sea and the air. Such creatures were not to possess a mind such as this.

[1] *Soliloquies,* i, 7.
[2] *The City of God,* xii, 23.

[3]Why is man superior to the animals? It is because he understands what he is doing. I am superior to the beasts only in that I am a rational living being.

[4]At this point I ought to refer to that place in which you,* in talking about the soul, have repeatedly used my name and said, "We cannot allow the soul to be immaterial as well as a spirit, as the clever bishop Augustine declares." So let us first discuss whether the soul is to be thought of as immaterial, as I said, or as material, as you say. . . . And first I should like to know how you define a body. For, if the essential characteristic of matter is that it consists of fleshly parts, then neither the earth, the sky, a stone, water, stars, nor anything of the sort will be a body. But if a body is whatever consists of larger and smaller parts, which occupy larger and smaller spaces, then all the things I have mentioned are bodies. Air is a body, this visible light is a body, as are all "the heavenly and terrestrial bodies," as the Apostle calls them (I *Cor.* 15:40).

Whether the soul is a body in the sense that air and light are bodies has been the subject of very detailed and subtle investigation. However, you declare that God is not a body, and for this I heartily congratulate you. But you worry me again when you say, "If the soul is immaterial, then, as some people think, it consists of an empty void, of an airy and tenuous substance." For by these words you seem to indicate a belief that everything which is immaterial is an empty sub-

* The reference is to Vincentius Victor, an adherent of a sect of the Donatists known as Rogatists. Vincentius had charged Augustine with heresy in regard to his views on the origin and nature of the soul. Augustine's reply is contained in the treatise, *The Soul and Its Origin,* from which this excerpt is taken.

[3] *The Principle of Order,* ii, 49.

[4] *The Soul and its Origin,* iv, 17–18.

stance. If this is so, how do you dare to say that God is immaterial without fear that the consequence may be that He consists of an empty substance? Furthermore, if God is immaterial, as you have already agreed, it would be far-fetched for you to say that He also consists of an empty substance. For it does not follow that whatever lacks body consists of an empty substance. Thus, if a man holds that the soul is immaterial, it does not follow that he wishes it to appear to be of an empty and tenuous substance; for he is declaring that God, who is certainly not something empty, is at the same time immaterial. There is, then, a big difference between what I am saying and what you think I am saying, for I say that the soul is not of an airy substance. Otherwise I would be declaring that it is a body, because air is a body according to all who know what they are talking about when they talk about bodies. However, because I said that the soul was immaterial, you interpreted me as saying, not only that the soul consists of an empty void, but also that for this very reason the soul is an airy substance. On the contrary, I said that, because it was not a body, as are air and what is filled with air, the soul cannot be something empty. Even the example of your wine skins was not able to convince you. When they are inflated or contracted, what is inside them other than air? They are so obviously not empty that their fullness can even support weights laid on them. But in case you think that breath is something different from air, in spite of the fact that, when it is stirred, air itself becomes a breath, as can be demonstrated by agitating a small fan, then take any concave vessel which you imagine to be empty. So that you may know that it is, in fact, full, press its mouth down into water and observe that no water can enter the vessel, for the reason that the air with which it is filled is holding the water back. However, when the vessel is turned over or placed on its side, it admits any water that is poured in or finds its way in since the air can now escape through the open mouth. This is more quickly and easily demonstrated by action than it is in writing. But we must not delay longer on this point. Whether you understand that the nature of air is material or not, you ought not to imagine that I see the soul as consisting of air. On the contrary, I have declared that the soul is entirely immaterial. This is what you also declare God to be, because you do not dare say that He is an empty void. However, you cannot deny that He consists of an all-powerful and unchanging substance. Therefore, when we declare that God is immaterial but is not an empty void, why do we fear that, if the soul is immaterial, it may be nothing but an empty void?

[5]AUGUSTINE: Do you think that your soul is anywhere else than in your body?

EVODIUS: I think it is in my body.

AUGUSTINE: Do you say that it is only inside, so that it fills out the body like a bag? Or is it outside the body like a cover? Or is it both inside and outside?

EVODIUS: In my opinion it is both inside and outside. For unless it were inside, there could be no vital force in our inner parts. Unless it were outside, we could not feel even a gentle prick on our skin.

AUGUSTINE: Why then do you continue to ask how big the soul is when you see that its size corresponds to the size of the body?

EVODIUS: If this is what reason teaches, then I ask for nothing more.

[5] *The Greatness of the Soul*, 7–9.

AUGUSTINE: You do right in asking for nothing more than reason teaches. But does this reasoning seem to you to be foolproof?

EVODIUS: Yes, since I can find no other explanation. At a suitable moment I shall put a question which disturbs me a good deal: that is, whether the soul retains the same shape when it leaves the body. For I remember that I put this last among the subjects to be discussed. But because I think the question of the number of souls is relevant to the size of the soul, I think that this question should not be overlooked at this point.

AUGUSTINE: Your view has something to be said for it. But first, if you please, let us deal with something which still disturbs me, relating to the size of the soul so that, if it is clear to you, I also may learn something.

EVODIUS: Ask whatever questions you please, for your pretense of doubt causes me to entertain real doubts about what I had thought was already settled.

AUGUSTINE: Tell me, then, I beg of you. Don't you think that "memory" is really a name devoid of meaning?

EVODIUS: Who could possibly entertain this view?

AUGUSTINE: Do you think that memory belongs to the soul or the body?

EVODIUS: It would be ridiculous to question this. Is it possible to imagine or to understand that a lifeless body remembers anything?

AUGUSTINE: Do you remember the city of Milan?

EVODIUS: I do indeed.

AUGUSTINE: Now that mention has been made of it, do you recall its size and features?

EVODIUS: I certainly do; no memory is fresher or more complete.

AUGUSTINE: Therefore, since you are not seeing it with your own eyes, you must see it in your mind.

EVODIUS: Yes.

AUGUSTINE: You also imagine that you remember how far away from us the city is now.

EVODIUS: This also I remember.

AUGUSTINE: Then you also perceive in your mind the extent of space separating different places.

EVODIUS: I do.

AUGUSTINE: Then, since your soul is here where your body is and does not extend beyond its spatial limits, as our argument has already shown, how does it perceive all these things?

EVODIUS: By memory, I think, since the soul is not actually present in these places.

AUGUSTINE: Then the images of these places are contained in the memory.

EVODIUS: So I think, for I do not know what is happening in these places at this very moment. Yet I would know this if my mind were extended out to these places and saw what was happening.

Augustine: I think you are right. But there is no doubt that these images are of physical objects.

Evodius: It must be so, for cities and lands are nothing but physical objects.

Augustine: Have you ever looked into small mirrors or into the pupils of another person's eyes and seen your own face?

Evodius: Often.

Augustine: Why does it appear much smaller than it actually is?

Evodius: What explanation do you expect other than that it is seen in proportion to the size of the mirror?

Augustine: The images of bodies must look small if the objects in which they are reflected are small?

Evodius: Yes indeed.

Augustine: How then, since the soul occupies as small a space as the body, can such great images be represented in it, for example, cities and wide areas of territory, and as many other huge objects as can be imagined? I ask you to reflect a little more deeply on the great size and number of objects contained in our memory—contained that is, in the soul. What a depth, what a vast expanse, what a huge extent the soul must have to contain these objects, although our previous argument tended to show that it is of the same size as the body!

VODIUS: I have nothing to reply to this and cannot adequately explain how all this perturbs me. I laugh at myself for giving such quick assent to our former conclusion that the size of the soul should be limited to the size of the body.

UGUSTINE: Do you think that the soul is something like the wind?

VODIUS: No. For although air, whose movement is, with good reason, conceived as wind, can fill the whole world, it is possible to imagine within oneself innumerable worlds of a similar nature and size and I cannot imagine a space big enough to contain all these images.

UGUSTINE: See then whether it is not better to believe, as I said before, that the soul is neither long nor broad nor high, just as you agreed with regard to justice.

VODIUS: I would quickly agree if I were not even more perplexed as to how the soul can contain countless images of such great extents of space while having no length or breadth or height of its own.

AUGUSTINE You can find nothing among the virtues of the soul which is more perfectly proportioned than goodness, just as among plane figures there is

[6] *The Greatness of the Soul*, 27–28.

nothing more perfect than a circle. If a circle is superior to other figures, not for its physical size, but because of its special degree of symmetry, how much more is goodness to be valued? For goodness excels all the other qualities of the soul, not by its greater physical extension, but by a certain proportion and harmony founded on reason. For instance, when a boy makes gratifying progress, in what is he said to be making progress if not in goodness? Don't you agree?

EVODIUS: That is obvious.

AUGUSTINE: Therefore, you should not think that the soul develops by growing as the body does. It advances by growing toward goodness, which, as we all agree, is beautiful and perfect, not because of physical extension, but because of the dynamic strength which it possesses. If "bigger" and "better" are not the same thing (which you have already conceded), then whatever progress the soul makes with age, and however much it develops its use of reason, it does not seem to me to be a matter of growing bigger but of growing better. If the size of the limbs were the cause of this growth, then the taller and stronger a man were, the more prudent would he be. This is not the case, and I am sure that you would agree.

EVODIUS: Who would deny this? But, since even you agree that the soul develops with advancing years, I wonder how it comes about that the soul, which has no size, is helped by the passage of time although not by the increasing growth of the limbs. . . .

[7]EVODIUS: I am not sure that we have followed through all the matters which usually cause me concern. Perhaps there are some points which escape my memory. However, let us give thought to a problem which has just come into my head, namely, that a baby does not speak and yet, as he grows, he acquires the ability.

AUGUSTINE: The answer is easy. You know that everyone speaks the language used by the people among whom he was born and reared.

EVODIUS: Everyone is aware of that.

AUGUSTINE: Then imagine someone born and reared in a place in which men do not talk but instead express their thoughts by nods and physical gestures. Do you not think that a man who never heard anyone speak would not speak either?

EVODIUS: I would like it better if you did not question me about an impossible situation. How could I imagine such people or any children they might have?

AUGUSTINE: So you did not see in Milan a young man of good appearance and great charm of manner who was dumb and deaf so that he could not understand others except by physical gestures and could not communicate what he wanted in any other way? He is well known. I also knew of a man living in the country who was able to speak and had four or more children (the exact number escapes my memory) from a wife who was also able to speak. The children were of

[7] *The Greatness of the Soul,* 31–40.

both sexes but were all deaf and dumb. They were recognized to be dumb from the fact that they could not speak and to be deaf from the fact that they understood no signs except by sight.

EVODIUS: Yes, I know him well and I accept the other examples you mention. But why do you bring up this question?

AUGUSTINE: Because you said that you could not imagine anyone being born among such people.

EVODIUS: I say that again. For, if I understand you rightly, you said that the children were brought up among people who could speak.

AUGUSTINE: I admit that. But, since we agree that there are such people, I ask you to think about this. If a man and a woman who were both deaf and dumb were to come together and then both be removed to some desert place where they were nevertheless able to survive, and if they produced a child who was not deaf, how could that child communicate with his parents?

EVODIUS Only by using gestures to give signs to his parents, just as his parents gave signs to him. However, a small child could not even do this. So my argument remains intact. What does it matter whether the child, as he grows, develops the ability to speak or to make gestures, since both are functions of the soul and we do not want to admit that the soul grows bigger.

AUGUSTINE: Now you apparently think that a man who can

walk on a tightrope has a bigger soul than one who cannot.

EVODIUS: That is another matter. No one would deny that tightrope-walking is an art.

AUGUSTINE: Why an art, I ask you? Because he has learned it?

EVODIUS: Yes indeed.

AUGUSTINE: Why, then, don't you think that something else which a man learns is also an art?

EVODIUS: Yes, anything which is learned is an art – I admit it.

AUGUSTINE: Did not the child we were talking about learn to make gestures from his parents?

EVODIUS: He certainly did.

AUGUSTINE: Then you should not attribute this to the growth of the soul but to the art of imitation.

EVODIUS: This I cannot allow.

AUGUSTINE: So not everything which is learned is an art, contrary to what you have just admitted.

EVODIUS: It is a question of art.

AUGUSTINE: Therefore, the child did not learn gesture – for you had also admitted this.

EVODIUS: He did learn it, but it is not a matter of art.

AUGUSTINE: Yet you have just declared that anything which is learned is an art.

EVODIUS: Well, then I agree. Both speech and gesture are matters of art in that we have learned them. Yet there are some arts which we learn by observing other people and other arts which are put into us by teachers.

AUGUSTINE: Which of these do you think the soul acquires by getting bigger? Both of them?

EVODIUS: Not both; only the former sort.

AUGUSTINE: Don't you think that walking on a rope belongs here? For those who do this acquire their skill by observation, I think.

EVODIUS: I agree. Yet not all who observe and make a careful study of it can master it, but only those who are exposed to teachers of the art.

AUGUSTINE: Well said. This is the answer I would give about speech. There are many Greeks who hear us speaking more often than they witness tightrope-walking. But in order to learn our language they go to teachers, just as we do when we want to learn their language. This being so, I wonder why you wish to call it an increase of the soul when people speak but not when they walk the tightrope.

EVODIUS: Somehow or other you are confusing the issue. The man who goes to a teacher to learn our language already knows another language, namely his own, and I think he learned that through an increase in the size of his soul. But when he learns another language, I say that it is not due to the growth of the soul but to an art.

AUGUSTINE: What if someone born and bred among deaf-mutes later in his youth encountered other people and learned their language without previously knowing any language? Would you say that his soul had increased in size at the time that he learned to speak?

EVODIUS: I would never have the temerity to admit this. So now I yield to reason. I do not think that the fact that we speak is any evidence of the growth of the soul; otherwise, I may be forced to admit that the soul has acquired all the other arts by a process of growth. If I were to say that, it would lead to the following absurdity: that the soul grows smaller whenever it forgets something.

AUGUSTINE: You have a good grasp of the problem. In actual fact it is correct to say that, in a sense, the soul grows by learning and, on the other hand, shrinks when it forgets something. But this is in a metaphorical sense, as we said before. We should certainly take care that we do not see the soul as occupying a larger space when we speak of it as growing. Rather, it has a greater power of action when it is educated than when it is uneducated. Yet the things which the soul learns and from which it appears to derive its growth make a great difference. As with the body, there are three kinds of growth, of which only one is necessary for the natural, harmonious development of the body's parts. The second is a superflous growth which introduces a physical disharmony, by developing one particular part of the body, while the health still remains intact. For example, it sometimes happens that people are born with six fingers or something similar. When they deviate too far from the normal, such growths are called "monstrosities." The third is a malignant growth which is called a "tumor." Here, too, the parts of the body are said to grow, and they do in fact occupy a larger space, but to the detriment of good health.

In the soul there are also natural "growths" (so to speak), through which the soul is said to be increased by application to subjects that are valuable and that are directed to good and happy living. But when we learn things that are matters of curiosity rather than of usefulness, even though they can always be used for something, they can be regarded as superflous "growths." For example, if a flute player, like the one we hear about in Varro, so delights the people that he is made king, nevertheless we should not imagine that our souls must be increased by application to that art. We would not want to have teeth abnormally large if we had heard that someone so equipped had killed an enemy by biting him. There is also the malignant kind of art which impairs the health of the soul, for example, being skillful in judging sauces by smell and taste, knowing in what lake a fish was caught, or being able to judge the date of a wine—all of these are skills of little value. When the soul appears to be increased by such skills and turns toward the senses while the mind is neglected, this can be classed as a tumor or even a wasting away of the soul.

EVODIUS: I thoroughly agree with what you say, but I am

a little troubled that the soul of a new-born child, insofar as we can observe it, is ignorant of everything and completely unskilled. If it is eternal, why has it brought no art along with it?

AUGUSTINE: The problem you raise is indeed an important one—in fact, I know of none more important. Opinions about it are so conflicting that, on the one hand, you hold that the soul brings with it into life no art, while I, on the other, hold that it brings with it all of the arts and that what is called learning is nothing more than remembering and recalling to mind. However, can you see that this is not the right time to ask whether this is so? For at the moment we are concerned to show, if we can, that the soul is not called small or great in virtue of the extent of space it occupies. As to the soul's external existence, if it has one, it will be appropriate to inquire about this when we begin to examine the fourth question you put forward, namely, why the soul was given to the body. What difference does it make, insofar as the soul's size is concerned, whether it has always existed or not, whether it will always exist, or whether it is without knowledge at one time and with it at another? Indeed, we have already shown that, even in bodies, duration of time is not the cause of size. It is also well known that skill may be entirely lacking to people as they are growing, while at the same time it may be present in those who are old. Many other arguments have been put forward, and in my view these are enough to show that the soul does not increase in size with the body's growth, which comes about with the passage of time.

Let us, then, if you please, analyze your other

argument that the sense of touch is exercized by the soul over the whole area of the body, although we deny that the soul occupies space.

EVODIUS: I would be agreeable to taking up this question, were it not that I think something must be said about strength. How is it that the body, as it grows larger with age, endows the soul with increasing strength, if the soul does not grow along with it? Of course, virtue is usually attributed to the soul and strength to the body. Yet I would never deny strength to the soul, for I note that there is no strength in bodies without souls. Of course, it must be admitted that it is through the medium of the body that the soul shows its strength. In the same way, the soul employs the senses through the instrumentality of the body. However, since strength and sense perception are functions of a living person, we cannot doubt that they belong to the soul rather than to the body. Therefore, seeing as we do that greater strength belongs to older children than to infants, and that adolescents and young men increase their strength from day to day until it is again diminished by the onset of old age, we have an impressive demonstration, it seems to me, of the soul increasing along with the body and thus growing old along with it.

AUGUSTINE: Your statement is not completely absurd, but I usually think of strength as consisting less in physical size and advancing years than in the training and development of the limbs. So that I may prove this to you, I ask this question: Do you think that it is evidence of greater strength when one man walks farther than another and is less fatigued?

EVODIUS: I do.

AUGUSTINE: If increase of strength is the result of advancing years and a simultaneous growth of the soul, why is it that as a boy, when I used to do a good deal of walking in the course of bird-watching, I could cover a much greater distance without fatigue than I could as a young man when I had taken to pursuits of a more sedentary nature? Then also, in wrestling, trainers look not so much for sheer weight and size as for bulging biceps, supple muscles and harmonious proportions of the body as a whole. These are the qualities from which they gather evidence of strength. Yet all of this is of no avail unless technique and practice are added. Also, there are many occasions when we observe men of great physical size being defeated by small or short men in contests of moving or carrying weights, or even in wrestling. Everyone knows that a champion of the Olympic games tires more quickly on the road than a peddler who wanders from market place to market place, although the athlete could knock the peddler down with one finger. Thus, we cannot call all strength "great" in the same sense, but can only speak of it as better for this purpose or that. Furthermore, the features and forms of bodies are of greater importance than their sheer size, and practice is so vital that we have the common belief that, if a man lifts a calf every day, he will be able to hold it up when it has become a bull without realizing that it has slowly increased in weight. On these grounds increase of strength with the years by no means proves that the soul grows with the body.

However, if animals with bigger bodies have

a greater endowment of strength because they are bigger, the reason is that lesser weights give way to bigger weights by the law of nature. This is so not only when they are carried by their own impulse to their own proper places, as, for example, moist and earthy bodies are carried to the spot which is most exactly beneath them, while bodies consisting of air and fire go in the opposite direction. The same law also holds when bodies are launched by some machine, which either hurls or shoots them or causes them to rebound, that is, when they are not moved by their own volition but are under the control of a force outside themselves. If you simultaneously drop two stones of unequal size from a height, the larger one reaches the ground first.* However, if the smaller one is firmly attached to the larger, it gives way to the larger and reaches the ground with it. And if the larger stone is dropped and the smaller one is thrown up from below to meet it, then when they meet, the smaller one drops back, because it has been repulsed by the larger. If you think this happens because the smaller one is forced against its nature to move upward, while the other is moving toward its own place with greater speed, then suppose that the larger is thrown up and meets the smaller on its way down to the ground. You will still observe that the smaller one is knocked back and forced upward, but that on its rebound it falls in another direction and comes down where it is unimpeded. Now, if the two are thrown against each other and meet

* Augustine did not test this experimentally, as Galileo did when he dropped the stone from the leaning tower of Pisa.

in mid-air . . . surely the smaller will yield to the larger and will move in the direction from which the latter has come, that is, the direction in which the larger stone is moving. Therefore, since smaller weights give way to heavier ones, as we have said, the force with which they meet is an important consideration. For instance, suppose that a smaller stone is thrown by a powerful machine with greater force than is a larger stone, which has been thrown with less force or is losing its impetus, and collides with it; then even if the smaller stone rebounds from the larger one, the larger will nevertheless slow it down or even drive it back according to the force of the impact and the relative weights of the two bodies.

Now that we have reviewed these preliminary considerations as far as our present inquiry demands, let us ask if what is known as strength in animals agrees with our reasoning. Everyone would say that the bodies of all animals are endowed with a specific weight, which, when it is activated by the impulse of the soul and brought to bear on something, is capable of achievement in proportion to its mass. The soul's impulse uses the sinews like thongs to move the weight of the body. . . .

Therefore, if what we call "strength" is made up of an impulse of the soul, a nervous mechanism, and the weight of the body, it is the will which supplies the impulse. This impulse is sharpened under the influence of hope or courage but is blunted by fear and much more by despair. Yet fear can cause an apparent upsurge of strength, provided there is still some hope left. The mechanism is controlled by physical coordination; well-regulated health keeps it in order and diligent exercise strengthens it. The limbs' bulk, which is developed by the passage of time and by nourishment but renewed by nourishment alone, gives the body weight. The person who possesses all these attributes is adequately endowed with strength, and one man is weaker than another in proportion to the lack of these things. Often a man who is endowed with small physical weight defeats another man of greater bulk through the smaller's persistent effort and more subtle strategy. Again, the bulk is sometimes so great that, although it is used with a weaker effort, it nevertheless crushes a small opponent who is putting out a much stronger effort. However, when it is neither the weight of the body nor the control of the muscles but the impulse itself, that is, the soul, which fails, and in consequence a stronger man is defeated by a distinctly weaker man because the former is more timid while the latter has more courage, I do not know whether the victory can be attributed to strength. Perhaps we can say that the soul has its own reserves of strength, from which it draws boldness and confidence. Because the weaker man possesses these qualities and the stronger man does not, we can see how far superior the soul is to its body, even in the activity which it carries out through the agency of the body....

If the soul does grow, think how foolish it is to find support for its growth in the body's strength rather than in the soul's own increasing store of knowledge; for the soul merely supplies the impulse for physical strength while knowledge is the soul's own exclusive possession.

[8]What shall I say about truth and also about wisdom, which excels all the powers of the soul, since the soul, which is found to be changeable, is not physically extended in space? Whatever consists of gross matter of any kind must necessarily be divisible into parts, each one of which occupies a different place. . . . In fact, there cannot be any physical thing, whether in the heavens or on the earth, whether consisting of air or of moisture, whose parts are not smaller than the whole, or which can possibly have one part simultaneously in the same place as another part. . . . On the other hand, we do not find that the soul is extended in space or that it has any bulk, even if we dismiss its power of perceiving truth and consider only its inferior power of holding the body together and of sense perception in the body. When the soul experiences feeling in any one part of the body, it is present in its entirety in that part. A smaller part of the soul is not in the finger and a larger part in the arm even though the finger is smaller than the arm. The soul is the same size everywhere, because it is everywhere present in its entirety. Thus, when the finger is touched, the whole soul feels it, although the sensation does not extend throughout the whole of the body. No part of the soul is unconscious of the touch, and this would not be so unless the whole soul were present in the finger. Yet, when the finger is touched, the soul is not present in the finger or in the sensation in such a way that it abandons the rest of the body or gathers itself into the one spot where the sensation occurs. For although the soul is present in its entirety in a finger of the hand, when another spot is touched, for instance, the foot, the soul does not fail to be wholly present in this sensation too. Therefore, it is present in its entirety in different and separate places without leaving one place in order to be present in its entirety in another. Nor does the soul occupy each place in such a way that each place possesses only a part of it. By this power of showing itself to

[8] *In Reply to the Letter of the Manichaean*, 20–21.

be simultaneously present in its entirety in each of several places, experiencing feeling in its entirety in each place, the soul sufficiently proves that it is not bound by conditions of space.

Now let us consider the mind's power of remembering material objects rather than intelligible things, a power which we see also in animals. Cattle, for instance, unerringly find their way through familiar territory and return to their resting places. Dogs recognize their masters and, when they are asleep, often growl and sometimes even bark, which they would not do unless their minds retained images of things which had been seen or perceived through one physical sense or another. Who can adequately conceive where these images are contained, kept or formed? For if they can be no larger than the size of the body, it might be said that the mind shapes and retains them within the body's physical space. But, as things are, the body occupies a very small area, while the mind turns over images of vast areas of heaven and earth with no want of room, although the images come and go in great crowds. By this the mind shows that it has no physical extension. Instead of the mind being engulfed by images of the largest spaces, it engulfs the images. However, it does not store them in some physical hiding place, but seizes them by a mysterious faculty or power which enables the mind to increase or diminish them as it pleases, to contract them within narrow limits or to expand them indefinitely, to organize or disorganize them at its pleasure, to multiply or reduce them to a few or to one.

What then shall I say about the faculty by which truth is perceived and by which a vigorous resistance is made to any images derived from physical sensation which contradict truth? By this faculty we observe the difference between the real Carthage and the Carthage which a person calls up in his mind and alters at his own pleasure with the greatest ease. The same faculty shows us that the countless worlds of Epicurus, in which his fancy roamed numberless times, arise from this same imaginative power. . . . What then is the faculty which sees these things? Try to fit this faculty into physical space, to give it physical extension, to blow it up into an infinitely large bulk. If you think well, you find you cannot do this. You observe that whatever spaces or masses occur to you can be divided into parts by thought alone; for in thought you can make one part smaller and another larger, as you please. But you find that the faculty by which you judge all such things, is over and above them all, not in physical height, but in its own exalted nature.

Thus, we discover that the soul is often subject to change owing to its throng of varying desires, its emotions which vary according to the abundance or shortage of physical provisions, the endless sports of its fancy, its forgetting and remembering, its states of knowing and not knowing. We find that the soul is very changeable owing to these and similar movements, but that it is not diffused or extended in space, and that it has a power which surmounts all such physical limitations. In view of all this, what are we to think or conclude about God, who remains superior to all intelligent beings in His freedom from disturbance and change, and who has given everyone his due? The soul ventures to express Him in words more easily than it ventures to look upon Him. And the more clearly it is able to see Him, the less it can say about Him. Yet if, as the Manichaean fancies spread it abroad, He were limited in extension in one direction and unlimited in others, He could be measured by so many subdivisions or fractions of greater or smaller size according to the whim of every thinker. If this were the case, a part of Him extending to two feet would be eight feet less than a part extending to ten feet. This is the characteristic of all natural objects, for they have extension in space and therefore cannot be present in their entirety in every single place. We do not find that this is true of the soul, and yet this perverted and degrading belief is held by people who do not have the ability to investigate such matters.

The Body-Soul Relationship

[9]This mode of union by which bodies and spirits are bound together and become living beings is thoroughly marvelous and beyond the comprehension of man, although it is this union which is man.

[10]Even if a soul is not wise, even if it is not just, it is still a soul. Even if it is not devout, it is still a soul. To be a soul is one thing, but to be a wise, just and devout soul is another. Therefore, when the soul is not yet wise, just or devout, it still is not nothing since it has life. The soul shows itself to be alive by certain functions, even if it does not show itself to be wise, just or devout. Unless the soul were alive, it would not move the body. It would not command the feet to walk, the hands to work, the eyes to see, the ears to hear. It would not open the mouth to give voice to sounds nor move the tongue to articulate speech. Therefore, it is by these functions that the soul shows itself to be alive and to be superior to the body. But is it by these functions that it shows itself to be wise, devout or just? Surely, even foolish, wicked and unjust men walk, work, see, hear and speak. It is when the soul raises itself up to something which is other than itself, which is above itself and from which the soul itself originated, that it assumes wisdom, justice and devotion to God. When it lacked all this, it was dead, and it had no life by which it should live, but only life in virtue of which it gave life to the body. For the element in the soul by which the body is animated is one thing but the element by which the soul itself is given life is another. The soul is superior to the body, but God is superior to the soul. Therefore, the soul is the life of the body, however unwise, unjust or contemptuous of God it

[9] *The City of God,* xxi, 10.
[10] *Tracts on St. John's Gospel,* 19, 12.

may be. Because it is God who is the life of the soul, He, who is present in the soul, endows it with wisdom, with devotion to Himself, with justice and with love. In like manner, when the soul is in the body, it endows the body with vigor, comeliness, movement and the service of its limbs. Thus, what the soul gives to the body is quite different from what God gives to the soul. The soul gives life, and also receives it; if it is not roused to life, it gives life, even though it is itself dead. Thus, when the Word comes and is instilled into those who hear so that they not only hear it but also obey it, the soul rises up from its death to its life, that is, from wickedness, foolishness and neglect of God to Him who is its wisdom, justice and clear light.

[11]Let us then ask what is better than man. It is indeed hard to find the answer unless we have first considered and discussed the question "what is man?" But I do not think that a definition of man is required of me at the present moment. Almost everyone agrees—or (and this is sufficient) at least those with whom I am now involved agree—that we are made up of soul and body. Therefore, the question which seems to me to be more in need of attention at this point is the following: "What is man himself?" Does he consist of each of the two parts I have mentioned; or is he a body only or a soul only? Although soul and body are two things, and although neither without the other would be called man—for the body would not be a man without the soul, nor again would the soul be a man if there were not a body animated by it—it is still possible that one of these may be held to be man and may be called such. What then do we say that man is? Do we say that he is soul and body—like a pair of horses yoked together or like a centaur? Or do we say that he is a body only, which is in the service of a soul which rules it? In this way the word

[11] *The Practices of the Catholic Church,* 6.

"lamp" denotes not the light and the container together but only the container, although we call it a lamp on account of the light it gives. Or do we say that, because the soul rules the body, man is nothing other than a soul? In this way, by "horseman" we mean, not the man and the horse together, but the man only, for the reason that he is made to control the horse. This is not an easy issue to resolve, and if it were easy to resolve it by reason, it would still take a long time to resolve it in words. However, there is no need to incur this expenditure of labor and time. For whether the name "man" refers to each of the two or to the soul alone, the chief good of man is, not the chief good of the body, but rather the chief good of the body and soul taken together or of the soul alone.

[12]Sensation is not a function of the body but of the soul acting through the body. (*Sentire non est corporis sed animae per corpus.*)

[13]TEACHER: We must give careful consideration to the question of whether hearing is really a matter of something being done to the soul by the body. Now, it is the height of absurdity to suppose that the soul is in any way subjected to the body in the way in which materials are subjected to the craftsman. For the soul is never inferior to the body as the craftsman's materials are inferior to the craftsman. Thus, the soul is not controlled by the body in the way in which the materials are controlled by the craftsman. However, this would be the case, if some of the rhythmical measures present in the soul were

[12] *The Literal Interpretation of Genesis,* iii, 7.
[13] *On Music,* vi, 8–13.

produced by physical causes.* When we hear, however, such measures are not really produced in the soul by those measures which we come to recognize in sounds.

I think that the soul, rather than suffering anything by the action of the body, does what it wills with the body and in the body, which by divine decree is subjected to the soul. Whenever physical things are taken into the body or impinge upon it from the outside, they produce an impact not upon the soul but upon the body, inasmuch as they either hinder or assist its functions. Therefore, when the soul resists an intruder and finds it difficult to make the body, which is subjected to it, persevere with the action laid down for the body by the soul, this very difficulty causes the soul to give closer attention to its function. When this difficulty does not escape the notice of the soul, it is called "feeling" (*sentire*), or more exactly "grief" or "labor." When the body feels a lack of what it needs to restore its losses, it becomes impoverished and the soul becomes more attentive because of its difficulty in functioning. The body's labor does not escape the notice of the soul, and the result is called "hunger" or "thirst" or something of the sort. In like manner, when the body has consumed too much food and its functions are therefore impeded, the soul becomes aware of it, and the result is indigestion. Hence, the soul acts with conscious

*The Latin word "*numerus*," here translated "rythmical measures," is frequently used by Augustine with reference to the rhythms and harmonies of music because these are founded on numerical relationships. For Augustine the study of Music is essentially the study of absolute number, which is given within the human soul and not introduced into it by sense impression.

intent when it ejects what is superfluous. This may be done either gently, that is, pleasantly, or roughly, that is, with pain. . . . So in brief, it seems to me that, when the soul experiences physical sensations, it is not being affected by the body, but rather it is acting with more deliberate attention than usual because of what the body is experiencing. The body's actions, whether easy, because of a condition of harmony, or difficult, because of a condition of disharmony, do not escape the notice of the soul. This is precisely what is meant by sense perception. The function of sensation, which is in us even when we are sensing nothing, is one of the body's instruments, which the soul employs with restraint so that it may be better prepared to give conscious attention to physical conditions, that is, to join like to like and repel what is harmful. . . . When a change occurs in the body, the soul gives more conscious attention to the situation, in which case we are said to see, hear, smell, taste and touch. Thereby the soul joins things that are congruent and fiercely opposes what is incongruent. These are, as I see it, the soul's reactions to what the body experiences, for the soul does not have the body's experiences impressed upon it.

But, since the present discussion is concerned with sound and it is aural sensation which is being debated, we must not wander too far astray. Therefore, let us return to the question at issue and see whether a sound produces some effect in the ears. Do you deny this?

PUPIL: No.

TEACHER: You would agree, then, that these ears are physical organs endowed with life.

PUPIL: Agreed.

TEACHER: Therefore, when that element in the ears which is similar to air is moved by vibrations in the air, surely we cannot think that the soul, which before the sound occurred was by a vital movement silently imparting life to the ears, no longer keeps in motion these organs which it endows with life? Or are we to think that, when the air within the ears has been externally set in motion, the soul continues to impart motion to this air in the same manner in which it was doing this before the intrusion of the sound?

PUPIL: No, it must be done by some other sort of movement.

TEACHER: Then surely we must conclude that this other sort of movement is characterized by positive action and not by passive endurance.

PUPIL: We must.

TEACHER: Then it is not absurd for us to believe that the movements of the soul, its actions or adjustments or whatever more suitable name we care to apply to them, do not escape the soul's notice when the soul experiences sensation. Now these "adjustments" are called up in response to physical experiences which precede them; for example: when visible shapes interrupt the light of our eyes, sound enters our ears, smells enter our nostrils, tastes affect our palate or some solid physical object is applied to the body from outside it, when something inside the body moves from one position to another, or when the whole body is moved by its own weight or by the weight of something else. The soul makes the kinds of adjustments we have described in response to these physical experiences, which give pleasure to the soul when it assimilates them but pain when it resists them. Hence, when, as a consequence of its own operations, the soul has an experience, the experience is derived from itself and not from the body. Of course, it goes without saying that, when the soul accommodates itself to the body, it is reduced in its own estimation, because the body is always something less than the soul.

Therefore, when the soul turns away from its Lord to its servant the body, it is necessarily in a condition of decadence. When, on the other hand, it turns from its servant toward its Lord, it necessarily improves itself and confers on its servant an easy existence very little disturbed by trouble and effort. Because of the body's peaceful condition, which is called good health, no attention is diverted to it; in fact the condition requires no attention, not because the soul is doing nothing in the body, but because no effort is required of the soul. For in all the work that we do, our concentration must be in direct proportion to the difficulty of the task. . . .

The Powers of the Soul

[14]Let us then put aside for the moment the other functions of the mind, which the mind takes for granted, and deal with the three that we have singled out for special consideration: memory, understanding and will. It is under these three functions that we discover and study the capacities of

[14] *The Trinity,* x, 17–18.

children and the ability they display. The more tenacious and ready a boy's memory, the keener his understanding; and the more eager his will to learn, the more his ability is praised. However, when a person's scholarship is in question, we do not so much ask what strength and readiness of memory he displays or how keen his understanding is, as what he remembers and what he understands. And seeing that a person's mind is considered worthy of praise, on grounds not only of his learning but also of his goodness, we take note not only of what he remembers and understands but also of what he wills. We do not look merely at the intensity of his will; we first look to see what he wills and then how much he wills it. For a person who loves intensely deserves praise only when what he loves is what ought to be loved intensely. Therefore, when we note these three attributes—ability, scholarship and the use to which a person puts his ability and scholarship—we first give consideration to a person's capacity in memory, understanding and will. In the second place, we want to see what a person has stored in his memory and understanding and to discover where his eager will has led him. But the third attribute, that is, the use a person makes of his abilities and knowledge, refers only to the will, which surveys the content of the memory and the understanding, using this content either as a means toward some end or as an end in which it may rest content. "To use" is to put something at the disposal of the will, whereas "to enjoy" is to use a thing with satisfaction, which is no longer a matter of hope but of actual reality. Thus, all enjoyment is a kind of use, since it puts something at the disposal of the will for the delight it brings. But not all use is enjoyment; for example, there is no enjoyment when the thing is put at the disposal of the will has been sought, not for its own sake, but for the sake of something else.

Now these three—memory, will and understanding—are not three vital functions but one; not three minds but one; it follows, then, that they are not three substances but one. "Memory," when understood as life, mind and substance, is an absolute term. But "memory" is used with a specific reference, and the same can be said of "understanding" and "will," which are also used in relation to some specific object. But life, mind and essence always exist absolutely in themselves. Therefore, these three functions are one, inasmuch as they constitute one life, one mind, one essence. Whatever else can be said of each of them singly can be said of all of them together, with a singular and not a plural reference. Yet they are three, inasmuch as they are related to one another. If they were not equal, not only each to each, but each to all, they certainly could not each include one another as they do, for in fact, not only is each one included in each other one, but all of them are included in each. I remember that I possess memory and understanding and will; I understand that I understand and will and remember; I will my own willing and remembering and understanding; and I remember simultaneously the whole of my memory and understanding and will. Whatever I do not remember as part of my memory is not in my memory, and nothing can be so much in my memory as memory itself. Therefore, I remember the whole of it. Again, whatever I understand, I know that I understand, and I know that I will whatever I will. But whatever I know, I remember. Therefore, I remember the whole of my understanding and the whole of my will. Similarily, when I understand these three, I understand all three as a whole. For I understand everything which is capable of being grasped by the understanding with the exception of those things of which I have no knowledge, and I neither remember nor will the latter. So when I do not understand something which is open to the human understanding, it follows that I neither remember it nor will it; conversely, when I do remember and will any of the things which are open to the understanding, it follows that I understand them. Furthermore, my will includes the whole of my understanding and the whole of my memory while I am using the whole of what I understand and remember. Therefore, since all three are included in each other, both singly and as wholes, the whole of each is equal to

Conclusion: memory, understanding, will are terms used to label 3 aspects of mind

the whole of each of the others, and the whole of each is equal to the whole of all of them together. These three are one thing, one mind, one essence.

[15] AUGUSTINE: It is obvious that you exist, and this could not be obvious to you unless you were alive. Therefore, it is clear that you are alive. Do you understand that all of this is true?

EVODIUS: I do.

AUGUSTINE: Therefore, it is also clear that you are capable of understanding.

EVODIUS: Yes, this is clear.

AUGUSTINE: Which of these do you think is best?

EVODIUS: The capacity to understand.

AUGUSTINE: Why?

EVODIUS: Existence, life and understanding are three things. A stone exists and an animal lives, but I do not think that a stone lives or that an animal understands. However, it is very certain that the being who understands both exists and lives, so I do not hesitate to conclude that the being which has all three qualities is superior to that which lacks one or two of them. What lives surely also exists, but it does not follow that it also has the capacity to understand. As I see it, the life of animals illustrates this distinction.

[15] *The Free Will*, ii, 7–10.

Furthermore, it does not follow that what exists also lives and understands. For instance, I can say that dead bodies exist, but nobody would say that they are alive. Much less does an inanimate object have understanding.

AUGUSTINE: Therefore, we conclude that of these three functions the corpse lacks two, the animal lacks one, and man lacks none.

EVODIUS: This is so.

AUGUSTINE: We also conclude that of these three functions the best is the one man possesses along with the other two—understanding. Because he possesses this function, it follows that he both exists and lives.

EVODIUS: This is certainly our conclusion.

AUGUSTINE: Now tell me whether you know that you possess the ordinary physical senses: sight, hearing, smell, taste and touch.

EVODIUS: I am certain of this.

AUGUSTINE: What do you think belongs to the sense of sight? That is, what do you think that we sense by seeing?

EVODIUS: Physical objects.

AUGUSTINE: We do not perceive hardness and softness by sight, do we?

EVODIUS: We do not.

AUGUSTINE: What then properly belongs to the eyes? What is it that we see with their help?

EVODIUS: Color.

AUGUSTINE: What is proper to the ears?

EVODIUS: Sound.

AUGUSTINE: And to the nose?

EVODIUS: Smells.

AUGUSTINE: To the taste?

EVODIUS: Taste.

AUGUSTINE: To the touch?

EVODIUS: The soft and the hard, the smooth and the rough, and many other such sensations.

AUGUSTINE: Well, then it seems, doesn't it, that we perceive the shapes of physical objects, that is, big or small, square or round, and so on, both by touch and by sight? So all this cannot properly be attributed to sight or touch alone but must be attributed to both together.

EVODIUS: I understand.

AUGUSTINE: You see, then, that some things have their own special sense which conveys information about them while other things belong to more than one sense?

EVODIUS: I see this too.

AUGUSTINE: Surely, then, we cannot determine what belongs to each of the senses, what belongs in common to all or to some of them taken together, by the use of any of the senses?

EVODIUS: By no means. This is determined by some other sense inside us.

AUGUSTINE: Is this, perhaps, the rational capacity which animals lack? For I am of the opinion that we understand sense data by the use of reason and that it is in this way that we come to know that sense data are as they are.

EVODIUS: I am rather of the opinion that by reason we discover the existence of an interior sense, to which all sense data are referred by those five well-known senses. For instance, in an animal the sense of sight is different from the power by which he either avoids or seeks the things which he perceives by sight. The former lies in his eyes, the latter deep in his soul. It is by the use of this latter sense that animals either seek with pleasure and accept, or avoid with displeasure and reject, the things which are seen or heard or experienced with one of the other physical senses. This sense can be said to be neither sight, hearing, smell, taste nor touch, but is some other sense which is set above all the others. Although we understand about this sense by means of our reason, as I said, I still cannot call it reason since it is clear that animals also have it.

AUGUSTINE: I agree that there is such a faculty, whatever it may be, and am quite ready to call it the interior sense. But, unless the data that the physical senses refer to it go beyond that sense, they cannot become knowledge, for whatever we know, we grasp and hold by reason. We know that colors are not perceived by hearing nor voices by sight, and when we know this, we know it neither by means of the eyes, the ears nor by that interior sense which the animals also have. We cannot believe that they know that light is not perceived by the ears nor a voice by the eyes, since we get to know this because we can rationally observe and can think.

EVODIUS: I cannot say that I have quite understood this. What if animals do perceive by means of that interior sense which you agree they do possess, that colors cannot be perceived by hearing or voices by sight?

AUGUSTINE: Surely you do not think that they can distinguish clearly between a color which is perceived, the sensation which is in the eye, the interior sense in the soul, and the faculty of reason by which all these things are individually defined and classified?

EVODIUS: By no means.

AUGUSTINE: Thus, reason could not distinguish between these four and mark their boundaries unless the perception of color were reported to it by the visual sense and then by the interior sense, which is set over and above the visual sense; the interior sense would then report the perception directly to reason. This is, of course, to assume that there is no other intermediate step.

EVODIUS: I see no other possibility.

AUGUSTINE: You see, then, that color is perceived by sight, but that sight is not perceived by itself. It is not, therefore, through the agency of that sense by which you perceive color that you come to know the sense itself.

EVODIUS: I see that clearly.

AUGUSTINE: See, then, if you can make a clear distinction between the following two things. You do not deny, I believe, that color is one thing and seeing color is another; moreover, it is another thing altogether to have the sense organs by which color can be seen when it is presented to us, even if color is absent at the time.

EVODIUS: I see the difference and admit that these are all distinct things.

AUGUSTINE: Do you see any of these three things except color with the eyes?

EVODIUS: No.

AUGUSTINE: Tell me, then, just how you can see the other two, for you could not make a distinction between them if you had not seen them.

EVODIUS: I do not know how I can see the distinction. I know that I can see it, and that is all.

AUGUSTINE: Therefore, you do not know whether you see it by reason or by that living function which we call the interior sense, which is set over the physical senses, or by some other means.

EVODIUS: I do not know.

AUGUSTINE: But you do know that the distinction can only be made by reason, and that reason cannot make it unless the material to be examined is presented to it.

EVODIUS: This is certain.

AUGUSTINE: Therefore, everything else by which all that we know can be known is but the function of reason, to which everything that affects us is offered and reported. The result is that sense perceptions can be classified within their own limits and understood only if sensing is supplemented by knowing.

EVODIUS: This is so.

AUGUSTINE: So reason itself distinguishes between its servants (the senses) and what they present; it also knows the difference between sense data and itself and realizes that it has more power than they do. Does reason understand itself by anything other than itself? Could you know that you have reason in any way other than by perceiving that you do by the use of reason?

EVODIUS: I could not.

AUGUSTINE: When we perceive color, it is not with the sense of sight that we know that we are perceiving;

when we hear sound, we do not also hear our hearing; when we smell a rose, we do not at the same time smell our smelling; in tasting something we do not taste our taste; and when we touch something, we do not also touch our sense of touch. It is clear that the five senses cannot be sensed by any one of these senses, although all physical objects are sensed by them.

EVODIUS: This is clear.

AUGUSTINE: I think that it is also clear that the interior sense not only perceives the data supplied by the five senses of the body, but that it also perceives the senses themselves. An animal would not bestir itself either to seek or to avoid something unless it were aware of its perceptions. This awareness is not a first step toward knowledge but is merely preliminary to the movement and the awareness itself surely does not come from any one of the five senses. If this is obscure, we can shed sufficient light on the subject if you think of how one of the senses—for example, sight—works. An animal could not open its eyes and, because of what it sees, move toward what it desires unless it were aware that sight depends upon opening the eyes and moving them toward some object. If the animal knows that it is not seeing while it is not, it must necessarily know that it is seeing when it is. . . . Our conclusions are as follows: physical objects are perceived by the physical senses; the physical senses cannot become aware of themselves; the interior sense can perceive physical objects through the agency of the senses and can also be aware of the senses themselves; and by reason everything else is known, including reason itself, and brought within the scope of knowledge. . . .

AUGUSTINE: Are my physical senses the same as yours, or are mine exclusively mine and yours yours? It is because our senses are exclusively our own that with my eyes I can perceive things that you cannot see.

EVODIUS: I quite agree, that, although our senses are of the same kind, nevertheless, yours are yours and mine are mine. . . . One person can not only see, but can also hear what another person does not. It is the same with all the other senses. One man can perceive something which another cannot. From this it is clear that your sense is yours, and yours alone, and that mine is mine.

AUGUSTINE: Will you say the same about the interior sense, or is it different?

EVODIUS: It is exactly the same. My interior sense is aware of my perceptions, and yours is aware of yours. At times I am asked by someone who sees something whether I also see it, because I am the one who realizes that I see it or do not see it, whereas the questioner cannot have this knowledge with reference to me.

AUGUSTINE: Well then, does each of us have his own reason? There are times when I understand something which you do not understand. You cannot know whether I understand it but I know that I do.

[16] *Free Will,* ii, 15–19.

EVODIUS: It is clear that each of us has his own rational mind.

AUGUSTINE: You would not say, would you, that each one of us sees different suns, moons, stars and such things, even if we each see them with our own private senses?

EVODIUS: Of course not.

AUGUSTINE: Many of us can see one thing at the same time, because each of us has his own individual senses by the use of which we all perceive the thing which we are simultaneously seeing. Thus, although my sense is one thing and yours is something else, nevertheless, what you and I both see are not different things but one thing, which is present to each of us and which is seen by us both at one and the same time.

EVODIUS: That is clear.

AUGUSTINE: We can also each hear one voice at the same time. Although my sense of hearing and yours are separate, the voice which we both hear at the same time is the same voice for both of us. It is not that one part of the voice is heard by my sense and another by yours, but that whatever the sound is, it is present as a whole to both of us and is heard by both of us at the same time.

EVODIUS: This also is clear.

AUGUSTINE: Note then what we have to say about the other physical senses. In the matter we are discussing, what is true of seeing and hearing is not true, although not entirely untrue, of the other senses. You and I can fill our lungs with one air and experience its effects by smelling. We can also both taste one piece of honey, or any other food or drink, and savor it. The object is one thing, and yet our senses are different, yours being yours and mine mine. Although we both experience the same odor and the same taste, the result is that you do not experience it with my taste or I with yours. There is no sense which is our common property. My sense is exclusively mine and yours is yours, even though one odor or taste is experienced by both of us. From this point of view, the senses of taste and smell are found to have a similarity with sight and hearing. But, although we both take in the same air with our nostrils, or taste the same food, the difference is that I do not inhale the same particles of air nor eat the same part of the food as you do. I eat one part and you another. So again, when I breathe in the air, I inhale what is enough for me and you inhale another part of the same air which is sufficient for you. Although one food is consumed by each of us, it still cannot be consumed as a whole by both me and you in the way both of us hear a word as a whole or see the whole of a form presented to our eyes. One part of food and drink must necessarily pass into me and another into you. Do you understand?

EVODIUS: I agree that this is well-established.

AUGUSTINE: Do you think that the sense of touch is like vision and hearing in the point at issue? Both of us can experience one object by touching it; but you can also touch the same part as I so that we can both experience through the sense of touch not only the same object but the same part of it. It is not like food set before us, of which we cannot both consume the whole when we are both eating it, although with the sense of touch you can touch the same thing that I am touching and we can both touch the whole of it. You do not touch one part of it and I another; we each touch the thing as a whole.

EVODIUS: I admit that from this standpoint the sense of touch is very similar to the first two senses we considered. However, as I see it, the difference between them is that both of us can see something in its entirety at the same time. But at any one moment we must each be touching different parts of it. We cannot both be touching the same part at the same time; I cannot touch the part you are touching unless you move away.

AUGUSTINE: You have given a very careful answer but must pursue the matter further. We have said that some of our perceptions are experienced by both of us in common, whereas others are experienced by each of us separately. For example, each one of us must experience his own sensations for himself; I cannot experience your sensations nor you mine. When we perceive certain objects through the physical senses and find that both of us cannot experience them together but only separately, it is because we cannot make them our own unless we are able to take them into ourselves and change them, as, for example, food and drink, of which you cannot consume the same part as I do. . . . When my palate experiences something with an agreeable taste, it irrevocably claims part of it for itself, even if it is a small part, and turns it into something which suits the constitution of my body. If this were not so, no taste would remain after what has been chewed was put out of the mouth. The same can be said about the particles of air which we draw in through our nostrils: you can inhale some of the air which I breathe out, but you cannot breathe in those parts which have gone to nourish me, for I cannot breathe them out again. . . . But all the other sensible things, which we experience without breaking them down and making them part of our bodies in the act of experiencing them, can be experienced by both of us, either simultaneously or successively, since the whole or part which I experience is also experienced by you. Examples of this are light, sound, and all physical objects which we do not actually destroy in the act of experiencing them.

EVODIUS: I understand this.

AUGUSTINE: Therefore, it is clear that the things we experience with the senses without changing them are of quite a different nature from our physical senses themselves. The reason why these things are common to both of us is that they are not changed and transformed, as it were, into our special and private property.

EVODIUS: I quite agree.

AUGUSTINE: I mean by "special and private property" what belongs to each one of us exclusively, what each experiences in himself alone, and what properly belongs to his own nature. By "common" and figuratively "private" property I mean what is experienced by all perceiving inner man, outer man

> beings without being broken down and changed.*

[17] The outer man,** endowed as he is with physical sense organs, perceives material objects. As we can easily observe, there are five physical senses: sight, hearing, smell, taste and touch. However, it would take a good deal of time to inquire into all we want to know about these five senses, and it is not necessary to do so. What we discover about any one of them also applies to the others. Let us, therefore, make particular use of the evidence we got from our eyes, since sight far excels the other senses; for in the subtlety of its character, it approximates more closely than the others the vision of the mind.

When we see a material object, the following three things are to be considered and distinguished; and it is very easy to do this. First, there is the object itself which we see—for example, a stone, a flame, or any other thing which can be seen—which can certainly be in existence even before it is seen. Then there is the act of seeing (*visio*), which does not exist before we perceive the object presented to the sense. Thirdly, there is the element which keeps the sense fixed on the object for as long as it is seen; this is called the attention of the mind (*animi intentio*). These three are not only clearly to be distinguished from one another; each has also its own distinct and separate nature. In the first place, the visible object (*corpus visibile*) is of a very different nature from the visual sense (*sensus oculorum*), which produces vision by making contact with the object. Thus, by "vision" we mean

* This passage is continued under "The Basic Significance of Number" in Chapter 4.

** The "outer man" (*exterior homo),* man in his physical aspect, is contrasted with the "inner man" (*interior homo*), man in his spiritual aspect.

[17] *The Trinity,* xi, 1–5.

the sense "informed"* by the object perceived. There is no vision if the visible object is withdrawn, nor can there be any vision at all if there is no object to be seen. Yet the object, by which the visual sense is formed when the object is seen, and, on the other hand, the form itself, which is imprinted by the object upon the sense, are not of the same substance. For the visible object has a separate existence, but the capacity for sense perception was already in the living person before it could see any visible object which it might encounter. The capacity for sense perception corresponds exactly to the vision produced by the object when it is brought into contact with the sense, that is, when the sense is informed from outside. This capacity belongs to the nature of the living person and is quite different from the object which we experience through sight. . . . Furthermore, the attention of the mind, which keeps the sense fixed on the object we see and connects them, not only differs from the visible object in its nature (the one is mind and the other is body), but also differs from the sense and from vision itself. This attention is an attribute of the mind alone. The sense of the eyes is called a physical sense only because the eyes are members of the body. Although an inanimate body does not perceive, the soul, when mingled with the body, perceives through a physical instrument which is called sense. This sense is cut off and extinguished by physical injury when someone is blinded. The mind, however, remains the same, even though, when the eyes are lost, the mind's attention does not have the physical sense which it may link to an external object for the purpose of seeing and by which it may fix its gaze upon the object when it is seen. The mind's very effort shows that even its attention can neither have perished nor have been diminished although the

* "Informed" *(informatus)* is used with a particular connotation throughout the argument which follows. When the sense makes contact with the "form" *(forma)* of the object sensed, that form is "impressed" (or "imprinted") on the sense. Thus, the sense is said to be "informed" by the object sensed. See the analogy later in this argument of the seal impressing itself on the wax.

physical sense is taken away, for a kind of desire to find out whether sight can be achieved or not remains unimpaired. Thus, these three – the object which is seen, the act of vision itself, and the attention of the mind which joins the other two – are clearly to be distinguished, not only because of the particular properties of each, but also because of the difference of their natures.

Although perception does not proceed from the object which is seen but from the body of the living being who perceives – that body with which the soul is fused in some marvelous way of its own – vision is nevertheless produced, that is, the sense is "informed" by the object which is seen. Therefore, we now have, not only a sense which can exist unimpaired even in darkness, provided that the eyes are sound, but also a sense that is actually "informed"; this sense is called "vision." Vision, then, is produced by a thing which is visible, but not from it alone, for a seeing person must also be present. Therefore, vision is produced by a thing which is visible and by a seeing person. The sense of sight exists in a seeing person, and the capacity for paying attention exists in the person who looks and sees. Yet the informing of the sense, which is called "vision," is imprinted only by the object which is seen, that is, by some visible thing. When this thing is taken away, the form, which was in the sense as long as the visible object was present, no longer remains. Yet the sense itself, which existed even before anything was perceived, remains. In the same way an impression made in water remains only as long as the object itself, which is impressed on the water, remains in it. If the object is taken away, its impression will no longer be there, even though the water, which existed before it took on the impression, remains. Therefore, we certainly cannot say that a visible thing produces sensation. However, it does produce a form, that is, its own likeness, which is reproduced in the sense when we perceive something visually. But we do not employ this same sense to distinguish between the form of a visible object and the form which is produced in the viewer's sense by the form of that object. The union of these two forms is so close that we cannot see them separately. However, reason tells us that we could not see them at all if some likeness of the visible object were not reproduced in our own sense. For instance, when a signet ring is pressed in wax, it does not follow that an image has not been produced because it cannot be seen until the wax has been separated from the ring. After they have been separated, the image remains and can be seen. Therefore, it is easy to see that a form impressed in the wax by the ring already existed before they were separated. On the other hand, if the ring were pressed down on a fluid, no image would appear when the ring was withdrawn. However, reason ought to tell us that, before the ring was withdrawn, it was imprinting its form in the fluid, and that this form can be distinguished from the form which belongs to the ring. This is the original form, from which the other form, which disappears when the ring is withdrawn, was produced in the fluid. The form of the ring, that is, the original form from which the second form was produced, continues to exist in the ring.

Hence, it is a mistake to say that, during the time the object is being looked at, the visual sense does not possess an image of the visible object, on the ground that the image does not remain when the object is removed. Because of this misconception, it is hard to convince people of duller understanding that the image of a visible object is formed in our sense when we are looking at the object and that this same form is vision. But those who pay attention to what I am going to say will not have any difficulties of this sort. After gazing at lights for some time and then closing our eyes, we often find that bright colors, which continually change and gradually diminish in brightness until they entirely fade away, seem to move before our eyes. These colors should be seen as the remains of the form which was produced in our sense while we were looking at the shining object, the variations taking place as the colors slowly and gradually fade away. If by chance we have been looking at latticed windows, the lattice work often appears in the midst of the colors. It is clear for this reason that this whole impression was produced in our sense by the object we were seeing. Consequently, the impression existed even while we were looking, and then it was clearer and more exactly defined, although so closely joined to the appearance of the visible object that the impression and the form could not be separated. In fact, the impression constituted the very act of vision. . . .

This being so, let us remember how the following three things are fused into a kind of unity, although they are different in nature. In the first place, there is the form of the visible object; secondly, there is the object's image impressed on the sense, that is, the vision or, in other words, the sense "informed"; thirdly, the mind's will, which applies the sense to the sensible object and retains the vision in the sense. The first of these, that is, the visible object, is not a part of ourselves as living beings, except when we are perceiving our own bodies. But the second is part of ourselves because it is produced in the body and, through it, in the soul. That is, it is produced in the sense, which exists only in association with a body and a soul. However, the third, the will, belongs to the soul alone. Therefore, although these three are very different in substance, they coalesce into such a complete unity that the first two can be distinguished from each other only with difficulty, even when reason intervenes to act as a judge. By the first two I mean the form of the object which is seen and its image produced in the sense, that is, the vision in the mind. The will combines these so powerfully that, when the sense is to be informed, the will not only applies the sense to the object perceived but also holds the sense on the object when the sense is informed.

[18] When the form of an object perceived by the physical senses is withdrawn, the object's likeness remains in the

[18] *The Trinity,* xi, 6–8.

memory, and the will can later direct its gaze toward the memory to be informed by it from within. This takes place in the same way that the sense was informed from the outside by the presentation of the object to be sensed. Thus, we have a trinity made up of memory, the internal vision, and the will which unites the first two. When these three are gathered into one, the process is called "thought." The three are all of the same substance, for in thought we no longer have the sensible object, which is no part of our nature as living beings; nor is the physical sense informed so as to produce vision; nor does the will act so that, when the sense is to be informed, it applies the sense to the sensible object and retains the form of the object in the sense. In thought, the physical form, which was perceived in the outside world, is replaced by memory, which holds on to the form which the soul has absorbed through the physical sense; the external vision which was produced when the sense was informed by the sensible object, is replaced by a similar internal vision when the gaze of the mind is informed by what the memory holds, that is, when physical objects are thought of in their absence. When the mind indulges in recollection, the will directs the mind's attention to the memory in order that the mind may be informed by what the memory has retained and that a similar vision may arise in thought. This is like the way in which the will, when the sense is to be informed, applies the sense to an externally presented object and, when the sense is informed, unites it with the object. Reason distinguishes between the visible form, which informs the sense, and the likeness of that form, which, when the sense was informed, was produced in the sense so as to bring about vision. Thus, when the mind thinks of the form of an object it has seen, its image consists of both the likeness of the object stored in the memory and the likeness formed from that in the remembering mind. However, this image gives the impression of being one single thing, and thus only by the judgment of reason can we find that there are in fact two separate things. Reason tells us that what remains in the memory when we are thinking of something else is different from what is produced when we recall something, that is, when we go back into the memory and discover the same form there. If this form were no longer in the memory, we would say that we had forgotten it and could not remember it; also, if, in the act of recall, the mind were not informed by the thing which was retained in the memory, the thinker could not experience vision. But the close union of these two things—what the memory retains and what is drawn from the memory so that the mind of the person who remembers is informed—makes them appear to be one since they are very much alike. However, when the thinker's attention is turned away and he has stopped "looking at" what was perceived in his memory, no part of the form which had formerly been impressed on it will remain in his mental sight, which will now be informed by the new thing to which it has turned so that another thought may be brought into being. However, what has been left in the memory continues to exist there, and the mind's attention can be directed back to it; when we recall it, and after we turn back to it, the mind can be re-informed by it and become one with it again. . . .

An object's likeness existing in the memory is to the mind's attention what an object located in a particular place is to the physical senses. A thinking person's vision is to an object's image established in the memory, i.e., the image which informs the mind's attention, what the vision of a person looking at an object is to the object's form by which the sense is informed. Similarily, the mind's effort in joining the visible object to vision so that a unity of three things which are different in their natural constitution takes place, is parallel to the will's effort in joining the image stored in the memory, i.e., the form which the mind's attention conceives when it returns to the memory, to the vision of the thinking person. Here a unity of three things takes place; but these three things are no longer different in their nature but are now one and the same substance. This is because the whole is within us and the whole is one single mind.

Now when the form and appearance of an object have disappeared, the will cannot focus the viewer's sense on it again. In the same way, when its image in the memory is forgotten, the will has nothing on which it can focus the mind's attention so that the mind can be informed. The mind, however, has a great power of imagining not only what has been forgotten but also what has never been perceived or experienced; it does this by increasing or diminishing the size of things which it still remembers or by changing or arranging them according to its fancy. Therefore, the mind often either imagines things to be different from what it well knows that they are or else, when it thinks of them, passes beyond what it knows for certain about them. In these cases we have to beware lest the mind give false information and deceive others or lest it form an opinion by which it deceives itself.

[19] What the memory has stored up and retained is quite different from what is derived from it in a person's thought when he recollects, although they appear to be the same when they are combined. The difference results from the fact that we can remember only as many physical forms as we have actually perceived, and we remember their size and shape exactly as we have perceived them, because the mind draws these forms into the memory through the physical senses. On the other hand, the things that are seen in thought are multiplied and varied in innumerable – indeed infinite – ways, although they are drawn from what is in the memory. For example, I remember only one sun, which is all I have ever seen. But if I wish, I can think of two or three suns, or as many as I please. When I think of many suns, my mind forms them from the original memory of only one sun. And the size of this sun in my memory exactly corresponds to its size as I

[19] *The Trinity,* xi, 13.

actually saw it. If I remember it as larger or smaller, I am no longer remembering what I have seen; in fact, I am not practicing memory at all. Although, if I do remember it, I remember its size as I actually saw it, I can still think of it as larger or smaller if I please. Indeed, I can think of it as moving exactly the way I want it to move, as standing still when I want it to rest or as coming or going in any direction I want. I can think of the sun as square, although I actually remember it as round, or I can give it any color I please, although I have never seen a green sun and therefore do not remember such a thing. And, as with the sun, so with everything else.

[20]The person who describes to me a mountain stripped of trees and clothed with olives is talking to someone who actually remembers the appearance of mountains, trees and olives. If I had forgotten them, I would not know what the person was talking about, and therefore I could not think of what he was describing. Thus, everyone who thinks of physical objects has recourse to memory, whether he himself is imagining something or he is hearing an account of past events or a prediction of things to come. In the memory he finds the limit and measure of all the forms at which he gazes in thought, for nobody can think of a color or a physical form which he has never seen, a sound he has never heard, a flavor he has never tasted, a scent he has never smelled, or the feel of an object he has never touched. Therefore, if no one can think of any physical thing unless he has actually perceived it, thinking is limited to the content of memory, as perception is limited to the range of physical objects. Our senses derive the form from the object we perceive; the memory receives this

[20] *The Trinity,* xi, 14.

form from the senses and, when we indulge in thought, the sharp vision of the mind receives the form from the memory.

[21] Thus, starting from the form of an object and finally arriving at the form produced in the vision of the thinker, we find four forms, each one giving birth, as it were, to the next. From the form of the visible object there arises the form in the senses of the viewer; from this form there arises the form produced in the memory; from the form in the memory comes the form in the vision of the thinker's mind. Therefore, the will makes three links between what we may call a parent and an offspring; first, the mind unites the actual form of the object with the form produced in the physical senses; this form is then linked with the form produced from it in the memory; finally, the form in the memory is joined with the form produced from it in the vision of the thinker's mind. The second of these links is more like the third than like the first, although it is closer to the first. There are two sorts of vision, the first being the vision of the perceiving person and the second the vision of the thinker. Now when the vision of thought takes place, something is produced in the memory which corresponds to something existing in the vision of the perceiving person. In thought the vision of the mind turns itself to this image in the memory, exactly as in perception the vision of the eyes turns toward an object. This is why I wanted to bring to your attention two trinities in this category: the first appearing when the vision of the perceiving person is informed by the object perceived; the second when the vision of the thinker is informed by the memory. There is another trinity which comes between these two and which appears when the form produced in the senses of the per-

[21] *The Trinity*, xi, 16–17.

ceiving person is given to the memory, but I have left it out because we do not usually refer to it as vision.* However, in every case the will is the agent which unites parent and offspring, as it were. Therefore, whatever the origin of the will itself, it cannot be called either a "parent" or an "offspring."

Now if we remember only what we derive from sense perception and can think only of what we actually remember, why do we often think things that are false, when we certainly do not falsely remember what we have perceived? The reason is that the will, which to the best of my ability I have already shown to be the agent which joins together and separates things of this kind, according to its pleasure leads the thinker's sight, which is to be informed, through the secret places of memory. To produce thought about what we do not remember, the will prompts the mind to draw from the store of what we do remember, taking something from one place and something else from another. The fusion of these elements into one vision yields something which is "false" in that it either does not exist externally in the physical world or does not seem to have been drawn from the memory, since we do not remember ever having actually perceived such a thing.

For instance, who ever saw a black swan?** Therefore, no one remembers a black swan. But anyone can think of one since it is easy to join a shape which we have come to know by sight to the color black, which we have often seen in other objects. We remember the shape and the color because we

* The two psychological trinities to which Augustine refers are the following: 1) The form of the object perceived, the power of sense perception, the will which links (*copulat*) the two; 2) The form in the memory, the power of thought, the will which links the two. The trinity which Augustine omits is the process by which the form imprinted on the senses is transformed by the will into the form stored in the memory. There are four successive forms: the form in the object, the form imprinted on the senses, the form stored in the memory and the form realized in thought.

** Augustine could not know of the black swans of Western Australia.

have perceived each of them separately. I do not remember a bird with four feet because I have never seen one. But I can very easily call up an image of one by adding two additional feet, which I have seen, to a winged shape, which I have also seen. Therefore, it would seem that, when we assemble in thought elements which we remember having separately perceived, we are not thinking about things which we actually remember. Yet, in fact, we do this under the guidance of memory, from which we draw and assemble various elements in as many different combinations as we fancy. Without the help of memory we cannot think of objects of great size which we have never seen. When in thought we magnify the size of objects to the greatest possible extent, we make them as large as the vast areas of the world over which our eyes can travel. Reason then carries us forward into still vaster areas, where imagination can no longer follow. In the same way reason declares the infinite range of number, but infinity cannot be grasped by the vision of a person who thinks of material objects. We learn from reason that the most minute atoms are infinitely divisible. However, when we have reached those fine and minute particles which we remember having seen, we can no longer call up finer and more minute images, although reason can continue to pursue and divide them. Thus, we cannot think of any physical objects except those which we remember or which we have gathered from the actual content of memory.

[22] How is it possible for us to think of things which we have never actually seen? What explanation could you have except that we possess the power of taking away from or adding to things? This is a faculty which is planted in the mind and which the mind must necessarily carry wherever it goes. It has a particular application to numbers. Through its use a crow's image, for example, which has been exposed to our

[22] *Letter of 389 A.D. to Nebridius, vii, 6.*

eyes and which is well-known to us, can be changed to any image we please, even an image of something which we have never actually seen. It is this faculty which causes such shapes to come rushing seemingly unbidden into the mind when it is engaged in its customary activity of thought. Therefore, as I have said, the mind, by abstracting certain features from objects which the senses have brought to it and by adding others, can produce in the imagination something which was never perceived in its entirety by any of the senses. Nevertheless, the component parts of the image were all perceived, although they were found in a number of different objects. For example, when we were boys born and reared in the country, we could imagine seas after we had seen water, even in a small cup. Yet we could not think of the flavor of strawberries and cherries until we had actually tasted these fruits in Italy. So also, people who have been blind from their earliest years cannot answer questions about lights and colors, for those who have never experienced them through the senses cannot know them.

St. Augustine was particularly fascinated by the scope of the human memory and quotes it in many places as evidence of the unlimited power of the soul and therefore of its immaterial nature. The following selections include the most famous passage on this theme from the 10th book of the *Confessions:*

[23] While we exist, while we are alive, while we know we are alive, while we never doubt that we remember and understand and will, and while we boast that we have a considerable knowledge of our own nature, we are still entirely ignorant of the power of our memory, understanding and will. We once asked Simplicius, who had been my friend since my

[23] *The Soul and its Origin,* iv, 9–12.

youth and possessed an outstanding and wonderful memory, what were the second-last lines of each of the books of Vergil's *Aeneid*. He told us promptly and from memory. We asked him to repeat the lines which preceded each of these, and he did so. We believed he could recite Vergil backwards and asked him to do this, beginning at any point he chose. Again he succeeded. We asked him to do the same in prose with any speech of Cicero that he had memorized, and he did as much of this as we wanted. When we expressed our admiration, he called God to witness that before the experiment he had not known that he could do these things. Thus, through this experience he learned for himself about the scope of his memory. It was only by experimenting and putting himself to the test that he was able to discover his own powers. Surely he was the same person before he made the test. Why, then, was he ignorant of his own powers?

We often assume that we shall remember something and therefore do not make a note of it at the time when we are thinking about it. But later, when we want to recall it, we cannot do so. Thus, we regret the assumption that we could remember it and the fact that we did not write it down to prevent its escape. Then on some other occasion it suddenly comes into our minds when we are not searching for it. Surely we were not other than ourselves when we were thinking of it. Nevertheless, when we could think of it, we were not exactly what we had been before. How is it that somehow or other we are withdrawn from and denied to ourselves and then are introduced and restored to ourselves? When we are looking for what we have stored in memory and cannot find it, we are like different people removed to some other place. But we cannot return to ourselves as though from another place; when we find what we want, we cannot simply be finding ourselves. Where are we searching except within ourselves? And what are we seeking if not just ourselves?. . . .The other thing we are seeking is simply our own nature, not as it was in the past, but as it now is. Indeed, our nature is an object of inquiry rather than understanding. I have often thought that I would understand a particular question put to me if I thought about it; but I have thought about it and failed to understand it. Therefore, I certainly do not understand the powers of my mind. . . . We know that we want or do not want something. But, even when our will is good, unless we are deceiving ourselves, we do not know what the will can effect, what powers it has, to what temptations it yields or does not yield.

You see, then, the extent of our ignorance about our nature. I am referring not to what it has been in the past, but to what it actually is now; I am thinking, not only of the facts of our physical nature, but also of what belongs to our inner life.

[24] I shall pass beyond this function of my nature (sense perception), mounting step by step toward my Maker. Thus, I enter the fields and spacious halls of memory, the treasure house of countless images of all kinds, images brought there from all kinds of things by the senses. Here we lay up everything we think, whether we add to, take away from, or in some other way modify what the senses have touched. To memory we also entrust everything else which has not yet been swallowed up and engulfed by forgetfulness. When I am in this storehouse, I ask for whatever I want to have brought out. Some things come out at once; some take longer to find and are dragged out as though from more secret receptacles; others rush out in crowds and hurl themselves upon us, although we are searching for something else, they seem to say, "Are you not by some chance looking for us?" But I brush them from the face of my memory with the hand of my heart until what I do want is uncovered and comes into view from its secret hiding place. Other things suggest themselves easily and come out in orderly array as soon as they are sought. What comes out first gives place to what follows and is stored to come out again when I want it. All this happens when I say something from memory.

In the memory everything is kept distinct and in its own

[24] *Confessions,* x, 8–14.

classes. Each has entered by its own proper avenue. For example, light and all the colors and forms of objects enter by the eyes; all kinds of sounds by the ears; odors by the pathway of the nostrils; flavors by way of the mouth. From the sense of touch, which is spread over the whole body, come impressions of hard and soft, cold and hot, smooth and rough, heavy and light—whether they are gathered from outside or inside the body. All these are taken into the vast recesses of memory, with its secret hiding places beyond words to describe, and there they can be recalled and scrutinized when needed. Each enters by its own proper door and is stored. However, it is not the objects themselves which enter, but only the images of what we experience through the senses, and these images remain in the memory for thought to recall. But even though we know by which senses they were seized and stored within us, who can say how they are constructed? Even when I dwell in darkness and silence, I can at will call up color in my memory. I can distinguish between white and black and any other colors I wish. Sounds do not rush in to disturb the visual image that I am contemplating, even though sounds are also lying hidden in the memory, stored in some other place as it were. I can also summon these if I please, and they come to me at once. Although my tongue is at rest and my throat silent, I can still sing as much as I please. The images of colors remain in the memory, but do not intrude and rush in when another treasure, which came in through the ears, is being reviewed. Thus, I also recall the things which have been taken in through the other senses and stored up. I distinguish the scent of lilies from violets, even when I am smelling nothing. I prefer honey to new wine and what is smooth to what is rough. I can do this when I am tasting or touching nothing but am only bringing back memories.

I do all this inwardly in the great palace of my memory, where I have before me the heavens, earth, sea and everything which I have been able to observe in them with the exception of what I have forgotten. There also I encounter and recall myself: what I have done in the past, when and where I did it, how I felt when I did it. Everything I remember is to be found there, both what I have personally experienced and what I have accepted on the authority of others. From the same store I can weave into past events various likenesses of things, which I have either experienced or believed in consequence of what I have actually experienced. Starting from these, I can ponder future courses of action, consequences and hopes, and again I think about them all as if they were actually present. "I shall do this," I say to myself in my mind's vast recesses, which are full of images of so many great things, "and this or that will result." Or I say, "May this or that happen?" or "May God avert this or that!" I say such things inwardly, and, when I say them, the images of all the things I am talking about are before me, drawn from the same treasure house of memory. If the images were not actually present before me, I could not say anything about them.

Great is the power of memory, exceedingly great, my God, a spacious and infinite sanctuary within me. Who can penetrate its depths? Yet it is a function of my mind and a part of my nature. I cannot entirely understand what I am, and therefore the mind is too limited to contain itself. But where is that part of it which it does not contain? Is it outside the mind and not within it? How is it possible that the mind does not contain itself? At this thought a great wonder rises within me; amazement seizes me. Men go to admire lofty mountains, the mighty waves of the sea, broad flowing rivers, the encircling ocean and the courses of the stars, and yet they do not study themselves. When I mentioned all these things, people were not amazed that I was not actually seeing them with my eyes. But I could not have spoken of them unless inwardly I saw in my memory those mountains, waves, rivers and stars, which I have seen, and that Ocean, which I have believed in, all as vast and spacious as if I were actually seeing them. However, when I did see them with my eyes. I did not take them into myself; it is only their images which are within me. I also know by which of the senses each was impressed on me.

But these are not the only things which the measureless capacity of memory carries. Here also is all that we have learned and not yet forgotten of the liberal arts, removed as it were into some inner place, which nevertheless is not a place. But this time it is not the images of these but the realities themselves which I possess. Whatever I know of literature, of the art of discussion, of the various kinds of questions, is in my memory. I am not holding on to the image and leaving the reality outside. When I heard all this, it did not sound and pass away like a voice impressing itself on the ears and leaving behind it merely a trace by which it might be recalled, as if it were still sounding when it has ceased to sound. Nor is it like a fragrance passing away and vanishing into the wind, affecting the sense of smell and thence conveying into memory an image of itself which we can seek out again. Nor is it like food, which is no longer tasted in the stomach but which is still, as it were, tasted in the memory. Nor is it like something experienced by the sense of touch which, although remote from us, is imagined in the memory. All these are not actually brought into the memory, but only their images are grasped with astonishing speed, stored up in wonderful cabinets as it were and in marvellous ways brought out when we recall them to mind.

But, when I hear that there are three kinds of question—namely whether something exists, what it is and of what sort it is—I possess the images of the sounds making up these words, and I know that the sounds passed through the air with a noise and that they now no longer exist. On the other hand, I have not experienced with any of my senses the realities signified by those sounds; I have seen them only with my mind.* I have laid up in my memory the realities themselves and not mere images of them. Let these realities tell, if

* Augustine here makes his familiar distinction between words (symbols) and ideas (realities). The first principles of the liberal arts are absolutes, and in Augustine's view they are therefore not learned through sense perception but communicated to man directly and inwardly by God.

they can, by what path they came into me. I run over all the doorways of my flesh, and I cannot find any by which they could have entered. My eyes say, "If they are colored, then we declared them." My ears say, "If they sounded, then they were declared by us." The nostrils say, "If they have an odor, then they came in through us." The sense of taste says, "If they have no taste, then you need not ask me anything about them." Where then did these realities come from, and by what path did they enter my memory? I do not know. For when I learned them, I did not put my trust in the mind of anyone else. I recognized them in my own mind; it was I who judged them to be true and entrusted them to my mind, as if I were laying them up in a place from which I could bring them out when I wanted them. Therefore, they were in my mind, even before I had learned them; nevertheless, they were not in my memory. Where were they? When they were spoken about, how did I recognize them and say, "It is so. It is true," unless they were already stored in my memory? But they were far removed and hidden away as if in secret caverns so that if they had not been drawn out by some teacher, I might never have been able to think of them.

Thus, we find that the act of learning those things, whose images we have not drawn in through the senses but which we see inwardly as it were, without images, is only gathering together, so to speak, in thought what the memory already contains but in a scattered and uncoordinated fashion. By concentrating our attention on this knowledge, we place it close at hand, so to say, in our memory, so that it can now come to us, with an easy familiarity, while formerly it was hidden away, scattered and neglected. How many things of this sort my memory holds, things which have already been discovered and, as I said, placed ready at hand! These are all the things we are said to have learned and to know. If I stop recalling them in thought, even for a short period, they sink down—slip away as it were into more remote hiding places—and have to be brought out again in thought, as though they were new, from these same places; for they have no other dwelling place. If I am to know them, they must be gathered together again as if they had been scattered. . . .

The memory also contains the innumerable principles and laws of numbers and measurement, none of which are communicated by the physical senses since they are not colors, sounds, odors, tastes or tactual sensations. I have heard the sounds of the words by which these principles are signified when we talk about them. But the sounds and the realities they symbolize are completely distinct. Sounds signify one thing in Greek and another in Latin, whereas the realities they represent are neither Greek nor Latin nor the property of any other language. I have seen the finest possible lines drawn by a craftsman, lines as delicate as a spider's web; nevertheless, the realities are different; they are not the images of the lines which the eye of the flesh has shown me.* The realities are known by anyone who, without thinking of any material object whatsoever, has recognized them within himself. I have also experienced with all my senses the numbers we use in counting. But the numbers by virtue of which we have the power to count are different from these; they are not the images of material numbers and, therefore, they really exist. . . .

I hold all these things in my memory, in which I also retain the method by which I learned them. I have heard many false arguments used against them; these also I keep in my memory. The arguments are false, but the fact that I remember them is not false. I recall also that in the past I have distinguished between these truths and the misleading arguments used to oppose them. But realizing that I am making such distinctions at the present moment is different from remem-

* The "reality" is the idea or principle of a line, i.e., something possessing length but not width. Particular lines are seen "outwardly," i.e., through the senses; the principle of a line is seen "inwardly," i.e., through the pure intelligence.

bering that I made them in the past when I thought about them. Thus, I remember that I have often understood these things, and at this moment I am storing in my memory the fact that I am now making these distinctions and understanding the points at issue. I do this so that at some later time I may remember that I understood them at this present time. Thus, I remember that I have previously remembered; and if in the future I recall that at this moment I was able to remember these things, I will surely recall it by the power of memory.

The selfsame memory contains the emotions of my mind, not in the same way the mind itself has them at the moment of experiencing them but in a way which differs according to the peculiar power of the memory. I can remember having been happy even if I am not happy at the moment; even when I am not sad, I can remember past sadness. I recall that I was once afraid, but I am not now experiencing fear. When I am not actually feeling desire, I can bring to mind a past desire. On the other hand, at times I recall past sadness in a moment of joy or recall past joy in a moment of sadness. This would not be surprising if we were referring to the body, since mind and body are different. It would not be remarkable if in a moment of gladness I remembered some past physical pain. But mind and memory are one thing. When we ask someone to keep something in memory, we say, "See that you bear this in mind." And when we are forgetful, we call memory "mind" and say, "It was not in my mind" or "It slipped from my mind." Since this is so, how is it that, when in a moment of joy I recall past sadness, my mind is joyful while my memory is sad? My mind is joyful because of the joy that is in it; on the other hand, my memory is not sad because of the sadness that is there. Surely nobody would deny that the memory belongs to the mind. The memory is like the mind's stomach, and joy and sadness are like sweet and bitter food. When they are committed to the memory, they are stored there as though they had passed into a stomach where they no longer have any taste. The comparison is ridiculous, but the two circumstances are not completely unlike.

Thus, I call on my memory when I say there are four passions of the mind—desire, joy, fear, sadness. In my memory I find what I can say about each of these in distinguishing and defining it according to its own genus and species. I draw all this from my memory. But when I recall these passions to mind and remember them, I am not disturbed by any turbulence which belongs to them. The passions are there, even before they are recalled by me, and this is why they can be brought out in the act of recollection. Perhaps, when I recall them, they are brought out from the memory as food is brought out from the stomach in chewing the cud. But why isn't joy's sweetness or grief's bitterness experienced by the person who recalls them? Is this the point where the similarity breaks down? If he must necessarily become sad or afraid whenever he would speak of sadness or fear, who would willingly speak of such feelings? But we could not talk of these feelings, unless we could find in our memory not only the sounds of their names connected with images imprinted by the senses of the body but also the ideas of the actual realities, ideas which we have received through no physical sensation. The mind itself, being aware of these ideas through the feelings it has experienced, has committed the ideas to the memory; or the memory itself has held on to them, even when they were not actually committed to the memory by the mind. . . .

[25] The woman who lost a coin and looked for it with the help of a lantern* would not have found it if she had not remembered it. If she had forgotten it, how would she know,

* *Luke* 15: 8.

[25] *Confessions,* x, 18–19.

when she did find it, that it was the one she had lost? I recall many things I have lost, looked for and found. I know that, when I was searching for one of them and someone said, "Is this perhaps it? Or that?" I said, "No, it is not," until I was shown what I was looking for. But unless I had remembered it, it would have been impossible for me to find it, even if it were placed before my eyes; I could not recognize it. It is always that way when we search for and find something which has been lost. For, if something is taken away from the eye but not from the memory, as any visible object may be, its image is inwardly retained and the object is searched for until it is restored to sight. Then, when it is found, it is recognized because of the image within us. We do not say that we have found what has been lost if we do not recognize it; and we cannot recognize it if we do not remember it. The object is held fast in the memory, although it is indeed lost to the eyes.

Thus, when the memory loses something, as happens when we forget something and try to recall it, where do we search for it except in the memory itself? If something other than what we are looking for is by chance offered in its place, we reject it until what we are looking for confronts us. Then we say, "Here it is," which we would not say unless we recognized it; and we would not recognize it unless we remembered it. In such a case we had certainly forgotten it, although it is possible that the whole of it had not escaped us but that we still possessed one part while we were looking for another part. Our search for the lost part may have arisen from the possession of the one part, because our memory realized that it was not in simultaneous possession of everything that it formerly held together as one. Thus, our memory was limping because of the loss of its usual possession and was demanding that what was missing should be given back to it. When, for example, someone well known to us is seen or thought about and we forget his name and search for it, any other name which occurs to us is not connected with him because we have not been accustomed to associate the person with that name. Other names are rejected until the right name comes along, that is, the name which agrees with the usual association. Where does this name come from if not the memory? Even when we recognize the name because we are reminded by something else, the name still comes from the memory. We do not look on it as something new which we have learned; instead, when we recall it, we give it our approval as being correct. However, if the name has been completely wiped out of the mind, we cannot remember it, even when it is brought to our attention. The fact is that we have not completely forgotten what we can still remember having forgotten. We cannot even begin to search for what is lost, if we have completely forgotten it.

Chapter Four

The Learning Process

The selections begin with the distinction between scientific knowledge and wisdom, a distinction basic to St. Augustine's idealism. Learning begins with sense perception, that is, with "the rational knowledge of temporal things." But it must rise up to the higher intellectual level, that is, to "the intellectual knowledge of eternal things." It is on this level that absolute truth is to be found by the effort of pure thought.

It is the function of the curriculum of the liberal arts to set the intelligence of the learner free by leading him gradually from concentration on sense experience to purely intellectual inquiry. St. Augustine holds that the basic principles of the arts of grammar, rhetoric and dialectic (logic) are absolutes. Similarily, the study of arithmetic, geometry, music and astronomy in a liberal as distinct from a utilitarian or vocational context, leads to an understanding of the absolute nature of number. All of these liberal disciplines combine to show that cause and effect and orderly movement in the universe are reducible to numerical proportion. For example, the satisfaction to be derived from the study of music comes from the insights it gives into the nature of eternal reality. It is therefore as a theoretical study of the numerical relationships expressed in rhythms and harmonies that music is to be admitted into the liberal curriculum.

Learning must start from some solid ground of certainty, and St. Augustine finds this in the absolute assurance we have of our own existence. With a striking anticipation of Descartes' *cogito ergo sum* (I think therefore I), Augustine argues from the reality of thought, even when it is mistaken, to the certainty of the existence of the self. He employs the formula, *Si fallor, sum* (If I am mistaken, I am).

Learning begins with the knowledge of the self. It culminates in the illumination of truth by God to the questing soul. The doctrine of divine illumination is a point on which Augustine corrects Plato, who had explained learning on the level of spiritual realities as a remembering *(reminiscence)*. Plato's theory rested, of course, on the non-Christian assumption of the pre-existence of the soul.

From Sense Knowledge *(scientia)* to Wisdom *(sapientia)*

[1]I have undertaken the labor [of writing this book] simply so that young people, or people of any age whom God has endowed with good ability, might be led, under the guidance of reason and by a series of steps, away from the senses of the body and material letters, in which it is easy to become entangled. My desire is that they attach themselves with a love of unchanging truth, to the one God and Lord of all, who presides over the minds of men with no material object coming between.

[2]Action, by which we make good use of temporal things, differs from contemplation of eternal things; the latter is counted as wisdom (*sapientia*), the former as knowledge (*sci-*

[1] *On Music,* vi, 1.
[2] *The Trinity,* xii, 22–25.

entia). When we do anything with courage, temperance and justice, we are involved in that discipline or subject of study, by which we are guided to avoid evil and pursue good in our actions. This discipline is also made up of what experience has taught us to guard against or to imitate as well as the necessary proofs we have learned about the things which have been provided for our use.

I consider the above to be "knowledge," which is to be distinguished from "wisdom." For the latter deals with things which neither have existed in the past nor will exist in the future, but which simply are. Because of the eternity in which they are, they are said to have been, to be and to be about to be without any passage of time. They have not been in such a way that they should ever cease to be nor are they about to be in the sense that they are not actually in existence now. They have always had, and always will have, an absolute being; they continue to be, but not as physical objects localized in space. Rather, they are intelligible things with an immaterial nature and are open to the vision of the mind as visible or tangible objects in space are to the senses of the body. Intelligible and immaterial first causes of material objects* exists; the objects themselves are located in space, but their first causes occupy no space. Likewise, movements which take place in time have first causes which have being and are open to the understanding but not to the senses; these principles exist outside the passage of time, and to reach them with the mental vision is possible for only a few people. A person may come as close to them as possible, but he cannot remain with them; his mental vision is, as it were, repelled, and he is driven off. Thus, his thinking about what in itself is not transient is transient. But this thinking, which we study in the liberal disciplines by which the mind is instructed, is committed to memory; the mind, therefore, can return to it at

**Rationes rerum,* elsewhere *aeternae rationes rerum,* the eternal reasons or first principles of things, corresponding to the Platonic ideas or forms.

a later time, although it must turn away from it for the moment. If our thinking did not go back to the memory to find what has been entrusted to it, we would be brought back to it as though we were completely ignorant and along the same path by which we had been led there in the first place. We would come upon this knowlege (of first principles) where we had found it the first time, that is, in immaterial truth, from which once again it would be copied and fixed in the memory. For example, the immaterial and unchanging first principle of a square object does not continue to exist in the way in which the thought of man remains with it. . . . If we grasp the principle underlying the harmony of some attractive tune, which lasts through a period of time, we can think about that principle for at least as long as the sound can be heard, although the principle itself exists outside time in a remote and deep silence. But what the mind's vision, transient though it is, derives from the sound and stores in the memory, as if in a stomach, can be recalled and, as it were, chewed over by the mind, which can translate into systematic knowledge what it has learned in this way. However, if this knowledge is blotted out by absolute forgetfulness, then under the guidance of teaching we can return to what has completely dropped away, and it will be found exactly as it was before.

This was why the versatile philosopher Plato tried to persuade us that men's souls lived here even before they acquired bodies. From this he argued that what we learn is not new to us but already known; in fact, we recall it to mind. He has told us that a boy who was questioned about geometry replied as if he were perfectly acquainted with the subject. When cleverly planned questions were put to him one after the other, he saw what there was to be seen and reported what he saw.* Now if this had been a matter of remembering

*The reference is to Socrates' questioning of the slave boy in Plato, *Meno*, 81C-86B. By the method of questioning Socrates "teaches" the boy how to double the size of a given square. The demonstration is designed to establish that learning geometrical principles is a matter of remembering what the soul experienced in a former existence and has since forgotten.

what was previously known, certainly very few people would have had the same success when questioned in this manner; for not everyone was a geometer in his previous existence and in fact geometers are so few in number that it is hard to find one anywhere. It is better for us to believe that the intellectual mind is so constituted that it sees in a sort of immaterial light of a unique kind those things which by the disposition of the Creator are linked to intelligible things in a natural order. In this there is a resemblance to the physical eye, which sees the objects around it bathed in the material sunlight, to which the eye is made to be receptive. Now the reason why the physical eye sees the difference between white and black objects without being taught to do so, is not that it understood this difference before it was created in the flesh. Then why is it only when we are properly questioned about intelligible things that we can give answers to questions on any subject, even when we are not familiar with the subject? On the other hand, why can a person answer questions about sensible things only when he has experienced them in his own body or has accepted them on the authority of the words or writings of some knowledgeable person. Surely we should not believe the story that Pythagoras of Samos remembered some things of this sort which he had experienced when he had lived here before in another body. There are other similar reports of people who have had mental experiences of the same sort. We can say that their recollections were misleading and like those we often experience in sleep; for then we seem to remember doing or seeing things which we have never actually done or seen. We can guess that the minds of such people, even when awake, were affected in this way at the prompting of malignant and deceitful spirits wanting to confirm or sow a false belief about the transmigration of souls with the purpose of leading men astray. Our conclusion may be that, if people really remembered things they had previously seen in this life while occupying other bodies, many people, if not almost everybody, would have identical experiences. Those who believe in the transmigration of souls suppose that, as the dead come from the living, so the living come into existence from the dead by a continuous and uninterrupted process, as sleepers consist of those who were previously awake and as those who are awake were previously asleep.

Therefore, if the correct distinction between wisdom and knowledge is that the intellectual understanding of eternal things belongs to wisdom and the rational understanding of temporal things to knowledge, it is easy to decide which is to be preferred to the other. But, even if we must employ some other criterion by which to distinguish these two things, which the Apostle certainly teaches us are different when he says: "To one is given by the Spirit the word of wisdom; to another the word of knowledge by the same Spirit," still the difference we have established between these two is also a very clear one. The intellectual understanding of eternal things is one thing, and the rational understanding of temporal things another; nobody doubts that the former is better than the latter. Thus, when we leave behind the things that belong to the outer man and desire to mount up within outselves away from what we have in common with the animals, the rational understanding of temporal things confronts us before we can come to the things that are open to the understanding alone (i.e., the intelligible things). It is the latter which are of the greatest importance and eternal.

[3]REASON: Reason, who is conversing with you, promises to display God to your mind, as the sun is shown to your eyes. The mind has, as it were, its own eyes. The established truths of the liberal arts resemble the things that are lit up by the sun so that they can be seen, for example, the

[3] *Soliloquies,* i, 12–15.

earth and all that it contains. It is God who illuminates everything and I, Reason, am to minds what sight is to the eyes. To have eyes is not the same as to look; similarily, looking is not the same thing as seeing. Therefore, the soul needs three things: it must have eyes which it can use effectively; it must look; it must see. The soul's eyes consist of a mind free from every taint of the body, turned away and purified from all desire for temporal things. It is faith alone which first brings about this state. The mind cannot see unless it is healthy; therefore, God cannot be shown to a stained and sick mind. When the mind does not believe that health is the precondition of seeing, it pays no heed to its own health; however, if the mind comes to believe that its situation is as we have described it and that it will be able to see only if it is healthy, it will despair of ever being healed; then it will certainly give itself up and refuse to conform to the advice of the doctor.

AUGUSTINE: This is as you say, especially since it is inevitable that, by the very nature of its disease, the mind will find our advice painful.

REASON: Therefore, to faith must be added hope.

AUGUSTINE: So I believe.

REASON: What if the mind believes all this, hopes that it can be healed, and still does not love the light promised to it, thinking that for the present it must be satisfied with darkness, which by force of habit has become agreeable to it? Won't it then turn its back on the doctor?

AUGUSTINE: I agree.

REASON: Therefore, love is the third thing necessary.

AUGUSTINE: Indeed, this is the basic need.

REASON: Thus, without these three, no soul can be healed so that it will see its God, i.e., understand Him. But when its eyes are healthy, what then?

AUGUSTINE: It should look.

REASON: Reason is the vision of the soul. But it does not follow that everyone who looks sees; therefore, straight and perfect looking, i.e., looking which leads to vision, is called virtue; for virtue is simply straight and perfect reason. But looking cannot turn toward the light even eyes that are already healthy, unless the three things we have mentioned are present: faith, from which we derive our confidence that the thing toward which are looking must be directed, is sufficient to make us happy; hope, which offers the assurance that seeing will follow right looking; and finally love, by which the soul yearns to see and enjoy fully. When these are present, looking results in a vision of God, who is the goal of all looking, not in the sense that there is no more looking thereafter, but in the sense that the soul has nothing more toward which to direct itself. True and perfect virtue consists in reason arriving at its own proper end, which is the pathway to the happy life. Vision is the understanding which belongs to the soul; it is achieved by the combination of the knower's intelligence and something to be known, just as what is called eyesight is achieved by the combination of the sense of sight and the sensible object. If either is taken away, nothing can be seen.

Now let us consider whether those three things are still necessary when the soul has come to see God, that is, to possess a knowledge of Him. In what way will faith be necessary when the soul already sees? Or hope, when it already possesses what it hoped for? Only love will suffer no diminution; on the contrary, much will be added to it. For, when the soul actually sees the unique and true beauty, it will love it all the more; but, unless the soul fixes its eye on this beauty with a great love and never ceases looking on it, it will be unable to continue in that most happy vision. However, as long as the soul is in this physical body, the physical senses continue to carry out their own proper function, even though the soul enjoys that fullness of vision which consists in knowing God. Therefore, although the senses may have no power to deceive, they still have the power to confuse. Faith can be called that which puts up a resistance to the senses and persuades us that the world of mind is a better world. Thus, even in this present life the soul can become happy in the knowledge of God. However, it endures many physical distresses and so must hope that after death all these troubles will be no more. Therefore, hope does not desert the soul in this life. But after this life, when the soul betakes itself wholly to God, love remains to keep it there. The soul cannot be said to have faith in the truth of all this when it is no longer worried by any intrusion of falsehood; nothing remains to be hoped for when the soul rests securely in the possession of everything. Therefore, the following three things are necessary to the soul: it must be healthy, it must look, and it must see. But there are three other essentials: faith, hope, love. Of these the first and second are always necessary in this life so that the soul will be healthy and will be able to look; but if the soul is to see in this life, all three are necessary. After this life the only necessity is love.

Our present discussion now leads me to tell you something about God which arises out of the analogy between intellectual understanding and sense perception. God is indeed a being understood through the intelligence alone, and so are the demonstrations of the sciences; but there is a great difference between them. The earth is visible and so is light; but the earth cannot be seen unless it is illuminated by light. Everyone admits that scientific demonstrations are most certainly and indubitably true. But we must also believe that they cannot be understood unless they are lit up by something analogous to the sun, about which three facts should be noted: it exists, it shines, it illumines. Similarly, there are three corresponding facts about the most transcendent God whom you wish to understand: He exists; He is open to the understanding; He enables other things to be known.

[4]AUGUSTINE: We accept that there is wisdom or there are wise people. We also accept the fact that all men want to be happy. But where do we see this truth? I have no doubt that you see it and that it is true. Do you then see it as you see your own thought, which I cannot know unless

[4] *Free Will*, ii, 28–31.

you tell me about it? Can you conceive that I can understand this truth, even if you do not tell me about it?

EVODIUS: I am sure that you too could understand it, even if I did not want you to understand it.

AUGUSTINE: Then is the one truth, which each of us sees with his own mind, the same truth for both of us?

EVODIUS: Yes.

AUGUSTINE: To take the matter further, I believe you would admit that wisdom should be sought out; you would regard this statement as a truth.

EVODIUS: I am quite certain about it.

AUGUSTINE: Then can we deny that this truth also is one thing and commonly available to all who know it, although each person sees it with his own mind and not with mine or yours or anyone else's? Surely anything that is seen is open to the common inspection of all viewers.

EVODIUS: This must be accepted.

AUGUSTINE: This is also the case in statements like the following: we ought to live justly; the worse is not to be preferred to the better; like is to be compared with like; every man should be given what is his own. Wouldn't you say that these are truths and that they are open to the common inspection of you and me and all who see them?

EVODIUS: I agree.

AUGUSTINE: Can you deny that what is incorrupt is better than what is corrupt; that the eternal is better than the temporal; that what cannot be violated is better than what is subject to violation?

EVODIUS: Nobody would deny such statements.

AUGUSTINE: Can anyone claim that such truths are his own private property, since they are unchangeably open to the inspection of all who have the power to see them?

EVODIUS: Nobody could properly claim a proprietary right over such truths. Not only are they true, but they are the same for everyone and the common property of all.

AUGUSTINE: Again, who could deny that the soul ought to turn itself away from corruption and toward incorruption, that is to say, that it should love incorruption and not corruption? If we admit the truth of this, how can we fail to understand that it is an unchangeable truth open to the common contemplation of all minds that are capable of understanding it?

EVODIUS: This is very true.

AUGUSTINE: Furthermore, who could doubt that a life which no adversity is able to divert from the straight and honest way is better than one which is easily shattered and upset by temporal misfortunes?

EVODIUS: Nobody could doubt that.

AUGUSTINE: I shall not ask any more questions of this kind;

it is enough that you are at one with me in regarding what we may call those moral rules and lights as most firmly established. We are agreed that they are both true and unchangeable and that, whether singly or collectively, they are open to the common inspection of those who have the capacity to view them, each with his own reason and mind. But I ask whether you think these truths belong to wisdom; for I think you would agree that the wise man is one who has attained to wisdom.

EVODIUS: Indeed I would.

AUGUSTINE: Well then, could a man who lives justly continue in this way if he did not recognize the superior and the inferior so that he could subordinate the latter to the former? Without knowing the meaning of "belonging," could he conduct his life in such a way as to give every man what is his own?

EVODIUS: He could not.

AUGUSTINE: Will you then deny that the man who sees this has a wise understanding?

EVODIUS: I shall not.

AUGUSTINE: Surely a man who lives prudently chooses what is not corrupt and values this more than what is corrupt.

EVODIUS: Indeed he does.

AUGUSTINE: Therefore when such a man chooses to turn his soul toward what everyone would admit is the right thing to choose, can it be denied that he chooses wisely?

EVODIUS: I cannot deny it.

AUGUSTINE: Also, when he turns his mind toward what he chooses wisely, surely he shows wisdom.

EVODIUS: Yes.

AUGUSTINE: Then is there no doubt that the wise man does not reject what he wisely chooses and sets his mind on, no matter what terrors and punishments may threaten him?

EVODIUS: No doubt at all.

AUGUSTINE: Therefore, it is clear that what we have referred to as "moral rules and lights" belongs to wisdom. The more a man uses them in the conduct of his life and lives in accordance with them, the wiser his life and conduct are. There is nothing wisely done which can properly be said to be separated from wisdom.

EVODIUS: True.

AUGUSTINE: Therefore, as the rules of number are true and unchangeable – the principles and truths of number being, as you said, unchangeably presented to and shared by all who look on them – so the rules of wisdom are also true and unchangeable. When I questioned you about a few of them one by one, you replied that they were true, self-evident, and open to the common inspection of every person with the capacity to view them.

EVODIUS: I cannot doubt it. But I am very anxious to know whether wisdom and number are contained within one and the same class of things; you reminded me that they were mentioned together in the Holy Scriptures.* Alternatively, could it be that the one is derived from the other or contained within it? Could number be derived from wisdom or contained within it? I would not venture to say that wisdom derives from number or is contained within number. The explanation of the following fact eludes me: I am acquainted with many accountants or calculators, or whatever you may care to call them, who have a superior and quite marvelous skill in counting, but very few, if any, are wise. Thus, I am forced to the conclusion that wisdom deserves much more respect than number does.

AUGUSTINE: You mention a fact which I also have found surprising. When I ponder the unchangeable truth of numbers and what you may call their resting place, sanctuary, region or whatever other appropriate name you may like to give to the dwelling place or abode of numbers, I find myself far removed from the realm of physical objects. There is something for me to ponder, although I can find nothing to express in words: I therefore return wearily to the objects about us in order to express myself, and I give the usual names to the things which are before our eyes. This also occurs when carefully, attentively and to the limit of my capacity, I concentrate my thinking on wisdom. Number and wisdom

**Eccles.* 7:25: "I applied mine heart to know and to search and to seek out wisdom and the reason of things." The Latin word *ratio* translated "reason," is used in its original sense of "reckoning," "calculation," "computation."

are most mysteriously and certainly true, a fact supported by the evidence of Scripture, which, as I have said, links the two together. On this account I am surprised that to most people number is of slight value, while wisdom is held in high regard; but the reason for this may indeed be that the two are one and the same thing. . . .

God has given numbers to everything, even to the humblest things and the most remote. All physical objects have their own numbers, even if they exist on the outermost bounds of creation; but they have not been granted wisdom. Not even every soul has wisdom, but only rational souls, as if God had taken up his residence in them so that from them He might exercise control over all other things, even the loweliest, to all of which He has given numbers. This is why we find it easy to pass judgment on physical objects as belonging to a lower order of creation. We see in all of them the impression of numbers, which are also lower than we are, and this is why we set a small value on numbers. But, when we begin to examine these numbers from another stand-point, as it were, we find that they transcend even our own minds and rest unchangeably in truth itself. Also, since there are few who can be wise, whereas even fools are able to count, men admire wisdom and hold number in contempt. But, as for learned and studious men, the more they are removed from earthly decay, the more they behold both number and wisdom resting in truth itself and hold them to be valuable. By comparison with this truth, not only gold and silver and the other things men fight over but even their very selves come to be worthless in their eyes.

[5]If only the two of us* could put questions on this matter to a very learned man who is also outstandingly eloquent, wise, and perfect in the highest degree. In talk and discussion he could well explain the influence wielded by the soul in the body, the power the soul has over itself, and its relationship to God, to whom it is nearest when it is pure and in whom it finds its highest and complete good. But now, since there is no other person at hand to help in this, I take courage so that I will not fail you. There will be the advantage for me that, while in my ignorant state I am explaining to you the powers of the soul, I shall be able to test at the same time the extent of the powers I myself possess. However, let me cut off at the start any exaggerated or unlimited expectations you may be entertaining. You may think that I will be referring to every soul; in fact, I shall refer only to the human soul, which ought to be our exclusive concern if we consider our own welfare.

In the first place, it is easy to observe that the presence of the soul gives life to this earth-bound and mortal body. It makes the body a single organism, holding it together and not allowing it to decay; it carries nourishment to be equally distributed throughout all parts of the body, giving each part its proper share; it preserves the body's harmony and proportion, not only in beauty, but also in growth and reproduction. These powers are, of course, clearly shared by men and plants; for we talk of plants as living, since we see and declare that they retain characteristics of their own kind, take in nourishment, grow, and reproduce themselves.

Mount now to the second level and look at the soul's powers of sense perception, in which you can observe the function of life manifested more clearly and openly. Of course, we should pay no heed to the obviously crude misconception, which is more "wooden" than the very trees it uses in its defense, that the vine feels pain when a grape is

* That is, Augustine and Evodius, the two participants in the dialogue.

[5] *The Greatness of the Soul,* 70–76.

plucked; it is said that such things not only experience sensation when they are cut, but even see and hear. But this is not the time to discuss this sacrilegious heresy. For the moment, as I suggested, examine the soul's power in sense perception and in the movement of those living organisms which enjoy a higher level of existence; by this power we are clearly marked off from things which are attached by their roots to the earth.

The soul reaches out to the sense of touch and perceives and distinguishes hot and cold, rough and smooth, hard and soft, light and heavy. It also distinguishes innumerable different flavors, odors, sounds and shapes by taste, smell, hearing and sight. In all this the soul seeks out and takes to itself everything that agrees with the nature of its own body, rejecting and fleeing from what is harmful to it. At times the soul withdraws from the senses, and, by giving them what we may call a holiday, it recreates their functions. At the same time it ponders the images of things it has drawn in through the senses, grouping them together in many various combinations and associations. All of this is done in sleep and dreams.

Often too the soul takes delight in motion, making joyful gestures, indulging in spontaneous movements, and effortlessly coordinating the various parts of the body. In sexual union the soul performs what is has the power to do and fuses two natures in companionship and love. It engages in cooperative action, not only in begetting offspring, but also in rearing, protecting and nourishing them. The soul habituates itself to the environment in which the body acts and by which the body is sustained, and becomes reluctant to be separated from this, as if the environment were an integral part of itself. This force of habit, which is not broken even by the removal of these ties or by the lapse of time, is called "memory." But again no one would deny that even the animal soul has all these powers.

Raise yourself then to the third and distinctively human level. Think of memory, not as limited to what has been implanted in the soul by habituation, but as consisting of the innumerable skills developed and retained by observation and instruction – the many arts of the craftsman, the cultivation of the ground, the building of cities, structures and projects of so many varied and marvelous sorts. There is the invention of systems of signs in words and gestures, in various kinds of sounds, in pictures and creative works of all kinds. There is the multiplicity of languages and institutions, some of them original and some recreated; the many various kinds of books for preserving the records of the past and all the concern shown for future generations. There are hierarchies of duties, powers, prerogatives and ranks to be observed in families and public life, whether service is rendered in civil or military duties or in relation to secular or sacred institutions. There is the power of reasoning and reflective thought, the floods of rhetoric, the various kinds of songs, the untold varieties of mimicries for the purpose of play and jest; there is also the art of music, the accuracy of measurement, the discipline of arithmetic, the interpretation of the past and future from the present.* All these are great, and they are distinctively human. But to this point all of this profusion is shared equally by the souls of the educated and the uneducated, the good and the evil.

Look up then and take a leap to the fourth level, where goodness and all real value begin. For it is here that, in order to play its part in the universe, the soul ventures to set itself over and above not only its own body but also the whole body of the universe itself. It repudiates its claim to worldly goods, comparing them with its own beauty and thus marking them off from itself and holding them of small account. Therefore, the more delight the soul takes in itself, the more it withdraws itself from things that are unclean and keeps itself unspotted, clean and trim. It strengthens itself against every-

* St. Augustine has given a functional definition of each of the liberal arts of the medieval curriculum: grammar, rhetoric, dialectic (forming the *trivium*); music, geometry, arithmetic, astronomy (forming the *quadrivium*). See below, p. 258, for a further catalogue from *The Principle of Order*.

thing aimed at diverting it from its resolve and purpose, sets a high value on human fellowship, and wishes nothing to happen to another which it would not wish for itself. It follows the authority and precepts of the wise and believes that God speaks to it in this way. However, this noble bearing is not achieved without labor, and there is a great and bitter warfare against the annoyances and allurements of the world. In the work of purification there is an underlying fear of death, at times not great, but at other times very heavy. This fear is light when the soul has a strong faith, but to prove the truth of this is granted only to the purified soul. So great are the providence and justice of God in the government of the world that death cannot come to anyone as an evil, even if an evil person inflicts it. But on this level there is a strong fear of death because, the less firmly a belief is held, the more anxiety is shown in the search. When peace of mind is reduced by the presence of fear, things are also seen less clearly, for peace of mind is very necessary for the study of difficult problems.

Then, as the soul progressively develops an understanding of the great difference between its condition of purity and its former polluted state, the more it fears that, when it has laid down its body, God may be able to endure it even less than it was able to endure itself in its polluted state. However, there is nothing more difficult than to fear death and to turn one's back on the seductions of this world to the extent that the soul's dangerous situation demands. But the soul is so great that it is capable of even this with the help of the justice of the supreme and true God. By this justice the universe is sustained and ruled, and by it all things were brought into being and exist in such a way that they cannot be better than they are. To this justice the soul most reverently and securely commits itself for help and success in the very difficult task of self-purification.

But, when the soul is free from every corruption and washed clean of all stains, it is at last in possession of itself and has the fullness of joy; it has no fears for itself, and nothing distresses it. This is the fifth level. Since it is one thing to achieve purity and another to hold on to it, the activity by which the soul cleanses itself and restores its purity is different from the activity by which it prevents any further pollution of itself. On this level the soul understands how great it is in every respect. When it has grasped this, then indeed, with high and marvelous trust, it moves toward God, that is, to the contemplation of truth itself and that high and most transcendent reward for which it has labored so hard.

Now this activity—by which I mean the desire to understand what most truly and supremely exists—is the loftiest vision of the soul, and there is none more perfect, superior or more direct. This then is the sixth level of activity. Just as it is one thing to cleanse the soul's eye so that it does not look in an idle, aimless way and with distorted vision and another thing to guard and protect its health, so it is quite a different thing to direct one's gaze calmly and straightforwardly toward what is to be seen. Those who want to do this before they are cleansed and healed are so repelled by the light of truth that they see nothing good in it but, on the contrary, a great deal of evil. Thus, they deny it the name of truth and with a pitiful and lustful desire, cursing the medicine offered to them, they run for refuge into their own darkness, which is the only state their diseased condition can endure. Hence, the divinely inspired Prophet declares most appropriately: "Create in me a clean heart, O God; and renew a right spirit within me" (*Psalms* 50:12). Now the spirit is "right," I believe, when it sees that the soul cannot wander off the track and go astray in its search for truth. The spirit is not "renewed" unless the heart is "clean," that is, unless man's thought has withdrawn itself from every lust and drained away all the dregs of mortal things.

And now we are on the seventh and last level of the soul, which is the very vision and contemplation of truth. Indeed, this is not really a level at all, but rather a resting place to which all the lower levels have brought us. How can I tell of the delights which are there, the enjoyment of the highest and true Good, the serenity and eternity which breathes upon us? Great and pre-eminent souls have told us about it all, insofar as they have thought it right to speak of it, and we believe that they have seen and are continually seeing it. At the present I make bold to tell you this: if with great constancy we hold to the course which God prescribes for us and which we have undertaken to follow, then by the goodness and wisdom of God we shall come to that supreme cause, author or first principle of all things, whom we may call by whatever may be the most appropriate name for such a great reality. When we understand this principle, we shall indeed see how all things under the sun are "vanity of vanities" (*Ecclesiastes* i:2); for vanity is deception and the vain are either deceived or deceiving or both. With this understanding we are at liberty to see what a great difference exists between the things of this world and what really exists. Since all worldly things have been created by God, their Author, they are marvelous and beautiful considered by themselves; but by comparison with the things that are eternal, they are as nothing.

The Primacy of Intellectual Understanding

[6] Let us see how far reason can take us from things that are seen to things that are unseen, as it makes its ascent from temporal to eternal things. We should not idly look upon the beauty of the sky, the orderly arrangement of the stars, the brightness of the light, the alternations of days and nights, the monthly courses of the moon, the fourfold divisions of the year, equal in number to the four elements, the great potency of seeds bringing forth forms and numbers; everything preserves its own limits and characteristic nature according to the class to which it belongs. When we consider these things,

[6] *True Religion*, 52–57.

we should not indulge in any light-minded and unprofitable curiosity; instead, we should take a step toward immortal things, which remain forever. The first thing to notice is the nature of the life force which perceives all these things through the senses. Since this is what gives life to the body, it is of necessity superior to the body. For no physical mass of any sort, however brightly it shines with visible light, is to be held of much value if it is without life. Any living substance is to be preferred to a substance which is without life; this is the law of nature.

Nobody doubts that irrational animals live and feel. Therefore, the most excellent characteristic of the human mind is, not that it has sense experience, but that it has the power of making judgments about sense data; for many animals see more sharply than men and have a keener perception of physical objects in their other physical senses. Nevertheless, to make judgments about physical objects is a function, not only of the life of sense, but also of the life of reason. What the animals lack is precisely our excellence. It is very easy to see that the person who judges is superior to the object about which a judgment is made. Now the life of reason passes judgment, not only on sense data, but on the senses themselves; for example, reason knows why an oar dipped in water must appear crooked when in fact it is straight, and why it must seem crooked to the eyes. Eyesight can merely report a fact; it is unable to make judgments about it. Thus, it is clear that, as the life of sense perception is superior to the body, so the life of reason is superior to both.

Therefore, if reason makes its own unaided judgments, there is nothing superior to it, although there is no doubt that reason is changeable since it does not always show the same degree of skill. The more skillful reason is, the better judgments it makes, and the measure of its skill consists in the extent to which it participates in some art or discipline, or in wisdom. Hence, we must ask what is the nature of an art. I do not want you to think of an art as something which is attained by experience, but as something discovered by reason. What merit is there in a man knowing that stones are more firmly bound together by a material consisting of lime and sand than by mud alone? What is outstanding about a man who erects a building so tastefully that features which are repeated are equal to one another? Or about one who sees to it that single features are placed in the center of his building? Although this is sense knowledge, yet it comes quite close to reason and truth. We should certainly ask ourselves why it should worry us if two windows, located side by side and not one above the other, are unequal in size when they could have been equal; on the other hand, if they were placed one above the other, the inequality would not cause us so much annoyance, even if one were twice as big as the other. Why should we have little concern about the extent of the difference in size of the windows when there are only two of them? On the other hand, when there are three of them, sense perception seems to require either that they be equal or that the middle one be to the largest as the smallest is to the one in the middle. In this way nature itself is consulted, as it were, to find out what she approves. Here we must above all note that a thing which did not displease us much when we looked at it alone, is rejected when it is set against something better for comparison. Thus, we find that, in the popular view, an art is simply the memory of things which we have experienced and which have been agreeable to us, with the addition of some physical skill and activity. If you lack this skill, you can still make judgments about the products of the arts, and this is a much superior function, even if you yourself cannot produce such things.

In all the arts it is symmetry which is pleasing, which preserves unity, and which renders everything beautiful. Symmetry requires equality and unity, and this is found either in the similarity of equal parts or in carefully proportioned arrangements of parts that are unequal. Who can find complete equality or similarity in physical objects, and who would venture to say after careful observation of an object that it is truly and simply one? This is because everything is involved in a process of change, passing either from one form to another or from one place to another. Each object consists of parts, each of which occupies its own place and is differentiated according to the extent of space it occupies. Furthermore, true equality and similarity, and true and original unity, are not understood and seen by the physical eyes or by any of the senses, but by the mind. How could we look for equality of any kind in physical objects, and how could we be sure that the equality found there is so greatly different from perfect equality, unless perfect equality is seen in the mind? This is necessary if we are justified in describing as "perfect" something which has not been "made."*

The beauty of everything which appeals to the senses is set in the context of space and time, for example, the body and the movements of the body. But that equality and unity, which are known to the mind alone and according to which judgments about physical beauty are made on the basis of sense information, do not fill any space and do not move in time. We could not claim that this standard can be used to judge that a wheel is round but not a small jar; or that we can apply the standard to a jar but not to a small coin. It is also absurd to declare, with reference to the durations and movements of physical things, that years can be judged to be equal by this standard but that months cannot; or that months can but days cannot. Whether a symmetrical movement occupies larger periods of time or only hours or brief minutes, it is judged by the same standard of unchanging equality. Now if smaller and greater shapes and movements are all judged according to the same standard of equality, similarity or symmetry, then the standard itself is greater than them all—but greater in respect of its scope. In point of space or time, the standard is neither larger nor smaller. If it were larger, we

* In Augustine's definition the "perfect" is the spiritual, the immaterial, the uncreated. But the word literally refers to what has been "fully made" (*per-factus*). Augustine points to the illogicality of using the term "perfect" (*perfectus*) with reference to what has not been "made" (*factus*).

could not judge smaller things by the whole of it; on the other hand, if it were smaller, we could not judge larger things by it. As it is, we judge a square market place, a square stone and a square writing tablet or gem according to an absolute standard of squareness. And again, we declare the movements of the feet of a running ant or of a marching elephant to be symmetrical by the same absolute standard of equality. Who can doubt then that the standard itself is neither larger nor smaller in extent of space or time, although its scope is greater than everything else? This standard, which governs all the arts, is entirely unchangeable; but the human mind, which has the power to see the standard, can suffer change and fall into error. Therefore, it is clear that the standard itself is superior to our minds, and we give it the name "truth."

We should not doubt that the unchanging nature, which is set over the rational soul, is God; where the original wisdom is, there also is the original life and essence. In God is that unchangeable truth which is properly called the law, which governs all the arts and is the art of the omnipotent Creator. While the soul realizes that it cannot judge either the appearance or the movement of material objects from its own resources, at the same time it ought to observe that its own nature is superior to the nature of the objects it judges. The soul should also recognize that the nature, by reference to which it makes its judgments but which cannot itself be judged, is superior to itself. Because I delight in absolute equality, which I contemplate not with my physical eyes but with the eyes of my mind, it is quite possible for me to say why corresponding limbs on both sides of a body should be alike. For this reason I conclude that the things I see with my eyes are better insofar as they approach more closely, within the limits of their own nature, to the things which I understand with my mind. Nobody can say why the things of the mind are as they are, and nobody in his senses can say that they "ought" to be as they are, as if they could be in any way different from what they are. . . .

[7] Many people aim at merely human pleasure and have no interest in reaching toward higher things to find the reasons why visible things give them pleasure. Thus,I think that, if I ask a workman why, after building an arch, he erects a second one similar to it against the first, he will reply that similar parts of a building should be in corresponding positions. Furthermore, if I proceed to ask why he says this, he will claim that the result looks well, is beautiful, and gives pleasure to those who look at it. But he will go no further than that and will look down and lower his eyes, since he does not understand the point at issue. On the other hand, when I meet a man equipped with interior eyes, that is, one who can see things invisible to the physical eyes, I shall press him to say why the result is pleasing so that he may venture to make a judgment about human pleasure. When he makes such a judgment, he is carried above sensual delight and escapes from its clutches while he is judging it; his judgment is about pleasure, but he does not use pleasure as the criterion. In the first place I shall ask him whether objects are beautiful because they give pleasure or give pleasure because they are beautiful. To this I shall certainly get the reply that they give pleasure because they are beautiful. Then I shall ask why they are beautiful. If he is shaken by this, I shall ask if it is because their parts are similar to one another and united in one harmonious whole.

When he agrees that this is so, I shall ask whether objects fully achieve this unity, which they are found to be aiming at, or whether they fall far short of it and in a way falsify it. Of course, nobody who has been put on the alert can fail to see that every form or physical object of any sort has some trace of unity, while at the same time no object, however beautiful, can attain the unity it seeks, since its parts are necessarily separated by intervals of space. If this is granted, I shall then ask him to tell where he sees this unity or what is its source.

[7] *True Religion,* 59–60.

If he cannot see it, how can he know what physical forms imitate and what they cannot fully achieve? If he were then to say to physical objects, "You would be nothing unless you were held together by some unity; but by the same token, if you were that unity, you would not be objects," he could properly be asked, "Where have you gained your knowledge of that unity, by which you judge objects? If you cannot see unity, you cannot judge that these objects fall short of it. But, if you see it with your physical eyes, you could not truthfully say that the objects carry traces of unity and still fall short of realizing it; for with the physical eyes you can see only physical objects and therefore you see unity with the mind. But where do you see it? If you see it here where our body is, it could not be seen by a man passing judgment on physical objects in some eastern country. So the principle of unity is not located in space; it is present to everyone wherever he may be exercising the function of judgment. It is nowhere in space, but its power is everywhere."

The following passage occurs near the beginning of the first book of Augustine's treatise *On Music,* which takes the form of a dialogue between a teacher (Augustine) and an unidentified pupil. Music has been defined as "the knowledge of good modulation" *(scientia bene modulandi).* Augustine's purpose in the argument which follows is to refine this definition by making a clear distinction between art and imitation. Art implies knowledge, and knowledge is of the mind and not of the body; on the other hand, imitation is largely a matter of unthinking physical reactions. Therefore, if we include knowledge in our definition of music, we are seeing music as an art and defining it in terms of intellectual knowing rather than practical performance. To "know" music is one thing, while to "perform" music is a practical activity and therefore of a lower order. The musical performer is unlikely to "know" the first principles of music, which in Augustine's view resolve themselves into principles of numerical relationships. This dualism of mind and body, of thought on the one hand and practical action on the other, is basic to Augustine's view of reality. Its implications for education have been severely attacked by modern educational realists, e.g., John Dewey.

[8]MASTER: It remains for us to ask why we include "knowledge" in our definition.

PUPIL: Yes, indeed. I remember that the sequence of our argument demands this.

MASTER: Then tell me whether you think that the nightingale modulates her voice well in the springtime. Her song is rhythmical and very sweet; furthermore, unless I am mistaken, it suits the season of the year.

PUPIL: I entirely agree.

MASTER: Is she therefore skilled in this liberal art (music)?

PUPIL: No.

MASTER: Then you understand that the term "knowledge" is essential to the definition.

PUPIL: I do.

MASTER: Well then, please tell me this. Do you not think that all those people who, under the stimulus of sensation, sing well, that is, rhythmically and sweetly, are like the nightingale? They sing well, although

[8] *On Music*, i, 5-12.

they cannot reply when they are questioned about their rhythms or about the intervals between high and low notes.

PUPIL: I think they do resemble the nightingale.

MASTER: Then what about those people who do not have this knowledge and yet take delight in listening? Are they not like bears and elephants and such animals, which we see making movements to music, or like the birds we observe taking pleasure in their own voices? For there can be only one reason why birds put such effort into their music: they get pleasure from it.

PUPIL: I agree. But this is a reflection on almost all the human race.

MASTER: Not so. For great men, even when they have no knowledge of music, like to conform to the common people, who are not much different from animals and who are considerably in the majority. Such men do this with moderation and prudence; after the cares of business, they derive some pleasure from music in a restrained way in order to relax and recreate their minds.

To indulge in music occasionally is reasonable, whereas to be held captive by it, even from time to time, is low and unbecoming. But what is your opinion? Can those who play on the flute, the lyre or some such instrument be compared to nightingales?

PUPIL: No.

MASTER: What then is the difference?

PUPIL: In your players I observe the presence of art, whereas in the nightingale I see natural instinct alone.

MASTER: What you say is probable. But do you think it right to use the term "art," even when their performance is due to a sort of imitation?

PUPIL: Why not? For I see that imitation has such a great influence in the arts that, when it is removed, they are almost entirely ruined. For example, teachers offer themselves for imitation, and this is the essence of what they call teaching.

MASTER: Do you think that art is a sort of reason and that people who use art are using reason? Or do you disagree?

PUPIL: I agree.

MASTER: Then whoever does not use reason is not practicing on art.

PUPIL: I grant this also.

MASTER: Then either you would say that magpies, parrots and ravens are rational creatures, or you have rashly called "imitation" by the name of "art"; for we see that these birds frequently utter songs and sounds with an almost human skill and that they do this merely by imitation. Or do you disagree?

PUPIL I do not yet clearly understand how you have reached this point and how it contradicts my reply.

MASTER: I had asked you whether you said that players of

the lyre or flute or some such instrument were practicing an art, even when they got their effects by imitation. You declared that it was art and added that imitation had such great influence that, when it was removed, almost all the arts seemed to you to be in danger. From this we now conclude that everyone who achieves something by imitation is practicing an art, although perhaps not everyone who practices an art has achieved it by imitation. However, if all imitation is art, and all art is reason, then all imitation is reason. But an irrational animal does not employ reason, and therefore he cannot be practicing an art. On the other hand, an animal does employ imitation; therefore, art is not imitation.

PUPIL: I said that many arts involve imitation, but not that imitation itself is art.

MASTER: Then do you not consider that arts which call for imitation also involve reason?

PUPIL: Yes, I think they call for both.

MASTER: I do not quarrel with you. But where do you find knowledge? In reason or in imitation?

PUPIL: In both.

MASTER: Then you will allow knowledge to those birds who, as you admit, practice imitation.

PUPIL: No; for I said that knowledge lies in both reason and imitation, so that it cannot be found in imitation alone.

MASTER: Then do you think that knowledge can be found in reason alone?

PUPIL: I do.

MASTER: Therefore, you think that art and knowledge are different things, since knowledge can be found in reason alone, while art combines imitation with reason.

PUPIL: I do not admit this conclusion. I had not said that all arts combine both reason and imitation, but only that many arts do so.

MASTER: Will you bestow the term "knowledge" on what combines the two? Or will you allow knowledge to the function of reason alone?

PUPIL: I cannot see why I should not use the term "knowledge" when imitation is combined with reason?

MASTER: Since at present we are talking about the lyre player and the flutist, that is, about music, I would like you to tell me this: when these players accomplish something by imitation, are we to think of this as a physical function and put it down to obedience on the part of the body?

PUPIL: I think it should be attributed both to the mind and the body. But the expression "obedience on the part of the body" was well chosen by you, for the body cannot obey except at the command of the mind.

MASTER: I see that you show great caution in your unwillingness to concede that imitation belongs to the body alone. Will you then deny that knowledge belongs to the mind alone?

PUPIL: Who would deny this?

MASTER: Then, in the case of strings and flutes, you cannot attribute knowledge to reason and imitation simultaneously; for you agreed that there is no possibility of imitation without the body, while at the same time you declared that knowledge belongs to the mind alone.

PUPIL: I agree that this follows from what I admitted to you. But what of it? The flute player will also have knowledge in his mind. He will not lose what is in his mind when he indulges in imitation, which I said depends on the body.

MASTER: Indeed, he will not lose it. I do not say that all those who play these instruments lack knowledge, but only that they do not all have it. This enquiry is being directed to the end that we should understand, if we can, with what good reason the term "knowledge" has been included in our definition of music. If every player of the flute, the lyre, and so on, possesses this knowledge, then I think that nothing is more worthless or debased. However, attend as closely as you can so that we may clarify the matter we have been working at so long. You have certainly granted me that knowledge resides in the mind alone.

PUPIL: I did.

MASTER: Do you say that the sense of hearing belongs to the mind, the body or both?

PUPIL: To both.

MASTER: And memory?

PUPIL: To the mind, I think; for although we pick up

something through the senses and commit it to memory, we are not on that account to imagine that memory resides in the body.

MASTER: That is perhaps a big question and not relevant to this discussion. But it is sufficient for our purpose, and I think you cannot deny it, that animals have memory. Swallows revisit their nests after a year, and it has been truly said that "goats remember and return to their homes" (Vergil, *Georgics,* iii, 316). It is also told that a dog recognized his heroic master, who was already forgotten by his own people (Homer, *Odyssey,* xxiii, 291). If we want to, we can find innumerable examples to prove what I say.

PUPIL: I entirely agree, and I am eagerly waiting to see how it helps your case.

MASTER: This is the point. If you attribute knowledge to the mind alone and deny it to all irrational creatures, you place it neither in sensation nor in memory (for the former does not exist without a body and both are found in beasts), but in the understanding alone.

PUPIL: I am waiting to see how this helps you.

MASTER: This is it. None of those who follow sensation, commit to memory the pleasures they get from sensation, draw on their power of imitation and move their bodies in response to these pleasures, are in possession of knowledge. In however skilled and learned a manner such people seem to do many things, I say they do not possess knowledge unless with the purity and truth of the intellect, they grasp the thing itself which they profess to demonstrate. If reason shows that those music hall players of yours do not grasp this, then in my opinion there will be no reason for you to hesitate to deny them knowledge and, therefore, to deny that they practice music, which is the "knowledge" of modulation.

PUPIL: Tell me how this is.

MASTER: I believe you would attribute the difference between faster and slower fingering to practice and not to knowledge.

PUPIL: Why do you think so?

MASTER: Because you were attributing knowledge to the mind alone, whereas fingering is clearly a matter of the body, although it is done at the bidding of the mind.

PUPIL: But, when the knowing mind gives its commands to the body, I think that the action should be attributed to the knowing mind rather than to the limbs which are its servants.

MASTER: Surely you think it possible that one man may excel over another in knowledge, although the one who knows less may be able to move his fingers with greater dexterity and ease.

PUPIL: I do.

MASTER: But, if speedy and more dexterous finger movement is to be attributed to knowledge, the more knowledge a person has the better his finger movements will be.

PUPIL: I admit this.

MASTER: Listen to this too. I believe that you have sometimes noticed workmen striking the same spot again and again with an axe or a hatchet and placing their strokes on the exact spot to which their mind directs them. But, when we attempt it and cannot match them, they often laugh at us.

PUPIL: It is as you say.

MASTER: When we fail to achieve this, is it because we do not know what spot to strike or how much timber to knock off?

PUPIL: Sometimes we do not know, and sometimes we do.

MASTER: Imagine then that one man knows everything that workmen ought to do, and knows it perfectly, but is less effective on the job. At the same time he gives very shrewd directions to those who have the greatest practical skill. Do you deny that this is the result of practice?

PUPIL: No.

MASTER: Therefore, not only the speed and ease of movement but also the physical techniques can be attributed to practice rather than to knowledge. If it were otherwise, the more experienced a man was, the more skillfully would he use his hands. Thus, we should not imagine that, because what is accomplished on flutes and lyres with the fingers and joints seems difficult to us, it is the result of knowledge and thought rather than of practice and diligent imitation.

PUPIL: I cannot oppose this, for I hear that some very learned doctors are frequently inferior to less experienced men when it comes to cutting or binding limbs, i.e., using their hands or a knife. They call this kind of medical work "surgery," which refers to a practical technique of healing residing in the hands. So now let us pass on and conclude this particular question. . . .

MASTER: Why do you think that ignorant people often hiss a fiuteplayer who produces worthless sound but applaud a good player? In fact, the sweeter the playing, the more deeply and keenly are people moved. Must we attribute this to their "knowledge" of the art of music?

PUPIL: No.

MASTER: Then what is the explanation?

PUPIL: I think this appreciation comes from nature, which has given all of us the sense of hearing, by which such things are to be judged.

MASTER: You are right. But now consider this: Is the flute-player himself endowed with this sense? Because, if he is, then, when he plays his flute, he can move his fingers as he judges best, and can register and commit to memory the sounds which give him most satisfaction and which are approved by his judgment. Then by repeating these sounds, he can accustom his fingers to take their places without any hesitation or fumbling, whether he receives what he plays from someone else or composes his own music under the guidance and approval of that natural instinct we were referring to. Thus, memory follows sensation, and the fingers, being trained and prepared by practice, follow the dictates of memory. Therefore, when he wants to, he plays effectively and beautifully in proportion to his excellence in all those attributes which, as we have found, man holds in common with the animals, to wit, the appetite for imitation, sensation and memory. Have you anything to say to this?

PUPIL: I have nothing. But I would like to discover the nature of this discipline (music), which, as I can clearly see, you have most subtly removed from the understanding of the most worthless minds.

MASTER: What we have done is not enough, and I cannot allow us to proceed to the explanation of this without understanding the grounds for our assertion that, without a knowledge of music, players can give pleasure to the ears of the crowd. For by this we imply that players cannot be students of music or skilled in it. Tell me then which of the following should be regarded as of greater value: what is preserved in our understanding or what is conferred upon us by the arbitrary judgment of ignorant people?

PUPIL: Everyone would agree that the former is better. The latter should not really be counted as belonging to us at all.

MASTER: Then do you deny that all knowledge is preserved in the understanding?

PUPIL: It is impossible to deny it.

MASTER: Is music also in the understanding?

PUPIL: This follows from the definition of music.

MASTER: Furthermore, I suppose you agree that the applause of the crowd and all the rewards of the stage belong to the class of things which are placed in the lap of fortune and depend on the judgment of the ignorant.

PUPIL: My view is that nothing is more fortuitous, more exposed to chance or more subject to the caprices of the crowd, than these are.

MASTER: Then, would players sell their songs at such a price if they had a knowledge of music?

PUPIL: I am impressed by this conclusion, but I have something to say in reply. I do not think that the seller of a gold coin is the same as a musician; for, when the musician receives applause or money is showered on him, he does not lose the knowledge which he possesses, by virtue of which he has delighted the crowd. He goes home laden with money and buoyed up with the praises of men, but with his art safe and whole. He would indeed be a fool if he despised the prizes, without which his fame would be considerably reduced and his purse lighter, but which do not take away from his art.

MASTER: Let us consider whether this argument brings our discussion to the conclusion we wish. I think that you take the view that the end for which we engage in activity is much superior to the activity itself.

MASTER: Then, when a person sings, or learns to sing, only to be praised by the crowd, is he putting a higher value on the praise than the singing?

PUPIL: He is.

MASTER: Well, do you think that a man who makes a bad judgment about a subject knows the subject?

PUPIL: By no means, unless perhaps he has been somehow corrupted.

MASTER: Therefore, a man who really imagines that a thing is of higher value when it is certainly of lower value lacks a knowledge of it.

PUPIL: That is so.

MASTER: Therefore, when you either persuade or show me that a musician is skillful but has not developed his skill merely to please the crowd and become rich and famous, I shall agree that someone can have a knowledge of music and at the same time be a player. But if, as is highly probable, every player sets money or glory as the objective of his professional activity, we must declare either that musicians have no knowledge of music or that fame or some other accidental prize is a worthier aim for some people than understanding is for us.

PUPIL: I see that, because I have conceded the previous proposition, I must yield to this one too; for I cannot think of a stage performer who loves his art for itself without any extraneous advantages. But, if such a person exists or will exist, then musicians can be regarded as worthy of honor and not contempt.

Absolute Truth: The Influence of Plato

[9]Among the students of Socrates, Plato with good reason radiated the greatest glory, far excelling the others and completely eclipsing them all. He was an Athenian from a good

[9] *The City of God,* viii, 4–5.

family, and by virtue of his marvellous ability he far outstripped his fellow students. However, he came to the conclusion that he himself and Socrates' instruction were inadequate to bring philosophy to its completion, and so he travelled abroad in as many countries as he could, going to every place which was said to be outstanding for the study of some particular science.* Thus, in Egypt Plato learned all that was highly regarded and taught there; from Egypt he came into those parts of Italy where the fame of the Pythagoreans was celebrated and there, under the direction of the more outstanding teachers and with great ease, he mastered all the Italian philosophy which was then flourishing.

Because Plato had a special affection for his teacher Socrates, he made him a speaker in almost all of his dialogues, putting into Socrates' mouth all that he had learned from other people or grasped by the effort of his own great intellect, and tempering even his moral discussions with Socrates' charm. The study of wisdom is concerned with action and contemplation; therefore, one part of it can be called "active" and the other "contemplative." The active part has reference to the conduct of life, that is, the regulation of morals, and the contemplative part is concerned with the investigation of natural causes and with absolute truth. Thus, Socrates is said to have been superior in the active part of this study, while Pythagoras, with all the resources of his great understanding, paid more attention to its contemplative part. Similarly Plato is commended for having perfected philosophy by joining those two parts into one and then dividing the study into three parts: the first moral, which is principally concerned with action; the second natural, which is devoted to contemplation; the third rational, by which truth is distinguished from falsehood. Although the last is necessary both for action and contemplation, it is nevertheless contemplation which claims for itself the investigation of truth.

* The tradition of Plato's extensive travels rests on uncertain authority. From Plato himself, we learn only of journeys to Italy and Sicily. See A. E. Taylor, *Plato: The Man and His Work,* pp. 3–9 (Methuen, 6th ed., 1949).

Hence, this tripartite division does not contradict the other distinction, by which the study of wisdom is understood to consist of action and of contemplation.

It would take too long to discuss the nature of Plato's views on each of these parts of philosophy, that is, what he understood and believed to be the aim of all actions, the cause of all natural objects, and the light of all understandings. Certainly we should be careful not to make any rash statements about his views because Plato constantly followed the well-known method of his teacher Socrates, whom he represented in his books as engaging in discussion; this was the method of concealing his own knowledge or opinions, which was what Socrates also liked to do. For this reason it is not easy to discover Plato's views on important matters; nevertheless, we must recall some of the opinions he expresses in his writings and introduce them into this book without regard to whether he was giving his own views or those of other people which won his approval.... Plato is properly given a place of preeminence over all the other pagan philosophers, and it may be that those who are given credit for having understood him with unusual penetration and truth see God as the cause of existence, the ultimate principle of understanding and the rule in accordance with which life is to be ordered. Of these three, the first is the concern of natural philosophy, the second of rational philosophy and the third of moral philosophy.... Thus, if Plato declared that the wise man is one who imitates, knows and loves this God, and who is made happy through the fellowship he enjoys with God, what use is there in studying other philosophers? Not one of them approaches more closely to us (Christians) than the Platonists do.

[10]Those philosophers who by their merits are seen to be raised high above the rest in fame and glory, have realized

[10] *City of God,* viii, 6.

that God is no material object; thus, they have passed beyond all matter in their search for God. They have seen that whatever is changeable is not the most high God; therefore, they have gone beyond every soul and all changeable spirits in their search for the supreme God. They have also recognized that in every changeable thing the form which makes it what it is can derive its existence only from Him who really exists because He exists unchangeably; and this is true whatever the mode or nature of that form.

Consider then the whole mass of the world, its shapes, qualities and orderly movements; also its elements, from the heavens right down to the earth. Take note of all its forms of life: the life which gives nourishment and resists decay, for example, in trees; the life which has the added power of sense perception, as in beasts; the life which adds intelligence to all this, as in man; or that form of life which needs no nourishment but merely sustains, feels and understands, for example, that of angels. All these forms of life can derive their existence only from God, who simply exists. For in His case, existing and being alive are not two different things; He cannot exist without living. Thus, living and understanding are also the same for Him; He cannot live without understanding. Nor in Him is there any difference between understanding and being happy, as though He could understand without being happy. For God, to live, understand and be happy is to exist. The philosophers we are talking about have realized that it was by virtue of this unchangeable nature and simplicity that God made everything, but that He himself could not have been made by anyone. They considered that whatever exists is either matter or life, that life is superior to matter and that the form of matter is open to the senses, while the form of life is open only to the understanding. For this reason they preferred the intelligible form to the sensible form, the "sensible" being what we perceive by physical sight or touch, the "intelligible" what can be understood by the vision of the mind. Now the mind evaluates all physical beauty, whether found in the qualities of an object, e.g., its shape, or in movement, e.g., a song. This judgment would not be possible if there did not exist in the mind itself a superior form of these things; I mean a form without extension, without any vocal sound, and not located in space or time. But even with regard to these things, if the mind were not changeable, it would not be possible for one person to make better judgments about sensible forms than another. The clever person has better judgment than the person who is slow, the skilled than the unskilled, the man who is practiced than the one who is unpracticed. Also, the same person makes better judgments after he has gained experience than he did before. What is capable of being more or less is certainly changeable; accordingly able and learned men who are trained in such matters have easily concluded that the first form is not to be found in things whose form is found to be changeable. As they see it, both body and mind show varying degrees of beauty, but they would be non-existent if they were without any form. Therefore, such thinkers recognized that there does exist something in which the first form enjoys an unchanging existence and which on that account is not subject to degrees of comparison. Thus, with very good reason they assumed that the first principle of things, which was not itself created but out of which everything originated, is to be found in this "something." Thus, when those invisible things of God, which are understood through the medium of created objects, were seen by such men, God was displaying to them what is known to Himself.

[11] You cannot deny that there is such a thing as unchangeable truth, and that this includes everything which is unchangeably true. You cannot say that this truth is either yours or mine or the property of any one person; you must admit that it is open to everyone. To all who can see what is

[11] *Free Will,* ii, 33–34.

unchangeable and true it presents itself on equal terms, like a light which in some marvellous way is at one and the same time withdrawn and yet open to the public gaze. Who could say that anything which is open on equal terms to all reasoning and intelligent beings belongs to any one of them as his own private property? You recall no doubt what we were saying a little while ago about the physical senses. What we experience in common through the senses of our eyes or ears, for example, colors and sounds which both you and I see or hear simultaneously, is not the private property of our particular eyes or ears; it is open to the perception of both of us in common. So what you and I behold in common, each with his own mind, could never be said to belong to either one of our minds. You cannot say that what the eyes of two people see simultaneously belongs to the eyes of the one or the other. The fact is that the gaze of both people is directed toward a third thing.

Do you then think that the truth, which we have been talking about for so long and in which we see so many things, is more excellent than our minds? Or is it equal to them or inferior? If truth is inferior, then, instead of making our judgments in accordance with truth we would make judgments about truth, just as we make judgments about physical objects because they are inferior to us. About physical objects we do not merely say that they are so, or are not so, but that they ought to be so or not so. Similarly we not only know how our minds are constituted but how they ought to be constituted. We make judgments about physical objects when we say, "This is less white than it ought to be," or "less square" and so on. But with reference to minds we say, "It is not as effective as it ought to be," or "It is not gentle enough," or "not eager enough," according to our moral standards. And we make judgments according to those interior rules of truth which we see in common. But no one passes judgment on the rules themselves. For when someone says that the eternal is better than the temporal or that seven and three make ten, nobody says that it ought to be so. They simply know that it is so. We do not examine and correct the rules; we are simply pleased to have discovered them. Now, if truth were the equal of our minds, it would also be changeable. For our minds see truth to a greater or lesser extent at different times, and this fact shows that our minds are changeable. On the other hand, truth abides in itself, neither advancing when we see more of it nor falling short when we see less. It is whole and uncorrupted, and with its illumination it delights those who turn toward it and punishes with blindness those who turn away from it. We pass judgment on our minds by the standard of truth, but we do not pass judgment on truth itself. We say, "He understands less than he ought" or "He understands as much as he should." The more closely the mind can approach and cleave to unchangeable truth, the more it must understand. Thus, if truth is neither inferior nor equal to our minds, the conclusion is that it must be superior and more excellent. . . .

[12]It is in truth that we come to know and lay hold of the supreme good, and that same truth constitutes wisdom. Therefore, let us perceive the supreme good in truth and let us grasp it and enjoy it to the full. He is indeed happy who enjoys the supreme good, for it is truth which points the way to all the things that are truly good. When a man understands these according to his capacity, he chooses them for himself, either one by one or several together, in order to enjoy them. Think of those who in the sunlight single out something to look at with pleasure and rejoice in looking at it; among them are those who are endowed with more vigorous, healthy and strong eyesight and who turn their gaze with greater pleasure towards the sun, which lights up all those other objects in which weaker eyes take pleasure. Thus, when a stronger and more active mental vision sees many true and unchanging

[12] *Free Will*, ii, 36–38.

things in the light of sure and certain reason, it is turning itself toward truth, by which everything is revealed; it cleaves to this truth, forgetting as it were everything else and in this truth enjoying everything at once. For, indeed, whatever pleasure is to be found in other truths is pleasant by reason of its participation in absolute truth. . . .

The things which we touch, taste and smell do not bear such a striking resemblance to truth as do the things we hear and see. The reason is that every word is heard as a whole by everyone simultaneously, and at the same time as a whole by each person separately. So also every shape presented to our eyes is the same size for each person who looks at it at the same time. Hearing and seeing are similar, although there is also a considerable difference between them. A word is not spoken as a whole at exactly the same moment, for it is extended or prolonged throughout a period of time; one part of it is pronounced first and another part thereafter. In the same way every visible form is, as it were, spread out in space and is not present as a whole in any one place. Again, all such things can be taken from us against our will, and certain difficulties can prevent us enjoying them. Even if a sweet singer could continue singing forever, those who are anxious to hear him would be competing with one another to hear him. The more numerous they are, the more they would pack into the auditorium and fight for seats in a struggle to be closer to the singer. Also, when they hear him, they would be unable to hold on to what they hear, and every sound heard would be transient. If I want to gaze at the sun and can do this without flinching, it would abandon me when it sets or happens to be veiled in a cloud. These and many other obstacles could cause me unwillingly to lose my pleasure in looking at the sun. Finally, even though my pleasure in seeing the light and hearing the voice is uninterrupted, what great profit would the experience bring me, when even animals can share it with me?

On the other hand, when people approach the beauty of truth and wisdom and have the persistent desire to enjoy this beauty, it is not shut off from them by a close-packed audience thronging around it; it neither passes away with time nor moves from one place to another; it is not cut off by the fall of night, veiled in shadow or in subjection to the physical senses. Truth is near at hand and everlasting to everyone in this world who loves truth and turns towards it. It is nowhere in space; yet it is present everywhere. The suggestions it makes to man come from outside him, but its teaching takes place within him.* It changes for the better all who look upon it, but no one changes it for the worse. No man passes judgment on truth; nevertheless, without it no man has good judgment. This is why it is clear that truth is certainly superior to our minds. It is by truth alone that minds are each separately made wise and enabled to be judges, not of truth itself, but of everything else with the help of truth.

The Basic Significance of Number

[13]AUGUSTINE: Think carefully and tell me whether you can find something which all reasoning beings see in common, each with his own reason and mind. I mean something which is open to all to see, but is not changed when it is used by those to whom it is available, as food and drink are; something which remains incorruptible and whole, irrespective of whether people see it or not. Perhaps you think there is nothing of this kind at all.

EVODIUS: I see that there are many such things, but it will be enough to mention one of them. The principle and truth of number is open to all reasoning beings, in such a way that every calculator

* Succintly expressed in the Latin: "[*Veritas*] *foris admonet, intus docet*."

[13] *Free Will*, ii, 20–24.

may try to grasp it with his own reason and intelligence. One man can do it easily, another only with difficulty, while another cannot do it at all. But the truth of number is the same for all who have the power to grasp it; it is not changed and transmuted, so to speak, into nourishment for the person who takes it. Therefore, it is not truth which fails when someone makes a mistake in calculation; truth remains true and complete, and the less of it a man sees, the more he is in error.

AUGUSTINE: You are indeed correct. I see that you are not inexperienced in such matters and have been quick to find a reply. But, if someone were to remark that numbers are not impressed on our minds exactly as they are but that they are derived from the objects which we contact through our physical senses, what would you say in reply? Or is this in line with your own thinking?

EVODIUS: I could never subscribe to that opinion. Even if I do perceive numbers with the senses, I could never perceive with the physical senses the laws governing the divisions and interrelationships of numbers. It is by the aid of a mental light that I give the lie to anyone who has done some adding or subtracting and reached a wrong answer. In all that I experience through my physical senses, for example, the sky, earth and all the other objects I perceive there, I do not know how long such things will last. But seven and three are ten; this is so, not only at the present time but always. Seven and three were never at any time not ten; there will never be a time in the future when this will not be so. This is the incorruptible truth of number, which I said is common to me and to all reasoning beings.

AUGUSTINE: I accept what you say in reply since it is most true and certain. But you will easily see that numbers are not brought to us by the physical senses if you consider that every number gets its name from the number of times it contains unity. For example, if a number contains unity twice over, it is called two; if three times, then three; if it is ten times one, it is called ten. The name and value of any number depend on the number of times it contains unity. Now whoever really thinks about unity will see that it cannot be perceived by the senses. For whatever comes into contact with our senses is demonstrably not one but many. All such things are physical objects and therefore have innumerable parts. I shall not talk about parts which are of minute size and indistinct, but, however tiny an object is, it surely has a right side and a left side, a top and a bottom, parts that are on one side and parts that are on the other side, end parts and parts in the middle. All these parts must necessarily exist in an object, however small. Thus, we see that no physical object is truly and simply one; nevertheless, all these many parts could not be counted unless we could distinguish them one from another through our knowledge of unity. When I seek unity in my physical environment and am sure that I am not finding it, then surely I know what I am looking for and not finding. I must know that I cannot find it there or rather that it does not exist there at all. Thus, since I know that no physical object is a unity, I know what unity is;

if I did not, I could not add up the many different parts of an object. Wherever I have learned about unity, it is not through the senses that I have found it. Through the senses I have known only physical objects, which, as we have demonstrated, are not truly and simply one. Furthermore, if we have not perceived unity through the senses, then we have perceived no number through the senses, at any rate not those which we perceive with the understanding. For there is no number which is not defined in terms of a multiple of one, and unity is not perceived with the physical senses. The half of a tiny object can itself be divided in half, no matter how small the two halves which constitute the whole. The two parts are present in the object, but they are not themselves simply two.* On the other hand the actual number which is called "two," contains unity twice over. Therefore, its half, which is unity pure and simple, cannot again be halved and divided into three or any number of parts; for we are now dealing with unity pure and simple.

Going through the sequence of numbers, we see that the number two comes after one, and by comparing them we find that the former is double the latter. However, the double of two (four) does not follow in immediate succession; the number three comes in between. This principle extends through all the rest of the numerical series by a fixed and inviolable law. The number one, i.e., the first of all numbers, is immediately followed by the number which is its double (two). But after the second number, i.e., two, the number which is the double of two

* i.e., since they can be further subdivided.

follows two numbers later. After the third number, i.e., three, the number which is its double comes three numbers later. Once again it is the fourth number after four which is twice four. And so right through the whole series of numbers you will find the principle which was revealed in the union of the first two numbers, i.e., one and two; this principle is that the double of a number comes at exactly the same distance from it as it is from the beginning of the series of numbers. How is it possible for us to see this steady, firm and inviolable law passing through the whole range of numbers? How indeed? For nobody experiences all the numbers with his physical senses since they are infinitely numerous. How do we know that this principle extends through all the numbers? By what phantasy or image can such a sure and certain truth of number, running through such an unending series, be conveyed to us? In fact, we can know this truth only in that interior light of which the physical senses are totally ignorant.

By these and many other pieces of evidence, everyone who discusses the question, whom God has endowed with good ability and who is not clouded by obstinacy, is compelled to admit that the law and truth of numbers do not depend on physical sensation, but stand inviolate and pure, and are open to the common inspection of all rational beings. We can think of many other things, which are generally and, as it were, publicly exposed to rational beings. These are the things which are seen by the mind and reason of each one of us separately, and which nevertheless remain inviolate and unchangeable. But it pleased me that the law and truth of number came first into your mind when you wanted to find a reply to my questions. For it is with good reason that the Scriptures link wisdom and number together when it is said: "I applied my heart to know and to search and to seek out wisdom and number."*

[14]When we are filled with the desire to be wise, what are we doing other than focussing our whole souls with the greatest possible attention on what we are experiencing within our minds? We concentrate on this and persevere with it to such an extent that our soul no longer takes pleasure in any of the preoccupations which attach it to transient things. Putting off all its yearning for the things of space and time, the soul lays hold of what remains one and the same forever. . . . Wherever you turn, wisdom speaks to you from the impressions she has traced upon her handiwork; talking within you, she calls you back, when you are turning aside to the things of the external world. She does this through the forms of external things, leading you to see that all the material things which delight and woo you through the senses are characterized by number. You ask yourself how this can be; thus, you return within yourself and come to understand that you would not be capable of passing judgment on the data of sense unless within yourself you possessed certain laws of beauty, to which you may refer every beautiful object you perceive in the external world.

Turn your eyes to the heavens, the earth and the sea, to everything which shines brightly in or above them, which creeps, flies or swims. They all have forms, and this is be-

*See the footnote on p. 211 above. St. Augustine here follows the Greek text of *Ecclesiastes* 7:25, which reads "wisdom and number" *(sapientiam et numerum),* instead of the Vulgate reading, "wisdom and the reason of things."

[14] *Free Will,* ii, 41–42.

ause they have numbers*; take numbers away from them, nd there is nothing left. What is the source of all these things nless it is He who is the source of number, for they exist nly inasmuch as they are numerically proportioned? Indeed, nen who construct all physical shapes have numbers as the asis of their craft, and they make their products conform to hem. While they move their limbs and tools, they are refering the object being shaped outside themselves to the light of umbers within them until the object receives such perfection s is possible, and, being communicated to the senses, pleases ne internal judge who sees the transcendent numbers.

Thus, if you ask what moves the limbs of the craftsman, the nswer is "number," for even these move rhytmically. If the ands have no task to perform and the mind has no intention f making anything and if the movement of the limbs is solely or pleasure, then we call the activity dancing. If you inquire hat gives pleasure in dancing, number will reply, "Look, it I." Examine the beauty of a well-formed body; numbers re expressed there in spatial form. Study the beauty of hysical movement; there you find number expressed in temoral form. Penetrate to the art from which all these numbers roceed, and search there for space and time. You cannot nd them; nevertheless, number is alive there. Number's welling place is not defined by space nor its duration by ngth of days; when people want to become craftsmen and pply themselves to the study of their craft, they move their odies in space and time, but their minds in time only; for it is ith the passage of time that they develop their skill.

Therefore, pass beyond the mind of the craftsman to look pon eternal number; then wisdom will shine out for you om her inner dwelling place and from the secret recesses of uth. If truth repels your too feeble gaze, cast back the eye f your mind to that way where she graciously showed herself you. But keep in mind that you have merely deferred a

* All physical phenomena, e.g., shapes, movements in music and nce, are expressions of numerical proportion.

vision, which you will seek again when you are stronger an more healthy.

Human Progress and the Rise of the Liberal Arts

[15]As far as we have been able to investigate the matter, ou study has shown traces of reason in sense perception; in sigh and hearing we find reason even in the pleasure itself. As fo the other senses, they cannot be called "rational" on accou of the pleasure associated with them; rather they represe the action of a living being directed to some end. In visio beauty is generally attributed to a harmony among the part of an object; this harmony is said to be "rational." In hearin when we say that a harmony is "reasonable" and that rhythmical song is "rationally composed," we appropriatel refer to them as "sweet." But we do not usually employ th term "rational" with reference to a color which attracts us i beautiful objects, or when a chord is struck producing a pu and liquid sound. We should conclude, therefore, that in th pleasures of sight and hearing we are concerned with som thing rational, when we are in the presence of measure an rhythm.

Thus, when we look at the several parts of this building the sight of one of the two doorways located toward the sid and the other almost, but not exactly, in the middle mu certainly offend us. On examining a building and noticing a unequal relationship of its parts, which is not absolutely ne essary, we seem to suffer a sort of visual injury. On the oth hand, the three windows inside this building, one in th middle and the other two at the sides, pour light at equ intervals on the bath. What pleasure this gives us and how

* The discussion is taking place in the bath-house of Verecund country house at Cassiciacum.

[15] *The Principle of Order,* ii, 33–44.

ttracts the attention of our minds! The fact is evident and equires no long explanation. This is why architects talk bout a "plan," and say that parts unsymetrically arranged ave no "plan."*

The principle we have noted is very widespread and apears in almost all the arts and works of man. Everyone nows that measure is the cause of all the sweetness in songs, 1 which an element of reason is associated with the pleasure f hearing them. Now imagine a dancer, whose very gesture ; significant to those who watch him perceptively; although ne's eyes are delighted by the rhythmical movement of his mbs, which is an expression of the "measure" *(modus)* we ave referred to, we call the dance "reasonable" because it is n accurate demonstration of something quite different from ie sensual pleasure it conveys. Thus, if the dancer portrays a 'inged Venus and a cloaked Cupid, he does not seem to ffend the eyes, even if he depicts these with remarkable iovement and posture. Nevertheless, through the eyes he ffends the mind,** to which these signs are displayed. On ie other hand, if the movements were not gracefully made, ie eyes would be offended because gracefulness of moveient is associated with the visual sense, in which the soul xperiences delight because of its connection with the body.

Therefore, sensation is one thing and what is experienced irough the senses is quite another. Beauty of movement elights the senses, but the mind finds its pleasure only in the eauty of the meaning which the movement expresses. This so applies to hearing, which is attracted and charmed by veet sounds; but it is the mind alone which receives the eaning conveyed by the sounds, although the ears trasmit iem.

* The Latin word is *ratio,* reason.

** That is, he offends the Christian mind because of the pagan ;nificance of the dance.

Thus, when we hear the following lines:

> "Quid tantum Oceano properent se tingere soles
> Hiberni, vel quae tardis mora noctibus obstet."
> (Vergil, *Georgics,* ii, 480-48

> "Why does the sun in the winter descend with speed t
> the Ocean?
> What is the reason which makes the nights so slow i
> departing?"

it is one thing to praise the meter and another to praise th thought. We do not say, "It has a reasonable sound," in th same sense that we say "The sentiment it expresses is rea sonable."

Therefore, there are three kinds of things in which th rational principle is displayed: the first consists of purposef action; the second of speech; the third of pleasure. The fir suggests that we do nothing without thought; the second tha we teach well; the third that we enjoy the happiness of co templation. The first is concerned with good conduct; th other two with the disciplines we are now discussing. No the rational principle within us, i.e., the element which us reason and either produces or seeks after what is reasonabl has linked in a natural bond of fellowship those who sha reason as a common possession. Men could not effectivel associate with one another unless they were able to ta together and, as it were, pour out their minds and thoughts one another. Therefore, reason saw that names, which is say, significant sounds, must be given to things so that me could use sense perception as an interpreter to bring the into communication with one another, since they could n experience one another's minds at first hand. But still the were unable to hear the words of people separated from the by distance. Therefore, reason carefully marked and di tinguished all the sounds made by the mouth and tongue, th bringing into being the letters of the alphabet. But none these achievements would have been possible if the infinite number of things had appeared to stretch out indefinitely without any fixed limit. Accordingly the usefulness of counting was conceived out of a great need, and with the invention of letters and arithmetic the profession of copyist and calculator came into being; this was the infancy, so to speak, of grammar, which is the subject Varro* calls "letters" (*litteratio*), although at the moment I cannot quite remember what it is called in Greek.

Reason advanced further and observed that, of the sounds we produce when we speak, sounds which it had now designated by letters, some came from the mouth effortlessly and with clarity; they were produced with the lips parted in various shapes and were given an unobstructed passage. However, other sounds were made by a varying pressure of the lips, while lastly there were sounds which could not be heard at all unless they were joined to other sounds. Hence, reason called those classes of letters successively vowels, semi-vowels and mutes. Then reason took note of syllables, distinguished eight classes and forms of words, and carefully worked out the principles governing the correct usage and compounding of words. Then, remembering number and measure, reason applied the mind to the varying lengths of sounds and syllables, and found that in quantity** some were double the length of others. This also was noted by reason and brought under definite rules.

At this stage the subject of grammar could have been complete. But since its very name, "grammar," shows that it is concerned with letters (which is why in Latin it is called *literature*), whatever was committed to writing as worthy of being remembered necessarily became its concern. Thus, history was added to it. . . .

* Marcus Terentius Varro (116–27 B.C.) wrote an authoritative work on the liberal arts called *Disciplinarum Libri Novem (The Nine Books of Disciplines)*.

** "Quantity" *(quantitas)*, literally "extent" or "size," is here used in its grammatical sense with reference to vowel and syllable length.

After having completed and organized the subject of gram mar, reason was moved to inquire into and investigate th faculty by which the subject was brought into being; for b definition, classification and synthesis, reason had not onl organized and systematized the subject but had also protecte it against any intrusion of falsehood. Thus, reason could no go on to formulate other subjects of study unless it began b classifying, noting and organizing what we might call its ow tools and instruments, and bringing into existence that dis cipline of disciplines which people call "dialectic" (logic This is the discipline which teaches us how to teach and t learn; through dialectic, reason makes a display of herself an proclaims what she is, what she wills and what she has th capacity to do. It is the subject which knows what knowin is, which not only wishes to make man knowledgeable bu also has the power to bring it about. But foolish men, i pursuit of what they rightly regard as good, useful and hono able, often follow their senses and habits rather than th purest evidence of truth, which only the exceptional min beholds. Thus, it is necessary that men be not only instructe but also often deeply moved. Hence, reason gave the name o "rhetoric" to the subject which aims at bringing this about. I is a subject characterized more by necessity than by integrit whose lap is filled with seductive enticements which sh distributes to the people so that they may be led to what is t their own advantage.

This then is what was achieved through the liberal arts b that part of us which expresses itself by signs and is calle "rational." From this point reason wished to advance to th supremely happy contemplation of the divine, but, to avoi tumbling down from its high place, it looked for steps, worke out a path for itself through its possessions, and establishe an orderly procedure. Its desire was to gaze upon the sort o beauty which could be studied in all its simple purity withou the use of the eyes. But the senses were an obstacle to this therefore, reason turned aside a little to study the senses which with insistent clamor declared that they possesse truth and persisted in summoning reason back when it was hurrying toward some other goal. In the first place, reason turned its attention to the ears, which insisted that the very words out of which reason had constituted grammar, dialectic and rhetoric, were their own possession. But reason, being very skillful at making distinctions, came to understand the difference between a sound and what is signified by a sound. Thus, it realized that the only thing which belongs to the ears is sound, of which there are three kinds: the sound in the voice of a living being; the sound produced by breath in wind instruments; the sound which comes from percussion. Reason found that tragic and comic actors and choruses, and in general all who use their own voices to produce music, belong to the first class; flutes and such instruments to the second class; guitars, lyres, cymbals and all percussion instruments to the third class.

However, reason saw that all this was worthless unless sounds were grouped according to well-defined time measurements and in a variety of patterns of acute and grave accents.* It realized that this was the basis of what grammarians had called "feet" and "accents," after they had carefully studied syllables. In words themselves there was no difficulty in discovering that long and short syllables were distributed in speech in almost equal proportion. Therefore, reason tried to organize these feet and group them according to established patterns. In the first place, it was guided by the ears and established certain divisions which it called "phrases" and "clauses." So that the sequence of metrical feet might not be prolonged beyond the point where its pattern could still be discerned by the judgment, reason laid down a limit after which the meter would turn back again. Thus, it formed the conception of a line of verse. What is not marked by fixed limits but runs on in a rational system of organized feet became known as "rhythm"; in Latin it is simply called

* It is generally accepted that the "acute" and "grave" accents in Latin were accents of stress rather than of pitch.

"number" (*numerus*). In this way poets were brought into being by the work of reason, which, when it found them producing work of great significance not only in sound but also in words and content, gave them great honor and the freedom, within reasonable limits, to compose whatever fictions they wished. But, because poetry had its origin in the basic discipline of grammar, reason allowed grammarians to be the critics of poets. Therefore, reason came to understand that, on this fourth level,* whether in rhythms or modulation, numbers reigned supreme and completed the whole work. It carefully examined their nature and found them divine and eternal, especially since it was with their help that reason had formulated all its previous knowledge. But now reason became increasingly less willing that the splendor and serenity of number should be tainted by the physical elements of vocal sounds; for what the mind sees is always present and immortal, and number is included in this. On the other hand, sound is perceived by the senses, and therefore flows from the present into the past and is stored in the memory. Thus, now that reason was showing favor to poets, by a reasonable fiction it was supposed that the Muses were daughters of Jupiter and Mercury; accordingly, this discipline, which has its roots both in sense perception and in the intellect, was given the name "music."

Thus, reason proceeded to the function of sight. Surveying the earth and heavens, it saw that the source of all pleasure is found in beauty alone. Further analysis showed that the source of pleasure in beauty lies in form, that form is founded on measurements and measurements on number. Reason asked itself whether lines, circles and other physical forms and shapes, were similar to those comprehended by the intellect; it concluded that all such physical shapes were far inferior. Hence, reason found that what the eyes look upon

*This is the level of music, with which poetry was always closely associated in classical culture. The previous three levels were successively: grammar (including arithmetic), dialectic, and rhetoric. The list is concluded with geometry and astronomy, and the whole forms a catalogue of seven liberal arts.

cannot possibly be compared with what the mind perceives. Therefore, reason reduced these distinct and separate observations to a subject of study and called it "geometry."

Then the movement of the heavens caught the attention of reason and invited careful study. Here also, after marking the well-regulated succession of the seasons, the fixed and definite course of the stars and the unvarying intervals maintained between them, reason understood that measurement and numbers were in full control. Thus, in a similar way, by defining and separating these phenomena and bringing the data together in organized wholes, reason gave birth to astronomy, a great support for believers in religion but a torment to the curious.*

Thus, in all these subjects of study, reason found that everything was permeated by numbers, which showed themselves still more clearly in those proportions which, by thought and contemplation, reason saw as absolutely true. On the other hand, in the realm of sense data, it found merely the shadows or traces of these absolute numbers rather than the realities themselves. Thus, reason drew itself to a new height, conceived a high goal and took on the task of proving the soul immortal. Carefully reviewing everything, reason at once perceived that its powers were very great and that, whatever it could do, it was able to do by virtue of numbers. Then a marvellous idea inspired it, and it began to suspect that perhaps it was itself that principle of number by which everything is counted; but, if it were not that principle, then number perhaps lay there, at the goal of all its effort. With its whole strength then, as though Proteus** were in its hands,

*Augustine's suspicion of astronomy arises from its frequent association with the pseudo-science of astrology. In other lists of the liberal arts he leaves it out.

**Proteus, the old man of the sea, capable of assuming a variety of different shapes, whom Menelaus on his return from Troy seized and held fast until Proteus told Menelaus how to return to his home. Homer, *Odyssey,* iv, 354–569. Proteus is also referred to be Vergil in *Georgics,* iv, 388 ff. Alypius, an intimate friend of Augustine, was one of the company at Cassiciacum. The reference is to the dialogue *Against the Academics,* iii, 5, 11.

reason laid hold of that principle of number which was likely to be the index of absolute truth, that principle of which Alypius made mention when we were inquiring into the Academic philosophers. For the deceptive images of the physical objects we count, images which have their source in that secret principle by virtue of which we are able to calculate, seize upon our attention and often cause absolute number to slip away when it is already within our grasp.

The man who does not yield to these images and who reduces all that has been spread abroad throughout so many subjects of study to a simple, sure and certain unity, fully deserves to be called educated. When such a person inquires into divine matters, it is not in vain; for such matters are now not only to be believed but also to be contemplated, understood and retained. But whoever is still a slave to his desires and sighs after the things which are transient, will make all the mistakes which it is possible to make. This will be so, even if at last he abandons all temporal things and lives a pure life. He will make mistakes as long as he does not know the answers to the following questions: What is "nothing"? What is "formless matter"? What is an object which has form but is without life? What is meant by a "material body"? By "the form of a material body"? By "place" and "time"? What is meant by existing "in a place" or "at a time"? What is motion "in a place" and motion which is not "in a place"? What is "stable motion"? What is "eternity"? What does it mean to say that something is neither "in a place" nor anywhere at all? What is meant by "timeless" and by "always existing"? What do we mean by "existing nowhere" and "existing somewhere," by existing "at no time," and by "never not existing"? Whoever is ignorant of all this—and I am not referring to a knowledge of the supreme God, who is better known in ignorance—but who wishes to inquire about and discuss the soul itself, will go badly astray. But it will all be learned quite easily by the man who understands simple and intelligible numbers. Furthermore, these numbers will be understood by the man who is endowed with good ability, who possesses the leisure which is the privilege of age or the mark of some fortunate combination of circumstances, and who, being kindled with desire, has followed in adequate measure the sequence of studies which we have just described. Since all the liberal arts are learned partly for practical use and partly for the understanding and contemplation of reality, it is difficult for anyone to master them unless he is very able and from his boyhood has persistently and steadfastly directed himself to that end.

The Certainty of Self-Knowledge

[16]REASON: You who wish to know yourself, do you know that you exist?

AUGUSTINE: I do.

REASON: How do you know?

AUGUSTINE: I cannot tell.

REASON: Do you see yourself as simple or compounded?

AUGUSTINE: I do not know.

REASON: Do you know that you are capable of movement?

AUGUSTINE: I am not sure of that.

REASON: Do you know that you think?

AUGUSTINE: I do know that.

[16] *Soliloquies,* ii, 1.

REASON: Then it is true that you think?

AUGUSTINE: It is true.

[17]What is it that the mind loves when it eagerly searches itself out in order to know itself but is still unknown to itself? Surely the mind is seeking to know itself, and this is the desire with which it is inflamed. Therefore, the mind is in love—but with what? Is it in love with itself? How can this be, since it does not yet know itself and it is impossible for anyone to love what he does not know? Has the mind learned about its nature by hearsay, in the way in which we often hear about people in distant places? Then perhaps the mind does not love itself as much as what it imagines about itself, which may be quite different from what it really is. Or it may be that the mind imagines something like itself, and thus, before it comes to know itself, it loves itself in that image because it is looking upon something similar to itself. Because the mind comes to know other minds from which it can form an image of itself, it becomes known to itself as a member of a class. But why does the mind not come to know itself as it gets to know other minds, for nothing can be more present to the mind than itself? However, if the mind is like the eyes of the body, which have a better knowledge of other eyes than of themselves, the mind would be seeking itself without any prospect of finding itself; for the eyes never see themselves except in a mirror. But, in the contemplation of eternal things, there must never be any question of thinking that the mind comes to know itself as in a mirror. Does the mind then see in the reason of eternal truth how good it is to know itself? Does it value this purpose and long for this self-knowledge to grow within itself? If this is so, the mind understands the value of knowing itself, although it is yet unknown to itself. But surely

[17] *The Trinity*, x, 5–6.

it is very surprising that, before the mind has actually come to know itself, it should realize the value of knowing itself? Could it be that the mind perceives some supremely desirable goal, i.e., security and happiness, by some secret memory which has remained in the mind although the mind has moved far away from it? Does the mind then believe that it cannot reach this goal unless it gets to know itself? Thus, while the mind loves the objective, it seeks itself, and, because of what it knows and loves, it searches for what is still unknown to it. But how can the memory of the mind's happiness endure while the memory of its own nature does not? Why should not the mind, which wishes to reach the goal, know itself as well as it knows the actual goal toward which it wishes to direct itself? When the mind longs to know itself, does it merely love the act of knowing? Is it not in love with itself, i.e., with something it has not yet known? Would it not be a bitter regret to the mind that it still lacks knowledge of itself although it desires to understand everything?

Now the mind knows what knowing is, and, while it loves this knowledge which it possesses, it also desires to know itself. Where does the mind learn that knowing is a function of itself if it does not know itself? Is it aware that it knows other things but that it does not know itself? Surely it is from knowing itself that the mind comes to know what knowing is. How does the mind recognize itself as knowing something if it does not know itself? For it is not another person's mind which it recognizes as knowing but itself; therefore, the mind knows itself. When the mind seeks to know itself, it is aware of itself as seeking; this is to say, it knows itself. Therefore, the mind cannot be entirely ignorant of itself, for as long as it recognizes this ignorance, it certainly knows itself. If if did not recognize its own ignorance of itself, it would not seek to know itself. Therefore, the fact that it seeks itself proves that it is more known to itself than unknown; for all the time it is seeking to know itself, it knows itself as seeking and as ignorant.

What then shall we say? That the mind knows itself in

some degree but not entirely? Surely it would be foolish to declare that the whole mind does not know what it knows. I am not saying that the mind knows the whole of what it knows, but merely that the whole of it knows what it does know. Therefore, when the mind knows something about itself, i.e., something which cannot be known except by the whole mind, it knows itself as a whole. Furthermore, it knows itself as possessing some knowledge, and it cannot know anything at all except with the whole mind; therefore, it knows itself as a whole. Again, what is there about the mind which is as well known to itself as the fact of its being alive? It cannot be mind and not be alive. . . . Therefore, as the mind is one whole mind, so it lives as a whole. But the mind knows it is alive; therefore, it knows the whole of itself. Finally, when the mind seeks to know itself, it already knows that it is a mind; otherwise it would not know whether it was really searching after itself, and its search could possibly be directed toward the wrong objective. . . . Therefore, when the mind inquires into the nature of mind, it must know it is inquiring into itself and must be absolutely certain that it is actually a mind. Furthermore, if it knows within itself that it is a mind and entirely a mind, then it knows itself as a whole. . . .

[18]What then is the meaning of the advice that the mind should know itself? It is, I believe, that the mind should reflect upon itself and live in accordance with its own nature. It should strive to order itself according to its nature, that is, under Him to whom it should be subordinated and over and above everything which should be subordinated to itself; it should be under Him by whom it ought to be ruled, and over and above everything which it ought to rule. Perverse desire often makes the mind act as though it has forgotten itself; it sees within itself beauties which belong to that more excellent

[18] *The Trinity,* x, 7.

nature of God, and its duty is to stand firm in the enjoyment of these. Instead, it conceives the desire to attribute these beauties to itself, and, although made in the likeness of God, it seeks to derive its existence not from God but from itself. Therefore, it turns about and moves away from God; under the impression that it is continually increasing, it resolves itself into something which continually diminishes. For the mind is not sufficient for itself, nor can anything else be sufficient for it when it withdraws from Him who alone is sufficient. Thus, through impoverishment and distress, it becomes too preoccupied with its own actions and the turbulent pleasures drawn from them. It is filled with a desire to acquire knowledge from external material objects, all of which it knows, loves and feels it may lose unless it holds on to them with great concentration. In this way the mind loses its security, and the less it thinks about itself, the more secure it imagines itself to be against the possible loss of itself.

Not to know oneself is different from not thinking about oneself; for we do not say that a man who is proficient in many branches of learning is ignorant of grammar just because at this particular moment he is not actually thinking about grammar but about the art of medicine. Therefore, although not knowing oneself and not thinking about oneself are two different things, so great is the power of love that what the soul has pondered long and lovingly will adhere to it as though glued, and the soul will still possess it when it comes back to think about itself. It has fallen in love with material things, with which the physical senses have involved it in a persistent familiarity; because it cannot take these material things into itself, into the realm, as it were, of immaterial nature, it gathers together and seizes upon images of them formed in itself and from itself. It puts something of its own substance into the making of these images, while at the same time it preserves something by which it can freely pass judgment on their forms. This "something" is mind, that is, the rational intelligence, which is preserved for the purpose of making judgments; for we realize that we share with the animals those parts of the soul which are impressed with the likenesses of material objects. . . .

[19]When the mind hears the command to know itself, if must avoid adding anything to what it actually knows itself to be. At least it knows for certain that the command is given to itself, i.e., to the self which exists, lives and understands. A corpse exists and an animal lives; but neither a corpse nor an animal understands. Therefore, the mind knows that its existence and life are the existence and life of understanding. For example, when the mind thinks it is made of air, it is supposing that air has the power of understanding; the mind knows it has the power of understanding, whereas it does not know, but only supposes that it is made of air. Thus, the mind must set aside what is pure supposition and determine exactly what it knows. It must cling to what has never been doubted, even by those who have supposed mind to be made of material of one kind or another.

Not all minds think themselves air; some have imagined themselves to be fire, some brain, and others this substance or that, as I have noted above; but all of them know that they understand, exist and live, understanding thus being related to an object understood, for existence and life are absolute conceptions. It is clear that nobody has understanding who does not live and that nobody lives who does not exist. It follows that the possessor of understanding has an existence and a life different from the corpse, which has no life, and from the sort of soul which has no power of rational understanding. The life of understanding is a life of a special and more excellent kind. Men also know that they have the power of willing and that nobody has this power unless he exists and lives; they relate the will to the thing they desire to bring about by means of that will. Then too, men know that they

[19] *The Trinity*, x, 13–16.

ave memory and that nobody remembers unless he exists nd is alive; but they also relate memory to something which ey remember by means of it. Of these three powers, memo- / and understanding are the two faculties which hold togeth- r our experience and knowledge of many things; on the other and, it is the will which determines our enjoyment or use of em. Of all the things we know, we "enjoy" those in which e will rests satisfied for their own sake; on the other hand, e "use" those things we refer to something else, that is, to mething which we ought to enjoy. It is wrong use and rong enjoyment which mark the depraved and blameworthy fe. But this is not the place to discuss that point.

Since we are talking about the nature of the mind, let us hut out from our consideration all knowledge drawn from utside us through the physical senses, and let us concentrate ur attention on what we have mentioned, that is, what every ind knows with certainty about itself. Whether the functions f life, memory, understanding, will, thought, knowledge and dgment are functions of air, fire, brain, blood, atoms or me fifth substance distinct from the familiar four elements, r whether these functions could all be produced by the omposition or harmonization of our fleshly substance, has ever been settled beyond human doubt. Various theories ave been maintained by different people, but nobody can oubt that he lives, remembers, understands, wills, thinks, nows and judges. For, even if a man doubts, he lives; if he oubts, he is remembering what has made him doubt; if he oubts, he understands that he is doubting; if he doubts, he ishes to be certain; if he doubts, he is thinking; if he doubts, e knows that he is ignorant; if he doubts, he judges that he ught not to be hasty in giving his assent. A man may have oubts on any other score, but he should not doubt any of ese facts because, if they were not true, he could not doubt nything.

Those who suppose that mind is either material or the com- ounding or commingling of matter, see all these functions as roperties of the subject. According to this view, the basic substance would be air, fire or some other material substanc which they suppose to be mind, and understanding wou belong to this material substance as one of its qualities. Tl material substance would be the subject, while the quali would be in the subject. Clearly then the subject would be tl mind, which they consider to be a material substance, wher as understanding and the other functions we have mention as clearly belonging to us, would be properties of the min Not very different from this is the view of those who der that the mind itself is material, but who see it as the cor position or commingling of matter. This view is different that, whereas the former people see the mind itself as tl substance and subject, of which understanding is a propert the latter declare that the mind itself is a property of tl subject, that is, of the material substance of which it is tl compounding and commingling principle. In consequenc such people think that understanding, is also simply a prope ty of that same material substance which is its subject.

All these people fail to take account of what we ha demonstrated, namely, that the mind knows itself in the ve act of seeking itself. Nothing can properly be said to known as long as its substance is unknown. Therefore, wh the mind knows itself, it knows its own substance; when it certain about itself, it is certain about its own substance. No everything we have said above confirms the view that tl mind is certain about itself, although it does not know wi certainty whether it is air, fire, or some material thing condition of matter. Therefore, it is none of these thing Thus, the whole purpose of the command that the mi should know itself is that the mind should establish beyo doubt that it is none of those things which it has certainly n proved itself to be, and that it should accept as certain on what it has clearly established about its own nature. This the rule followed by the mind when it thinks of fire, air or a other material object. But it would be impossible for it think of what it actually is in the same way as it thinks what it is not; for it thinks of all things such as fire, air, this that material substance or any part, composition or mingling together of matter by means of mental imagery. If the mind actually was one of these substances, it would think of that substance in a different way from the others. In fact, it would not employ the mental imagery we employ when we think of absent objects experienced by the physical senses, whether we are thinking of particular objects or objects of the same class. Instead, the mind would think of its own nature by a kind of inward presence, real and not imaginary, since nothing can be closer to the mind than itself. It would think of itself as it thinks of its own functions of life, memory, understanding and will, all of which it recognizes within itself and it would not employ imagery as though it had made some external contact with them through the senses in the way in which all physical objects are experienced. If the mind does not attach to itself anything derived from its thinking about material things, and thus avoids imagining itself to be of the same sort, whatever remains with reference to itself is actually itself.

[20]We exist, know that we exist and take delight in our existence and in our knowledge of it; in all this we are not plagued by any deceptive illusion of truth since we do not get this information through any of our physical senses, by which we perceive things in the external world; for example, colors by seeing, sounds by hearing, smells by smelling, tastes by tasting, hard and soft objects by touching. When we consider such sense impressions in thought, we are studying mere images, which very closely resemble the objects of sense perception but which are no longer physical in their nature. These images, retained in our memory, stimulate us to desire the objects themselves; but I require no deceptive representations or images of apparitions to assure me that I exist, know

[20] *City of God,* xi, 26.

that I exist, and take pleasure in that knowledge. With regard to these truths, I have no fear of the arguments of the Academics, who say, "What if you are mistaken?" For, if I am mistaken, I exist; the man who does not exist certainly cannot be mistaken, and, if I am mistaken, by this same token I exist. Therefore, since I exist if I am mistaken, how can I be mistaken in believing that I exist? For it is certain that I exist if I am deceived. Therefore, because I, who am subject to mistake, exist even though I am mistaken, certainly I am not mistaken in the knowledge that I exist. Consequently, neither am I mistaken in knowing that I know; for, as I know I exist so also I am certain that I know. Then, when I love these two assurances, my knowledge is augmented by this love as a third element of equal value. I am not mistaken about this love I experience because I am not mistaken about the things I love. Nevertheless, even if all this is false, it would still be true that I am in love with what is false; for how could I rightly be blamed and prevented from loving false things, if it were false that I loved them? However, since the facts I have just mentioned are true and real, who could doubt that, when they are loved, the actual love of them is also true and real? Furthermore, just as everybody wants to be happy, so everybody wants to exist. For how can a person be happy if he is nothing?

The Illumination of Truth

[21]There is a sort of intellectual light which defies description and is beyond the grasp of the understanding, although the common light of day may suggest the power and nature of that other light. Some eyes are so strong and vigorous that, as soon as they are opened, they can fearlessly turn themselves toward the sun itself. For them the light itself is, in a sense

[21] *Soliloquies*, i, 23.

their health; they need no teacher, but perhaps only advice. For them it is enough to believe, hope and love. But others are dazzled by the brightness which they so eagerly desire to behold and are often glad to turn back into their darkness without looking at it. There is danger in trying to show them what they are not yet strong enough to see, even if they may properly be called healthy. In the first place, they must be given training; also their desire must be deferred and at the same time nourished to their advantage. We must begin by presenting to their gaze things which do not shine with their own light, but which can be seen by means of light, for example, a garment, a wall and so on. Then they should be shown something which does not shine by its own light but which reflects light more brilliantly, without it being so bright that it hurts the eyes, for example, gold, silver and such things. Then perhaps fire should be carefully exposed to them, followed by the stars, the moon, the glow of the dawn and the splendor of the brightening sky. Thus, sooner or later, according to whether they pass through the whole range of experience or miss some of the steps due to a superior power of adaptation, they will look upon the sun fearlessly and with great satisfaction. This is the method followed by the best teachers with those who are most anxious to achieve wisdom, but whose eyesight is not yet keen although they do have the capacity to see. It is the function of good teaching to develop a gradual approach to wisdom, for, without this carefully planned progress, almost incredible good luck is required to attain it.

[22]If you do not grasp what I am saying or have doubts about the truth of it, at least decide whether you have any doubt about the fact that you are in doubt. If it is certain that

[22] *True Religion*, 73.

you are in a state of doubt, ask yourself why you are so sure about this; then you will surely conclude that this certaintly comes, not from the light of the sun, but from "that true light which lighteth every man that cometh into the world" (*John* i:9). This light can be seen neither with the physical eyes nor with those eyes which in thought scan the images that thrust their way in through the mind's eyes. The true light is seen by those eyes which say to the images, "You are not what I seek, nor are you the principle by which I set you in order, expressing my disapproval of what is base in you and my approval of what is lovely. The actual principle, by whose standard I express this approval and disapproval, is still more beautiful than you. Therefore, I set a higher value on it, ranking it above you and above all those physical objects I draw on to make you." So think of the rule in this way: Every man who understands that he doubts understands what is true (i.e., that he doubts), and he is sure of what he understands; therefore, he is certain about a truth. Thus, everyone who doubts whether truth exists has within himself one truth about which he has no doubt. Now a particular truth is true only to the extent that it derives from absolute truth. Accordingly, no one should entertain doubts about the existence of absolute truth, no matter what other doubts he may have. Wherever truth is seen, there is light exceeding all limitations of space and time and devoid of all physical images. Is it possible that truth could be in the least corrupted, even if every reasoning being were then to perish or grow old among the lower things of the flesh? Reasoning does not create truth but discovers it; therefore, truth exists in itself before it is found, and, when it is found, it makes us new.

[23]I searched for the grounds of my approval of the beauty of physical objects, whether they are found in the heavens or

[23] *Confessions,* vii, 17.

the earth, and for the principle which enabled me to pass valid judgments on changing things and to say, "This ought to be so; that ought not to be so." When I made such judgments and looked for the authority by which they were made, I found the unchangeable, true eternity of truth set over and above the changeable nature of my mind. Thus, step by step I passed from physical objects to the soul, which perceives through the medium of the body, and from this to the soul's interior faculty, to which the physical senses display external objects. Animals can go this far. Then I went on to the faculty of reason, to which all that is gathered from the physical senses is referred for judgment. I found that this faculty also was changeable in me, and so reason lifted itself up to an understanding of itself. It withdrew my thinking from the paths of habit, turning it away from the confusing crowds of images so that it might discover the nature of the light by which it was bathed. Then, with the utmost certainty, reason called out that the unchanging is to be preferred to the changing and told how it had made the acquaintance of the unchanging; for unless, by some means or other, reason had come to know the unchanging, it could not have preferred it to the changing. Thus, in the stroke of a trembling glance, reason arrived at what really exists; at that moment my gaze very truly rested on those things of thine which cannot be seen but are understood through the medium of created things. But I lacked the strength to keep my gaze fixed on them; my weakness was beaten back and I returned to my former paths, carrying nothing away except a loving memory and the desire for something whose fragrance I had sensed but which I still did not have the power to consume.

CHAPTER FIVE

The Encounter of Teacher and Pupil

In St. Augustine's view the pattern of teaching is to be found in the personal relationship through which God offers instruction to man. God's love for man and His commandment, "Thou shalt love the Lord thy God . . . and thy neighbour as thyself" give point and direction to the communication of teacher and pupil. The principle of personal concern and mutual involvement is basic to all the instructions about teaching given by St. Augustine. He holds that the teacher can influence his pupils to love the things he himself loves only by the impact of his own example. The teacher must himself be a "student" in the literal sense of one who "ardently desires" to attain an understanding of truth; he must be "in love with understanding."

In his dialogue called *The Teacher,* St. Augustine argues that teaching and learning are not separate activities but a single process in which teacher and pupils are mutually involved in teaching one another and learning from one another. The teacher cannot teach in the commonly accepted sense of transmitting knowledge directly from his mind to the minds of his pupils. Learning is always the result of the personal involvement and volition of the individual learner. Hence, teaching is not the technique of handing over knowledge to another person but the art of stimulating another person to learn for himself, i.e., to be his own teacher.

But, if the "external" human teacher can communicate knowledge only indirectly, through verbal symbols presented to the senses, there is nevertheless a teacher who can teach directly without the intervention of signs, verbal or otherwise. This is the "internal teacher" (*magister interior*), whose "word" (*logos*) is not a re-presentation or symbol of the thought of God but the actual thought itself. To gain an understanding of truth, the learner must, therefore, lay himself open to the teaching of God, who by an act of grace reveals the truth directly to the mind of the student who eagerly desires to grasp it.

The Teacher's Approach to his Task

[1]I have a greater liking for learning than for teaching, for this is the advice given us by the Apostle James (1:19): "Let every man be quick to hear but slow to speak." Thus, the sweetness of truth should move us to learn, whereas teaching is imposed on us by the necessity of love. We should therefore hope that the need for one man to teach another will pass away and that we shall all lay ourselves open to the instruction of God.

[2]There are many who learn peacefully but who teach in an agitated manner. Although they themselves have a patient teacher, they are harsh toward the learner. We all know how peacefully the Scriptures teach us. A man comes and reads

[1] *The Eight Questions of Dulcitius,* 3, 6.
[2] *Sermons,* 47, 9.

the precepts of God, drinking them in peacefully from a peaceful source; then, being approached by someone who wants to learn something from him, he storms and rages, accusing the learner of understanding too slowly and throwing him into confusion. The result is that the learner fails to get a sufficiently clear understanding of the lessons which the teacher himself has had the opportunity to hear in a more peaceful atmosphere.

The work *Concerning the Instruction of the Uninstructed (De Catechizandis Rudibus),* from which the following brief selections are taken, was written in response to a request from a deacon of Carthage, Deogratias, who had become dissatisfied with the effect of his own instruction of candidates for baptism. Much of the advice which St. Augustine gives him is of general value to teachers. For example, a lesson must be ineffective if the teacher does not establish a rapport with his pupils and adapt his content and method to the needs and capacities of the audience he is addressing. If the teacher is talking to a group, he must find out what sort of people are in it; if he is instructing one person, he must start by finding out something of his background and interests. Above all, the teacher must approach his task and his pupils with the divine love in his heart.

[3] Clearly there is one situation which we should not pass over. That is the case of a man coming to you to be instructed, who is well-educated in the liberal arts, has already made up his mind to be a Christian and has come with the express purpose of becoming one. It can almost be taken for granted

[3] *The Instruction of the Uninstructed,* 12.

What are some of the tactics St. Augustine proposes in working with students who are well advanced in liberal education?

that a man of this sort has already gained a considerable knowledge of our Scriptures and literature. Furnished with this, he may now have come simply to become a partaker of the sacraments; for it is usual for such men to look carefully into things, not just at the moment when they become Christians but before that. At an early stage they enter into discussion with anyone they can find, and argue about the opinions they hold in their minds. Therefore, with such people we must adopt a briefer method, avoiding the boring repetition of what they already know and passing over it with a light and discreet touch. We would say that we understand they are already familiar with this and that, and then rapidly review all the facts which need to be impressed upon the minds of the uninstructed and uneducated. We should try to teach in such a way that, if our man of culture is already familiar with some part of our subject matter, he does not hear it coming as though from a teacher. At the same time, we should see to it that, if he is still ignorant of something, he will learn it while we are going over points with which we understand him to be already familiar. Furthermore, there is certainly an advantage in questioning the man as to how he was induced to want to become a Christian. If you find that his decision was motivated by books, whether canonical writings or the compositions of reputable literary men, you may begin by saying something about these, expressing approval of each of them according to their merits in respect of their canonical authority or the painstaking skill of their interpreters. . . . We should draw from our inquirer some account of himself, so that we find out with what writer he is most familiar and what books he knows best; for it was by these that he conceived the desire to join the Church. When he has given us this information, we should gladly express our approval of these books if we are familiar with them or if we at least know that they are accepted by the Church as having been written by some Catholic of note.

[4] I have heard you repeating one complaint more than any other, namely, that you have the impression that, when you are instructing someone in the Christian faith, your talk is poor and spiritless. Now I am sure that this feeling results not so much from lack of content – I am well aware that you are sufficiently provided and equipped with that – or from poverty of speech, as from mental weariness, which may spring from the cause I have already mentioned, namely, that we find greater pleasure and interest in what we perceive in silence in our own minds. We have no desire to be called from that to a noisy verbal babble which falls short of representing our thought. Or it may be that, even when our talk is agreeable, we get more pleasure from hearing or reading things which have been still better expressed and which have been set out without any care or anxiety on our part, than from putting words together extemporaneously for other people to understand. The effects of such words remain uncertain; whether they adequately convey our meaning or have a beneficial effect on the hearer is problematical. Again, the reason for our dissatisfaction may be that we are now thoroughly familiar with our subject matter and no longer find it necessary to our own advancement; thus it annoys us to return frequently to subject matter that is taught to the uneducated. Our own minds have matured, and no longer move with any pleasure in the context of such well-worn and, as it were, childish knowledge. Also a sense of weariness is induced in a speaker when the person listening to him remains unmoved, either because in fact he feels nothing or because he does not indicate by any physical movement that he understands or is pleased with what is said. We feel like this, not because it is proper that we should be greedy for the praises of men, but because what we are offering belongs to God. The more we love those to whom we speak, the more we

[4] *The Instruction of the Uninstructed,* 14.

want them to like what is offered for their salvation. As a result, if we fail in this, we are pained, weakened and lose heart in mid-career as if we were expending our efforts to no purpose. There are also times when we are taken away from some business we want to puruse, which was giving us pleasure to transact and which appeared to be more than usually necessary. We are forced to give instruction to someone either at the command of a person we are unwilling to offend or because of the persistence of people we cannot get rid of. In such circumstances we come with minds already perturbed to a task which requires great calmness; we bewail the fact that we are not allowed to maintain the orderly sequence we want to obeserve in our occupations and the fact that we cannot possibly be adequate for everything we are asked to do. Thus, our talk becomes less acceptable because of our distress, and flourishes less exuberantly because it is drawn from the arid soil of our sadness. . . .

[5] We often feel it wearisome to go over and over again matters which are thoroughly familiar to us and better suited to little children. If this is the case with us, then we should try to meet our pupils with a brother's, a father's and a mother's love. Once we are thus united to them in heart, all this subject matter will seem new to us exactly as it will to them. For so great is the power of a sympathetic disposition of mind that our hearers are affected while we are speaking and we are affected while they are learning. Thus, we take up our dwelling in each other, and in this way they are, as it were, speaking within us what they are hearing, and in some way we are learning within them what we are teaching. Is it not a common occurrence for us that, when we show to people who have never seen them certain extensive and beautiful vistas either in a city or in the country, scenes which we have been

[5] *The Instruction of the Uninstructed,* 17–19.

Power of loving motives, sympathetic imagination, joy in being a wayshower

in the habit of passing by without any sense of pleasure simply because we have become accustomed to the sight of them, we find our own enjoyment renewed in their enjoyment of the novelty of the scene? We experience this more vividly in proportion to the intimacy of our friendship with the people concerned. Insofar as we are united to them by the bond of love, things which previously were old become new to us. But if we ourselves have made any considerable progress in the contemplative life, it is not our wish that those whom we love should simply be gratified and astonished as they gaze upon the works of men's hands. It becomes our wish to lift them to the contemplation of the skill and wisdom of their Creator, so that they should mount up to the admiration and praise of the all-creating God, in whom is the most fruitful culmination of love. How much more then ought we to be delighted when men come to us with the purpose already formed of obtaining a knowledge of God Himself, on whose account everything which ought to be learned is learned. How we ought to feel ourselves renewed in their newness so that, if our ordinary preaching is somewhat frigid, it may rise to fresh warmth under the influence of their unusual degree of attention! Our joy will also be increased by reflecting on the mortal error from which the person is passing over into the life of faith. We walk through streets, which are very familiar to us, with all the cheerfulness of well-doing, when we happen to be pointing out the way to someone in distress because he has lost his direction. Thus, when we practice the teaching which leads to salvation, how much more enthusiastically and joyfully should we tread and retread those paths, which, as far as we personally are concerned, need not be opened up any more! For we are dealing with a soul which deserves pity and is worn out with the devious wanderings of this world; and we are leading it along the paths of peace at the command of Him who has given that peace to us. illustration

In truth it is very difficult to continue talking until the set limit when we observe that our hearer is quite unmoved. It may be that he is restrained by religious awe and does not dare to signify his approval by voice or by any movement of his body; or he may be inhibited because by nature he is shy, does not understand what we are saying, or holds it as valueless. Since we cannot look into his mind and the exact reason must therefore be a matter of conjecture for us, it becomes our duty, when we speak, to try everything which might be able to stir him up and draw him out, as it were, from his place of concealment. An excessive fear, which prevents him expressing his views, should be dispelled by the influence of kindly exhortation; we should overcome his bashfulness by laying before him the conception of brotherly friendship; and by putting questions to him we should find out whether he is understanding what is said to him. We should instill a sense of confidence so that he may give free expression to any objection which suggests itself to him; at the same time we should ask whether he has already heard the same things on a previous occasion and whether perhaps they are failing to move him now because they are well-known to him and commonplace. We should thus shape our course in accordance with his answers, either speaking in a simpler style with more detailed explanation, or refuting some antagonistic opinion. Instead of attempting a more prolonged exposition of matters which are well known to him, we might give a brief summary of them and pick out some of those events which are handled in a mystical manner in the Scriptures, particularly in the narrative passages; by giving an exposition and explanation of these we may make our talk more attractive. But if our hearer is of a very sluggish disposition and deaf to all such sources of pleasure, then we must simply bear with him in a spirit of compassion. After briefly going over other points, we should then, in a manner calculated to inspire him with awe, impress upon him the truths which are most indispensable on the unity of the Catholic church, temptations and the Christian manner of living in view of the judgment to come. In this way we ought to say much to God on his behalf rather than much to him about God.

It also happens frequently that a man who has at first been

our attentive listener becomes exhausted, either by the effort of listening or by standing, and no longer opens his mouth to approve what is said but rather to yawn and gape; he even exhibits an involuntary desire to go away. When we observe this, it is our duty to refresh his mind by saying something seasoned with a decent cheerfulness and appropriate to the matter under discussion. Or we might say something wonderful and startling or perhaps even painful and distressing; whatever we say in this way will be all the better if it affects our hearer immediately so that a quick sense of self-concern may keep his attention on the alert. Nevertheless, it should not be of the sort which wounds his sense of shame by any harshness attached to it; rather it should be calculated to win him over by the friendliness it conveys. . . .

[6] There is a difference between the method of a person giving private instruction when there are no other people at hand to pass judgment, and the method of one teaching in public surrounded by an audience of people holding various opinions. Again, in the practice of teaching the effort will be of one sort when only one individual is being taught, while all the rest listen with the attitude of people judging and endorsing things well-known to them. It will be different when all present are waiting for what we have to set before them. And again in this same instance one technique is necessary when all are seated in private with the intention of beginning a discussion and another is necessary when the people sit silently with their attention focussed on a single speaker who is about to address them from a raised platform. Under these circumstances it will also make a big difference whether our audience is small or large, or whether it is composed of educated or uneducated people or of both. It will also matter whether they are city-bred, rustics or a mixture of both, or

[6] *The Instruction of the Unistructed,* 23.

love of one's subject and love of those to be ta

whether it is an audience in which all sorts of people are mingled. For different people must necessarily have different effects on the man who has to speak to them and teach them. The address we deliver will bear certain features expressive of the feelings of the mind from which it proceeds, and it will affect the audience in various ways in accordance with the speaker's frame of mind; at the same time the listeners themselves will variously influence one another by their mere presence together. But since we are now talking about the instruction of uneducated people, I can tell you from my own experience that I find myself differently affected according as I see before me for the purpose of instruction a highly educated man or a dull fellow, a citizen or a foreigner, a rich man or a poor man, a private individual or a man of honors, a person occupying some position of authority, a man of this nation or that, of this or that age or sex, a member of one sect or another, or one associated with this or that popular error. My talk always takes its start, proceeds and reaches its conclusion in accordance with the varying state of my feelings. Also, since the same medicine is not to be given to all, although to all the same love is due, so love labors hard with some people, becomes weak with others, is at pains to edify some, dreads being a cause of offense to others, stoops before some, lifts itself erect before others, is gentle to some, severe to others, an enemy to none, a mother to all.

The Self-Activity of the Learner

[7] Although the method of question and answer is the best of all methods for seeking truth, scarcely anyone can be found who is not ashamed of being defeated in an argument. Thus, a subject which lends itself well to discussion is always disrupted by an explosion of obstinacy accompanied by torn

[7] *Soliloquies,* ii, 14.

tempers, sometimes concealed, but at other times openly displayed. Therefore, it seemed right, as I see it, to seek truth in a harmonious and suitable spirit and with God's help. The plan was that I should ask you questions and that you should reply to them. Therefore, there is no reason why you should hesitate to go over a point again if you have made a rash admission and tied yourself in knots. This is the only possible way of escaping a difficulty.

[8] It is often easier for people to attain the objectives for the sake of which they study a subject than to pursue the very complicated and thorny study of the rules. For example, a man who wants to give you the rules for walking could warn you not to lift the rear foot before you set down the front foot; and he could go on to describe in great detail how the hinges of the joints and knees must be moved. What he says is true, and nobody can walk in any other way; but people find it easier to walk by carrying out the movements than by concentrating their minds on them while they are being performed or by understanding the movements should they be given a lesson on them. Furthermore, those who cannot walk care even less about such instructions because they cannot test them in action. Similarily a clever man is generally quicker to see that the conclusion of an argument is not justified than to grasp the reasoning which established the conclusion. On the other hand, a dull person does not understand the conclusion and finds still greater difficulty in grasping what he is told about it. All these rules are noteworthy for the pleasure they give us in the demonstration of truth rather than for their practical assistance in discussion and in the formation of judgments. It may be that the study of the rules produces a better trained intellect, although at the same time such knowledge may have the accompanying effect of making

[8] *Christian Education,* ii, 55.

the mind more prone to mischief or vanity. Those who have learned the rules may take on the desire to deceive other people by plausible talk and questions; or they may give the impression that they have acquired for themselves some powerful tool with which to establish their ascendancy over good and innocent people.

The following intensely human episode, taken from the beginning of the dialogue *The Principle of Order,* describes a learning experience developed according to what is now known as the "activity" or "problem" method of teaching. The dialogue is concerned with the problem of cause and effect in the universe, and the whole discussion springs from a question raised in the minds of teacher and pupils by a rather commonplace, if unusual, occurrence in their physical environment. If the principle of order in the universe is absolute, then even the most ordinary event must have its cause. The discussion, which grows out of such humble beginnings, quickly claims the interest and attention of Augustine and his pupils and leads them far from the humble mouse, which started it all, to an exploration of difficult philosophical issues. If learning is to be productive, the right moment must be seized whenever it occurs, even if, as in this case, teacher and pupils have already retired to bed for the night.

[9] When pains in my chest had forced me to give up my teaching appointment, I immediately went to the country house of my close friend Verecundus.* As you know, without any compulsion I had already been struggling to find my way

* In October, 386 A. D., three months after his conversion to Christianity, Augustine resigned his appointment as public teacher of rhetoric in Milan *(Confessions,* ix, 2). Verecundus was a teacher of grammar in Milan.

[9] *The Principle of Order,* i, 5-17.

into philosophy. . . . In this country house we had discussions on whatever subjects seemed worthwhile to us, and we took the trouble of having our proceedings recorded in writing. All this appeared to be good for my health, but, since I was a little worried about my voice, no very violent controversy crept into the discussion. At the same time, since the discussions were taken down in writing, there was no need to express them in different words or to be put to the trouble of recalling them if we wanted to report them in letters to other people. Those who were engaged in the discussions with me were: Alypius; Navigius, my brother; Licentius, who had suddenly developed a consuming passion for poetry; Trygetius, whom the army had restored to us and who had a veteran's love of history.*

One night according to my usual custom I had wakened from sleep and was turning over whatever came into my mind. Because of my desire to lay hold of truth, this had become a habit with me; when I was immersed in some problem, I would spend at least one half of the night pondering it and would not be diverted from my thoughts by the studies of the young men. At any rate, they were so preoccupied with these during the entire day that I thought it too much that they should also spend part of the night in the labor of study; thus, I used to advise them to find some occupation other than their books, and at the same time to develop the habit of reflecting on themselves. Thus, as I have said, I was awake when the sound of the water which flows behind the bathhouse claimed my attention and held it more persistently than usual. It seemed odd to me that the same water, running over the pebbles, should make a noise which fluctuated between a sharp and a dull sound. I began to ask myself what could cause this but no solution occurred to me. Then Licentius rapped on a part of his wooden bed to frighten away

Problem

* Alypius, a close friend not much younger than Augustine, had been a student of Augustine at Carthage; Navigius was a younger brother; Licentius and Trygetius were youths toward whom Augustine acted as tutor.

some persistent mice and in this way showed that he was awake. I said to him, "Have you noticed, Licentius, how the sound of the water in the channel is varying?" "Yes, I have," he said. "I woke some time ago, and, in the hope that the weather had cleared, I strained my ears to hear if the rain was coming down. The water was behaving exactly as it is now." Trygetius confirmed this, for he was also lying awake in his bed in the same room, although we thought him asleep; we were lying in darkness, which in Italy is almost necessary, even for the wealthy.

When I realized that our whole school, or what remained of it because Alypius and Navigius had gone to town, was awake and that the running of the water was inviting discussion, I said, "What do you think is causing the sound to fluctuate? Surely we do not think that at this hour anyone would be repeatedly interrupting the flow of the water either by crossing it or by washing something in it." "What else do you think could cause it," said Licentius, "except that at some point the leaves, which in autumn fall continuously and in large numbers, have lodged in the narrow channel and from time to time are overwhelmed and give way to the pressure of the water? Then, when the water has passed over them, they mass together again and bank it up. Or else some other condition, produced by the varied movements of the floating leaves, occurs to check the flow and then to release it." Lacking any other explanation, I thought this a probable one; therefore, I praised his ingenuity, admitting that, although I had spent some time searching for the cause, I had found no answer.

Then after a short silence I said, "You had right on your side when you were not overcome by astonishment and remained inwardly loyal to Calliope."* "Yes, indeed," he said, "but you have certainly given me good reason for wonder." "How so?" I asked. "Because," said he, "you yourself saw fit to wonder at this phenomenon." I said, "Where does wonder

* Calliope, the muse of epic poetry.

come from? What is it that begets wonder if not some unusual happening outside the normal run of cause and effect?" To which Licentius replied, "I approve of your expression 'outside the normal run of cause and effect,' for I hold that nothing occurs without a cause." At this I was buoyed up by a livelier expectation than is usual when I put questions to my students; the mind of the youth had so quickly conceived a significant idea, although it was only yesterday that he had begun to study this sort of question and we had never before broached such matters together. "Good," I said, "Well done! You have indeed produced an excellent and important idea, and have been very bold. Believe me, you have passed over and above Helicon* with a good deal of room to spare – Helicon, whose summit you are struggling to reach as if it were heaven. But I ask you to stand by your idea at the ready, for I am going to try to topple it. " "Please," he said, "will you allow me a moment's respite? For I am giving my whole attention to another matter." Being a little afraid that Licentius might be coming into the grip of his passion for poetry and might be carried far away from philosophy, I said, "It distresses me to see how devoted you are to singing and wailing out those verses of yours in every sort of meter. They are trying to erect a stouter wall between you and truth than was erected between your two lovers. For at least they had a small crack through which to breathe." At that moment, you see, Licentius had begun to sing about Pyramus.**

I had spoken to Licentius with a sterner voice than he expected, and he fell silent for a while. I had already given up the discussion we had started, and had turned again to my own thoughts, not wanting to make a vain and foolish attempt to force a mind that was preoccupied elsewhere. But then Licentius said, "Terence's words; 'Because of the evidence given by myself I am as unhappy as a mouse,'*** could be

* Mt. Helicon, the home of the muses.

** From Ovid's "Pyramus and Thisbe," *Metamorphoses,* iv, 55ff.

*** From Terence's comedy *The Eunuch,* Act 5, scene 5.

just as appropriately applied by myself to my own condition. But at least the outcome will be different. For Terence says, 'Today I am lost'; but in my case who knows but that today I shall be found? For if you do not despise the tendency of superstitious folk to receive omens even from mice, why should I not be instructed by that mouse or rat which revealed to you that I was awake? I frightened it off by the noise I made, and it showed wisdom in returning to its own resting place to commune with itself in peace. So why should I not be warned by the sound of your voice to indulge in philosophy rather than singing? For I am beginning to believe your daily advice to us that philosophy is our real and indestructible habitation. Thus, if it suits you and you think it proper, put any questions you please; I shall do my best to defend the fixed order of things, taking up the position that nothing happens outside the established rule of cause and effect. Indeed, I have become so impregnated with this proposition that, even if defeated in the argument, I shall attribute my defeat to cause and effect rather than to pure chance. It will not be the proposition which will be defeated but only Licentius."

Accordingly, with renewed pleasure, I again turned my attention to the boys and said to Trygetius, "What is your view?" He answered, "I am mainly on the side of cause and effect; but I am not sure of my ground, and hope that such an important question will be rigorously debated." "Your uncertainty," said I, "is something you share with Licentius and myself." "As for myself," said Licentius, "I am absolutely certain of my opinion. Why should I hesitate to demolish the wall you have mentioned before it has been completely erected? In fact, if I turn away from philosophy, the reason may lie not as much in poetry as in your lack of confidence in the possibility of discovering truth." Then Trygetius triumphantly said, "Now we have something of great significance, namely, a Licentius who is opposed to the Academics*; he has usually defended them with such enthusiasm." "Let this alone," said Licentius, "I beg of you, in case some seductive subtlety seizes me and turns me from a divine idea which has begun to display itself to me and to which I am eagerly clinging." At this point, seeing that my joy was overflowing more abundantly than I had ever dared hope, I uttered this line of verse:

> "So let Apollo, Father of the Gods, Apollo high and exalted,/Bring it about that you begin the battle."
> (Vergil, *Aeneid*, x, 874-875)

"For he will lead us right on to the end," I went on, "if we follow where he 'bids us go and take up our dwelling'; he who 'gives us this omen' and 'steals into our hearts.'** But it is not that 'high and exalted' Apollo we have to deal with, that Apollo who in caves, on mountain sides and in groves is roused by the odor of incense and the slaughter of beasts, and fills the minds of his frenzied worshippers; our business is rather with Another, who is very truly exalted and utters only the truth. To say it briefly, He is none other than Truth itself,

* The reference is to the skeptical philosophers of the New Academy, whose most notable representative was Carneades (214-129 B.C.) The 'Old' Academy of Plato and his successors had denied the possibility of acquiring knowledge through the senses; Carneades and his school also doubted the possibility of reaching certainty through purely intellectual understanding. Cicero's *Academica* was written in support of this skeptical principle, while Augustine's *Against the Academics* marshals the arguments against it.

** These words are a paraphrase of Vergil, *Aenied*, iii, 88-89, where Aeneas prays to Apollo in his temple at Delos, asking, "Where do you bid us go? Where take up our dwelling? Grant me an omen, O Father, and steal into our hearts." The pagan references are curious in this Christian setting. They show that in the period immediately following his conversion and baptism, Augustine did not feel the pangs of conscience about his love for Vergil, which he later was to express in Book 1 of the *Confessions*.

whose prophets consist of everyone who can attain to wisdom. Therefore, Licentius, let us advance to the attack as worshippers fortified by our piety, and let us stamp out under our feet the destructive smoky fires of our carnal desires."

"Now," said Licentius, "ask me questions, I beg of you, to see whether, with the help of your words and mine, I can give some explanation of this baffling problem." "Tell me first of all," I said, "why you think this water flows according to the principle of cause and effect and not in a purely random manner. The fact that it flows along wooden conduits, and is brought here for our use, can be attributed to cause and effect; for this was done by men using their reason, so that the same stream might serve both for drinking and for washing; also, because of the lie of the ground, it was inevitable that the water would flow this way. But with regard to the fact that these leaves, as you say, fell into the channel in such a way as to produce the phenomenon which has surprised us—how can you attribute this to cause and effect rather than to pure chance?" Licentius replied, "If a person is quite confident that nothing can happen without a cause, he cannot think that these leaves ought to have fallen, or could have fallen, in any other way than they did fall. Do you really want me to describe the exact location of the trees and their branches and, indeed, the precise weight nature has given to the leaves? What point is there in my inquiring into the motions of the air in which the leaves float, the density of the air through which they descend, and their various movements, which depend upon the condition of the atmosphere, their weight, their shapes and many other more secret causes? Such conditions elude our senses and are completely hidden from them. This alone is pertinent to the question we are considering and does not elude our mind: that nothing occurs without a cause. A persistent questioner might go on to ask why trees are planted here, and I would reply that men have utilized the fertility of the soil. What then if the trees do not produce fruit and have been accidentally begotten? To this I would reply that our knowledge is limited; nature, which brings forth trees, never acts in a random fashion. Do I need to labor the point further? Let me be shown something happening without a cause; if you cannot show me anything, then you must believe that nothing happens except in obedience to a strict law of cause and effect."

I answered Licentius as follows: "You may call me an annoying questioner since I launched an attack on you with a view to ending your dialogue with Pyramus and Thisbe; nevertheless, I shall proceed to put my questions. This 'nature,' which you want to appear so well ordered, has produced some trees here which bear no fruit. Now what advantage can there be in this?" While Licentius was thinking out his reply to this, Trygetius said, "Surely trees have other advantages to confer on man than their fruit. Many benefits come from their shade, timber and even from their branches and leaves." "Please," said Licentius, "do not give this sort of answer to our master's questions; for we could point to innumerable other things from which men derive no advantage; or at least the advantage is so hidden or insignificant that it cannot be unearthed and brought out in our defense. Let him rather teach us how it is possible for something to occur without being preceded by a cause." "We shall see to this later," I said, "for it is no longer necessary for me to play the part of the teacher, since you, Licentius, have declared that you had all the answers to this important problem; nevertheless, up to this moment you have in fact taught me nothing, although I am anxious to learn and have spent days and nights pondering this problem alone."

"Where are you leading me?" Licentius said, "Am I following you with as little resistance as those leaves of yours? They follow the winds, by which they are so effectively launched into the running water that they do not merely drop in but are also carried along by the water. This is surely what will happen if Licentius gives instructions to Augustine, particularly on matters central to philosophy." "Please," I said, "do not indulge in such self-abasement and exaltation of me. For I am also merely a child in philosophy; when I ask questions, I am not much concerned who is the channel through which God, who every day hears my own questioning, gives me His answers. I believe that one day you also will be His prophet, and this day is perhaps not far distant. Nevertheless, even those who are remote from studies of this sort can teach us something when they are brought together in a group of people engaged in discussion and linked to one another by what we may call the common bonds of question and answer. This 'something' they teach us is quite different from 'nothing.' Do you not see—I am choosing to use your own example—that those very leaves, which are carried along by the wind and float on the water, set up a resistance to the current as it hurries them along and that they thus declare to us the principle of order in the world—that is, if the principle you are defending is true?"

At this point Licentius leapt out of his bed for joy, saying, "Who would deny, O mighty God, that You govern everything according to a principle of order? Everything is so well controlled! By what unalterable sequences events are linked together. What long and numerous chains of causes have brought us to the point of talking together here and meeting with you [Augustine]! How did it happen that we woke from our sleep, that you became conscious of the sound of the water, started looking for its cause and yet did not discover the cause of such a simple little matter, if all this did not happen as a result of the orderly movement of things? The mouse came out so that I would betray my wakefulness; then your words, uttered perhaps without premeditation (for nobody is in full control over what comes into his mind), somehow or other took such a course that they taught me what I ought to reply to you. I also ask you this: if our discussions, being taken down in writing and spread abroad, become well known to people, won't this fame seem so important that some great seer or Chaldean must predict it long before it actually happens? If he does foretell this event, he will be called 'inspired,' and will be so exalted by the unanimous praises of all men that no one will dare ask him why a leaf fell

prediction

from a tree or whether a wandering mouse proved troublesome to a man lying in his bed. Surely there is no seer who would ever have predicted such events as these, whether voluntarily or at the request of a client. Nevertheless, if our prophet were to see it as inevitable that a book should become well known—if he did not see this, there would be no prediction—then whatever accounts for the fluttering of leaves in a field or the presence of the lowliest little animals in a house is just as much a link in the chain of cause and effect as the writings themselves are. For the writings are composed of words which could not in any way have entered the mind, issued from the mouth and been handed down to posterity, unless these lowly events came first. I now beg of you, therefore, let no one ask me why this or that happens; it is enough to know that nothing happens unless it has been produced or set in motion by some cause."

"It is clear, young man," I said, "that you are not aware how many arguments against divination have been put forward and what sort of men have advanced them. But for the moment do not tell me whether anything happens without a cause—for I see you do not want to answer on this point—but rather tell me whether this principle of order, which you have taken up, seems to you a good or a bad thing." He muttered to himself for a little and then said, "Your question is not one to which I can answer 'yes' or 'no,' for I detect here a sort of middle path. Order seems to me neither good nor bad." "What then," I said, "do you think is the opposite of order?" "Nothing," he replied, "for how could there be an opposite of something which comprehends and embraces everything? If something were to be the opposite of order, it must be outside order; now I see nothing outside order. Therefore, we must hold that nothing is the opposite of order." "Therefore," said Trygetius, "error is not the opposite of order?" "By no means," Licentius said, "for I see no one falling into error without a cause. Order entails sequences of causes and effects, and error is not only itself the product of a cause but also produces effects of which it is the cause. How then can error be contrary to order if it is not outside order?"

When Trygetius had fallen silent, I could not restrain my joy at seeing this young man, the son of a very dear friend, becoming my son also; and not only that, but he was growing and developing into a friend also. This Trygetius, in whom I had despaired of developing a taste even for literary studies of a moderate standard, was now plunging right into the heart of philosophy with every enthusiasm, as if it were his own domain. While I was quietly marvelling at this and glowing with joy, suddenly, as though seized by a sort of inspiration, Licentius exclaimed, "If only I could utter what I have in mind. I ask you, O words, where, where are you? Come to my aid. Both good and evil are included within the orderly arrangement of things. Believe this, if you wish, for I know not how to explain it." I remained in silent wonder. But Trygetius, seeing the fellow becoming approachable again and more amenable to discussion, as if he had been in a state of intoxication which was now dissipated, said, "What you say seems absurd to me, Licentius, and entirely contrary to truth. Bear with me for a moment, I entreat you, and do not interrupt with exclamations." "Say what you will," he said, "for I am not afraid that you can seduce me from what I see and have almost grasped." "Is it not possible," said Trygetius, "that you are moving away from the principle of order, which you are defending, and rising against God with such careless talk? For what could be more impious than to declare that evil is contained within the orderly arrangement of the world? There is no doubt that God loves order." "Yes, He certainly does," said Licentius. "It has its source in Him and dwells in Him. Consider within yourself whether there is anything more appropriate which can be said on such an important matter; for I am not yet capable of enlightening you further on this problem." "What am I to think?" said Trygetius. "I accept wholeheartedly what you say, and what I understand is enough for me. Certainly you have said that evil also is included in the principle of order, and that order itself has its source in God and is loved by Him. From which it follows that evil too comes from God and is loved by Him. . . ." (The discussion continues.)

Words and Things: The Problem of Communication

[10] When men listen to other men, what they understand is in fact given to them within; it shines forth and is revealed inwardly. What is achieved by men who teach externally? What am I accomplishing now when I am speaking? I am merely thrusting a noise of words into your ears. But what can I actually say or speak, if He who is within does not make a revelation? The person who cultivates a tree is outside the tree, but its Creator is inside. The man who plants and waters works externally, and this is what we do. . . . Because I am a man, who do I teach? Surely I teach the person who hears my word. If I, being a man, teach the person who hears my word, so the Father also teaches the person who hears His word.

The pages which follow present almost one half of the dialogue called *The Teacher (De Magistro),* in which the participants are Augustine and his natural son Adeodatus. The dialogue opens as follows:

[11]AUGUSTINE: What would you say is our purpose when we speak?

[10] *Tracts on St. John's Gospel,* 26, 7–8.
[11] *The Teacher,* I.

ADEODATUS: As far as I can see, our purpose is either to teach or to learn.

AUGUSTINE: The first alternative is clear, and I agree with it. When we speak, we obviously desire to teach. But how does learning come into it?

ADEODATUS: Surely, only when we ask questions.

AUGUSTINE: Even then I think we are merely desiring to teach. I ask you to consider this: don't you ask questions simply to teach the other person what you want to know?

ADEODATUS: This is so.

AUGUSTINE: Then you see that we employ speech merely for the purpose of teaching.

ADEODATUS: I am not quite clear about this. If speaking is simply uttering words, I find that we do this when we sing; and we often sing when we are alone, with nobody present who could learn from us; therefore, I cannot think that we have any intention of teaching anything.

objection

AUGUSTINE: Nevertheless, I think there is a kind of teaching which consists in reminding, and which is certainly important, as will appear in the course of our discussion. But, if you do not think we are learning when we remember something and if you hold that, when someone reminds us of something, he is not teaching us, I do not oppose you. Therefore, I now point to two reasons for speaking: to teach or to remind either other people or ourselves. This is also our objective when we sing; do you agree?

* things = images

ADEODATUS: Not exactly. It is quite unusual for me to sing in order to recall something to mind. I sing merely for pleasure.

AUGUSTINE: I see your point. But you surely understand that what pleases you in singing is a melody, which may or may not be associated with words; this means that speaking and singing are different things. We play flutes and harps; birds sing; there are times when we sing tunes without words. These sounds can all be called singing but they cannot be called speaking. Have you anything to say against that?

ADEODATUS: No indeed. . . .

[12] AUGUSTINE: Even when we do not utter a sound, we are thinking words and therefore speaking within our minds. By this sort of speech we are merely calling something to mind, since the memory, in which the words are embedded, turns over the words and thus brings to mind the * things themselves, of which the words are the signs.

ADEODATUS: I understand the point you are making.

AUGUSTINE: Then we are agreed that words are signs? | 1st generalization

ADEODATUS: Yes.

AUGUSTINE: Also, a sign cannot be a sign unless it signifies something, can it? | 2nd generalization

[12] *The Teacher,* 2–8.

ADEODATUS: It cannot.

AUGUSTINE: How many words are there in this line of verse: *"Si nihil ex tanta superis placet urbe relinqui."* [If it pleases the gods that nothing be left out of such a great city]*

ADEODATUS: Eight.

AUGUSTINE: Then there are eight signs?

ADEODATUS: Yes.

AUGUSTINE: I suppose that you understand the line.

ADEODATUS: I would say so.

AUGUSTINE: Tell me what each separate word means.

ADEODATUS: I understand what "si" ["if"] means, but I can find no other word to express its meaning.

AUGUSTINE: Then at least you would know where we should look for the thing signified by the word "si."

ADEODATUS: I think that "si" signifies doubt, and surely doubt is found in the mind.

AUGUSTINE: I accept this for the time being. Go on to the other words.

ADEODATUS: "Nihil" ["nothing"]—what else could this word signify, except what does not exist?

* Vergil, *Aeneid,* ii, 659.

"nihil" = nothing. Not a thing or image

AUGUSTINE: Perhaps this is so. But what you have just declared, namely, that a sign cannot be a sign unless it signifies something, makes me hesitate to agree. What does not exist cannot be "something." Thus, the second word in this line is not a sign since it does not signify something; therefore, we have come to the wrong conclusion that all words are signs, or alternatively that every sign signifies something.

ADEODATUS: You press me too hard. When we have no meaning to give to a word, it is surely very foolish to utter it. When you speak to me, I assume that any sound you make is meaningful and that by everything that comes from your mouth you are giving me a sign so that I may understand something. Therefore, when you speak, you should not utter these two syllables [i.e., *ni-hil*] if you do not mean something by them. On the other hand, if you see that the word is necessary for making some announcement and that we are taught or reminded of something when it sounds in our ears, then surely you also come to understand something I want to say, even though I cannot say exactly what it is.

AUGUSTINE: Where are we getting then? Are we saying that this word indicates a mental state rather than some non-existent thing? Could we describe this mental state in this way, namely, that the mind fails to see something and discovers that it does not exist, or thinks that it does not exist.

ADEODATUS: This is perhaps what I was trying to explain.

AUGUSTINE: However this may be, let us pass beyond this point lest we fall victim to an absurdity.

ADEODATUS: What absurdity is that?

AUGUSTINE: That "nothing" may hold us back so that we are delayed on that account.

ADEODATUS: Yes indeed, this would be ridiculous. Yet somehow I see that it can happen, and indeed that it actually has happened.

AUGUSTINE: At the right time we shall better understand this kind of contradiction if God is pleased to allow it. In the meantime, turn to the line of verse and try to explain to the best of your ability what the other words mean.

ADEODATUS: The third word is a preposition, "ex" ["out of"], instead of which I think we could put "de" ["from"].

AUGUSTINE: I am not asking you to substitute one equally well-known word for another well-known word which means the same thing, if indeed they both do have the same meaning. For the present, however, let us concede the point. If the poet had not said "out of such a great city," but "from such a great city," and I were to ask you what "from" means, you would say "out of," on the ground that these two words, i.e., signs, have the same meaning as you see it. But I want to know what is that one thing which is signified by these two signs.

ADEODATUS: My view is that they indicate the separation of one thing from something in which it had previously existed; the first thing is said to be "out of" the other thing. This other thing may not exist, as in the line of verse the city does not exist, and yet some Trojans were able to come "out of" it. On the other hand, the other thing may continue to exist, just as we say that businessmen in Africa are "out of" Rome.

AUGUSTINE: I shall agree with you about this and refrain from pointing out the many possible exceptions to the rule. But at least you can easily see that you have explained words by words, that is, signs by signs, well-known words and signs by equally well-known ones. I want you, if you can, to show me the things themselves of which these words are the signs.

ADEODATUS: I am surprised that you do not know, or rather pretend not to know, that by my answers I certainly cannot give you what you want. The reason is that we are talking together, and therefore we can give answers only in words. On the other hand, you are looking for things which are certainly not words, whatever they are; nevertheless, you are trying to get these things from me by the use of words. First, put your questions to me without using words, and then I can give my answers in the same coin.

AUGUSTINE: I admit you are right. But, if I asked the meaning of the three-syllable word "paries" ["wall"] when it is pronounced, surely you would be able to point with your finger so that I could immediately see the thing itself of which the three-syllable word is the sign. Then you would be showing me the thing itself without uttering any words.

ADEODATUS: I agree that this can be done, but only with nouns which signify material objects, and only if these objects are actually present.

AUGUSTINE: Do we call a color an object or rather a quality of an object?

ADEODATUS: A quality of an object.

AUGUSTINE: Then how is it that we can also point to a color with the finger? Are you in fact adding to material objects the qualities of objects, and showing that they also can be taught without words when they are actually present?

ADEODATUS: When I spoke of material objects, I intended to include everything material, that is, all that is perceived in objects.

AUGUSTINE: But consider whether some exceptions are to be made here also.

ADEODATUS: You advise me well, for I should not have said "all" material objects, but rather "all visible objects." I admit, of course, that sound, smell, taste, weight, heat and other qualities which relate to the senses other than sight, cannot be pointed out by the finger, although it is impossible to see them apart from material objects, which means that they themselves are material.

AUGUSTINE: Have you ever noticed that men hold a sort of conversation with deaf people by gesture and that the deaf ask questions and give answers in the same way? This is also how they make all their wants known, or at least the greater part of them. In this situation, there is certainly no use for words; nevertheless, not only objects are indicated, but also sounds, tastes and other such things.

ADEODATUS: I have nothing to argue against you except this: that I am not the only person who would be unable to tell you the meaning of the expression "out of" without employing words. Not even a professional dancer could do this.

AUGUSTINE: Perhaps you are right; but let us imagine that it is possible for him to do it. You do not doubt, I suppose, that, by whatever physical movement he tries to show me the thing signified by a word, he will not be showing me the thing itself but only a sign of it. Thus, although the dancer is not demonstrating a word by means of a word, he is nevertheless demonstrating a sign by means of a sign. So the monosyllable "ex" ["out of"] and the gesture he makes are both signs of exactly the same thing. And it is this one thing which I want you to show me without the use of a sign.

ADEODATUS: How could anyone do what you want—I ask you?

AUGUSTINE: In the same way as a wall does it.

ADEODATUS: But the course of our reasoning has shown that not even a wall can be demonstrated without a sign; for the pointing of a finger is surely not a wall. All that happens is that a sign is given by means of which the wall can be seen. Therefore, I see nothing which can be shown without signs.

AUGUSTINE: Well then, if I were to ask you what "walking" is, and you were to stand up and do it, would you not then be using the thing itself rather than words or any other signs to teach me?

ADEODATUS: I admit that is so, and I am ashamed that I did not see something which is so self-evident. Many things now occur to me which can be shown directly instead of through signs, such as eating, drinking, sitting, standing, shouting and very many others.

AUGUSTINE: Come then, tell me now whether, if I were ignorant of the meaning of the word "walk", and were to ask you what "walking" is while you were in the very act of walking, how would you teach me?

ADEODATUS: I would go through the motion a little faster so that, after putting your question, you would be instructed by the appearance of some new element in the situation. Yet nothing would be occurring other than what it is necessary to demonstrate.

AUGUSTINE: Do you know that walking and hurrying are different things? A man who walks does not suddenly hurry, and one who hurries is not necessarily walking. For we speak of "hurrying" with reference to writing, reading and countless other activities. Therefore, if after my question you speeded up the activity in which you were engaged, I would think that "walking" meant "hurrying"; for this would be the new element you had added and I would be misled by it.

ADEODATUS: I agree that we cannot demonstrate a thing without a sign if we are actually performing the action in question at the moment when we are asked about it. For, if we add nothing to what we are doing, the questioner will think we are unwilling to give a demonstration, that we are paying no attention to him and merely continuing to do what we are doing. But, if he asks us about activities which we are able to perform but in which we are not actually engaged at the moment, we can give a demonstration of them immediately after he has asked the question. In this way we can give the required demonstration by means of the thing itself rather than by a sign; unless at a moment when I am by chance actually speaking, our questioner should ask me to tell him what "speaking" is. Then, whatever I say in order to teach him, it is necessary for me to put it in words. From this starting point and without departing from the actual thing which he wants to have demonstrated to him, I shall continue to teach him until I clarify what he wants to know. I shall not be looking for signs with which to give this demonstration, but shall use only the thing itself.

[13]AUGUSTINE: Are you of the opinion that actions which we can quickly perform when asked about them can be demonstrated without a sign? Is there an exception to this?

[13] *The Teacher,* 29–36.

ADEODATUS: I am turning over in my mind all the actions which come under this definition, and as yet I have not discovered any of them which can actually be taught without a sign, except perhaps the act of speaking—and also teaching if someone were to ask me what that meant. For I see that, when someone puts a question to me and I do something in order to instruct him, the person concerned does not learn directly from the thing which he wants to have demonstrated to him. To take our previous example, if someone asks me what "walking" is at a time when I am doing nothing, and if I try to teach him what he wants to know without using a sign, that is, by immediately starting to walk, how can I guard against the misunderstanding that "walking" means covering exactly the amount of ground I have covered? If the other person comes to this conclusion, then he will be wrong. For he will be inferring that a person who walks a longer or shorter distance than I walk, is not walking at all. And what I have said about this one word covers all the others suggested. Nothing can be demonstrated without a sign, with the two exceptions which I have just mentioned.

AUGUSTINE: Well, I accept that. But you would agree, wouldn't you, that speaking and teaching are different functions?

ADEODATUS: Yes, indeed. For, if they were one and the same thing, nobody would teach without speaking. But we teach many things by non-verbal signs; therefore, nobody could doubt that there is a difference.

AUGUSTINE: Is there any difference between teaching and giving signs? Are they the same?

ADEODATUS: I say that they are the same.

AUGUSTINE: The person who says that we give signs in order to teach is right, isn't he?

ADEODATUS: Certainly he is right.

AUGUSTINE: Well then, if someone else were to say that we teach in order to give signs, surely what we have just said could easily be used to contradict him.

ADEODATUS: That is so.

AUGUSTINE: Then, although we give signs in order to teach, we do not teach in order to give signs. Therefore, teaching and giving signs are two different things.

ADEODATUS: You are right, and I was at fault in saying that they are the same.

AUGUSTINE: Now answer this for me. If a man teaches what teaching is, does he do it by giving signs or in some other way?

ADEODATUS: I do not see how he could do it in any other way than by giving signs.

AUGUSTINE: Therefore, what you said a little while ago is wrong, namely, that, if someone asks what teaching is, it can be taught directly without signs. For we find that not even this can be performed without giving signs since you have agreed that giving signs and teaching are different things. If they are different, as appears to be the case, and, if teaching cannot be practiced except by giving signs, then, contrary to what you thought, teaching cannot be demonstrated in a direct manner. Thus, up to this point nothing has been discovered which can be directly demonstrated except speaking, which, as well as signifying other things, signifies itself. But, because speech is itself a sign, it is not yet completely evident that anything can be taught without signs.

ADEODATUS: I have no reason to disagree with you.

AUGUSTINE: Therefore, we have reached the conclusion that nothing can be taught without signs and that knowledge itself should be valued by us more highly than the signs by means of which we get knowledge; however, we made the proviso that not everything represented by a sign is to be preferred to its sign.* e.g. "filth" "vice"

ADEODATUS: I agree.

AUGUSTINE: I ask you, do you recall the long circuitous path that we took to accomplish such a slight result? Since we began to hurl words at each other, which we have been doing for quite a long time now, we have labored to find the

* In sections 27-28 (omitted from this translation) it was argued that, although the knowledge of a thing is always more valuable than the knowledge of its sign, yet the signs of certain things are better than the things they represent; the two examples used are "filth" and "vice."

answer to three questions: first, is it true that nothing can be taught without signs? second, are certain signs to be preferred to the things they represent? third, is the knowledge of things better than the knowledge of their signs? But there is a fourth matter about which I would like to hear a few words from you: have you any doubts at all about the conclusions we have reached?

ADEODATUS: I would indeed expect that after such a winding, tortuous journey we would have reached some definite conclusions. But somehow this question of yours worries me and makes me hesitate to agree. For I imagine that you would not ask it unless you had reservations to bring forward. Also, the difficult nature of the problem does not permit me to see it as a whole and to give absolutely confident answers. I am afraid there is something lying closely wrapped up in the matter, and my mind cannot penetrate to it.

AUGUSTINE: I am pleased to note your hesitation; it shows a cautious mental attitude, which is the greatest protection of tranquillity. It is certainly very difficult not to be disturbed when what we have always held with an easy and ready acquiescence is toppled by contrary arguments, or, as it were, wrested from our hands. While it is right to yield to arguments which have been well considered and scrutinized, there is also a danger in accepting what is not known as though it were known. When something which we have always confidently accepted as certain to remain standing forever goes down in ruin, there is the possibility that we will fall into danger of distrusting reason when cherished beliefs are shattered — i.e. becoming cynical (or sk

such a hatred and distrust of reason that we will think we should not put our trust in truth, even when it is clearly established.

Therefore, let us push ahead and give further attention to the question of whether you are right to be hesitant about our conclusions. I ask you to consider the following situation: Imagine a man, ignorant of the method of trapping birds with the use of twigs and lime, meeting a bird-catcher equipped with his tools. This bird-catcher is not in the act of trapping birds, but is merely passing by. When the other man sees him, he follows close after him, searching around in his mind, as is natural, to discover the purpose of the bird-catcher's equipment. The bird-catcher observes his curiosity and, having the desire to give a demonstration, prepares his reeds, and with his rod and hawk captures a small bird which he has seen close by. Surely under these circumstances the bird-catcher would be teaching the spectator without giving signs but directly, by the action itself.

ADEODATUS: I am afraid that here we have a case analogous to that of the person who asks what "walking" is. I cannot see that the whole art of bird-catching has been shown here.

AUGUSTINE: It is simple to remove this scruple from your mind. Let us also assume that the spectator is so intelligent that he learns the whole nature of the art from observation of this one demonstration. It is sufficient to point out that some men, although not all men, can be taught without a sign.

ADEODATUS: I also have this to add to what you say: if a man is very well endowed intellectually, he can discover all there is to be known about walking if walking is demonstrated by only a few steps.

AUGUSTINE: I agree to this addition and positively approve of it. You see what the upshot of all this is: each of us has come to the conclusion that some things can be taught without signs and that our earlier views, to the effect that there is absolutely nothing which can be shown without signs, are wrong. Starting from these examples, we can think of not only one or two things but thousands, which are directly demonstrated without any signs being given. Why then, I ask you, should we doubt it? To pass over the countless performances of actors, who give direct exhibitions of things without a sign, we might consider that surely God and nature directly display to our sight the sun and the light, which permeate and cover everything, the moon and the other heavenly bodies, land and sea and the innumerable forms of life therein. Then, if you think about the matter more carefully, perhaps you may actually find that nothing can be learned from its appropriate sign. When a sign is given to me, it may find me ignorant of what it represents; then it can teach me nothing. But, if I know what it means, what do I learn from the sign? For example, when I read, "Their *saraballae* were not altered,"* the word *"saraballae"* does not

* *Book of Daniel,* Vulgate edition, 3, 94.

show me the actual thing which it symbolizes.* If the word is defined as some sort of "head covering," I surely do not learn when I hear this definition what "head" is or what "coverings" are. I knew all this before, and the knowledge of these things came to me, not when they were named by other people, but when I saw them for myself. The first time the syllables "ca-put" ["head"] came to my ears, I was as ignorant of their meaning as I was when I first heard or read "saraballae." But, after frequently hearing "caput" and marking the circumstances under which it was said, I observed that it was the word for a thing which was already very well known to me from sight. Before I made this discovery, the word was merely a sound to me; I learned that it was a sign when I discovered what object it symbolized. I learned about the object itself, not through signs, but by actually seeing it. Thus, it is better to learn the sign after the actual thing has been learned than to learn the thing after the sign.

So that you may get a firmer hold on this, imagine that at this moment we are learning the word "head" for the very first time. Not know-

* The word *"saraballae"* is neither a Latin nor a Greek word; both its form and meaning are uncertain. J. M. Colleran in his edition of *The Teacher* (Westminster Press, Westminster, Maryland, 1950, p. 233) notes: "Some mss. have *"quaedam pedum tegmina,'* that is, 'footwear of some sort' (instead of *'quaedam capitum tegmina,'* 'headwear of some sort')." He also notes that in various places "the word is rendered trousers, coverings for the limbs, garments, and even coat." The obscurity in the meaning of the word admirably reinforces Augustine's argument that the sign or symbol *(signum),* and the thing symbolized are entirely different things; therefore, the sign by itself can tell us nothing about the thing, which we can come to know only through direct experience of it.

ing whether it is merely a vocal sound or it also signifies something, we ask what "head" is. Remember that we desire to have knowledge of the sign itself and not of the thing represented by the sign. This is the knowledge we lack, as long as we do not know what the word signifies. If then, when we put the question, the thing symbolized is pointed out to us with the finger, we learn about the sign by seeing the thing; up to that point we had merely heard the sound, not grasped the meaning. Surely then we perceive the sound, not by means of the sign as such, but merely because the ear has been stimulated; on the other hand, we come to understand the meaning of the sign from the thing represented by the sign. Now the pointing of a finger can indicate merely the object toward which the finger is pointed; this object is not the sign but the part of the body called "head." Thus, by means of the pointing I cannot learn the thing (for I know that already); nor can I learn the sign because the finger was not pointed at that.

But I am not particularly concerned about the pointing of the finger, which seems to me to be a sign of the act of pointing rather than a sign of what is pointed out. It is exactly the same as uttering the exclamation "Look!" In fact, we usually point the finger when we say this, just in case one sign alone might not be sufficient. What I am particularly trying to bring home to you, if I can, is that we learn nothing through those signs which take the form of words. As I have said, we do come to understand the function of the word, that is, the meaning embedded in the sound, until after we have experienced the actual thing symbolized. We do not understand the thing simply as a result of hearing the sign.

What I have said about "head" applies also to "coverings" and innumerable other things. Although I already know what these are, I am nevertheless ignorant of the meaning of the objects known as "*saraballae*." If someone represents them to me by gesture, paints one of them for me, or shows me something to which they bear a resemblance, I cannot say that he is teaching me. I could easily establish this if I wanted to talk at somewhat greater length. But I do make the point that he would not be teaching me by the agency of words. If he should happen to see some of the things called "saraballae", and should advise me by saying, "Look, saraballae" when I am present, then I would learn what I did not know by the sight of the thing itself or by the agency of words. From seeing the thing I would get to know and grasp the meaning of the name. For, when I came to understand the thing itself, I did not trust the words of some other person; nevertheless, I may have trusted them to help me focus my attention and look for what I wanted to see.

The most that can be said is that words have the limited power of stimulating us to search after realities; but they do not show realities to us so that we may know them. If a person teaches me, it is because he presents to my eyes, or any of my senses or my mind, the things which I want to know. Therefore, through words we learn only words – in effect, merely their sound and noise. Although nothing can be a word unless it is a sign, nevertheless when I have heard a word, I cannot recognize it as a word until I know what it means. Therefore, the knowledge of words is completed only after the things they signify are understood. But, when only words are heard, not even words are being learned; for when we already know a word, we cannot be said to be learning it; and as for words we do not know, we cannot say we have learned them except when we have grasped their meaning. Meaning is learned not by listening to vocal sounds but by getting to know the things which are represented by the signs. Certainly it is well reasoned and truly said that, when words are uttered, we either know what they mean or we do not know. If we already know a word, it is more accurate to say that we recall it than to say that we are learning it. But, if we do not know it, we are not even remembering it, although we may perhaps be stimulated to ask about it.

AUGUSTINE: Now with those objects of knowledge which are open to the intellect,* we do not consult someone who utters sounds outside ourselves, but we consult truth, which presides over our minds deep within us; nevertheless, it may be that words motivate us to make the consultation in the first place. Our teacher is the consultant

* So far the argument has centered on "sensible" things, i.e., physical things which we get to know through the senses. It was agreed that we understand sensible things only through first-hand experience and not by listening to words. Now the argument switches to "intelligible" things, i.e., abstract truths, which can be grasped only by the intellect unaided by sense data.

[14] *The Teacher,* 38–46.

who is said to dwell within the inner man; this consultant is Christ, the unchangeable power of God and everlasting wisdom. He is the teacher whom every rational being consults; but to each man only as much is revealed as he is able to receive relative to the condition of his will, which may be evil or good. If someone falls into error, it is not because of any fault in the truth which has been consulted, any more than it is the fault of the light outside us when the physical eyes are deceived, as they often are. We are agreed that, with regard to physical objects, we consult this light so that it can show them to us insofar as we are able to see them. . . . In the same way, when we are concerned with the things which are grasped by the unaided intelligence, we consult the truth inside us with the help of reason. Therefore, what can be said in support of the view that words teach us something quite apart from their sound which strikes our ears? All that we perceive is perceived either with the senses or with the mind. The things we sense are called "sensibles," while the others are known as "intelligibles"; if we follow the alternate usage of our own Christian writers, the former are "carnal things" and the latter "spiritual things." When we are asked about the former, we can give an answer only if the things we experience through the senses are actually before us; for example, when we are looking at the new moon and are asked what it is made of or where it is. In this case, if the questioner does not see it himself, he merely believes my words, and often, in fact, he does not believe them. It is quite wrong to say that he learns unless he himself is seeing what is being spoken about. This is to say that he does not learn from the words which are uttered but from the things themselves and from his senses; for the same words sound in the ears of the person who sees a thing and of the person who does not see it. But, when we are questioned about things we have perceived in the past and not about things we are actually looking at, we are not speaking of the things themselves but of the images impressed by them and committed to memory. I do not know how we can speak of all these images as true when we see they are false,* unless we are speaking of them, not as things we actually see and perceive, but as things we have seen and perceived. Thus, we carry all these images in the deep recesses of our memory as proofs that we have seen the things themselves in some former time. When the mind contemplates these images, we can therefore speak of them in good conscience, knowing that we are not lying. However, these proofs belong to each one of us privately; if the person who listens to me has personally experienced the things themselves, he does not learn about them from my words, but merely recognizes them from images stored up within himself. On the other hand, if he has not personally experienced them, it is certain that he is merely believing my words and not really learning.

Thus, when we consider the things we perceive with the mind, that is, by means of the intelligence and reason, we are talking about what we are looking at *directly* in that interior

* He uses "false" here in the sense that we are viewing not the things themselves but merely images or representations of them in the mind.

light of truth by which what we call the inner man is enlightened and in which he delights. If at the same time the person who listens to me sees these realities for himself with his inner eye, he knows what I am talking about, not because he has listened to my words, but because he has contemplated the realities on his own account. Thus, even when I am speaking the truth and he is seeing it, I am not teaching him anything; for he is not taught by my words but by the things themselves which are made clear to him and inwardly revealed by God. This is the reason why he can answer questions about the matters at issue. There could be nothing more absurd than to suppose that he is taught by my speaking, since, even before I uttered a single word, he could have explained these same matters in answer to questions. It often happens that a person denies something when asked about it, but by further questioning is brought to admit it. The viewer's weakness of vision is the cause of this since he is unable to consult the inner light about the matter taken as a whole. He is encouraged to do this with the various parts of the problem when he is questioned separately about each of the elements constituting the whole problem—which he had been unable to see as a whole. If he is led along this path by the words of a questioner, he is not being taught by words; the words are merely raising questions which put him in a fit condition to learn inwardly.

For example, suppose I put a question to you on the problem we are considering, i.e., whether anything can be taught by words, and the question seemed ridiculous to you because you could not see the issue as a whole. Then I would have to ask questions adapted to your capacity to hear the inner teacher; so I would ask, "Where have you learned those things whose truth you admitted when I spoke to you about them and which you now say that you know?" You would perhaps reply that I had taught you them. Thereupon I would add this: "What if I were to declare I had seen a man flying? Would this verbal statement be as persuasive to you as the statement that wise men are to be preferred to fools?" You would at once deny that the former statement was equally credible; you would say that you did not believe the first statement or that, even if you did believe it, you did not "know" that it was true; on the other hand, you would declare that you were absolutely certain about the truth of the second statement. From this example, you would no doubt understand that you learned nothing from my words, either about what you did not know when I spoke of it or about what you knew very well. If you were asked about each of the statements separately, you would swear that the first indicated something you did not know, while the second stated something you did know. But at this point you would be admitting the whole proposition which you had rejected; the reason would be that you would now have a clear and certain view of the various elements constituting the problem, which may be summed up as follows: whatever statement we make, a person listening to us either does not know whether it is true or knows that it is false or knows that it is true. In the first case, he either accepts the statement on faith, or holds an opinion, or is in a state of uncertainty; in the second case, he opposes and denies the statement; in the third case, he testifies to the truth of it. In not one of these cases does he actually learn anything. The man who has no first-hand acquaintance with the reality we have been talking about is in exactly the same position as the person who knows that what he has heard is false and the one who, when questioned, could give the same answers which issued from us in the form of statements. None of these can be said to have learned anything from my words.

Thus, with the things that are seen by the mind, it is useless for someone who does not himself see them to listen to the talk of someone who does see them. Of course it may be useful to believe such things, even if one does not actually understand them. But the person who can see them for himself is inwardly a pupil of truth and outwardly a good judge of a speaker, or rather I should say of what a speaker says; for such a person often knows what has been said even when the speaker himself does not. For example, someone who believes the teaching of the Epicureans that the soul is mortal, might give an exposition of the arguments employed by wiser men in support of the immortality of the soul. If someone who has the capacity to see spiritual things is listening to him, he judges that our Epicurean is speaking the truth. Nevertheless, the speaker does not know whether he is speaking the truth and indeed imagines that he is telling big lies. Are we then to think of him as teaching something which he himself does not know? Certainly he is using the same words which would also be employed by someone who knows what he is talking about.

Therefore, words are not to be credited with even the function of indicating the mind of a speaker, for we can never be sure that a person really knows what he is talking about. There are also liars and cheats; as you can clearly see, they are so far from revealing their minds by the words they use that they actually conceal their thoughts. Of course, I do not question that the words of those who speak truth aim at, and so to speak declare their intention of, revealing the mind of the speaker. They would achieve this intention by universal agreement if only liars were not permitted to speak. Of course we have often found, both in ourselves and in others, that words do not exactly express our thinking. To the best of my knowledge, this can come about in two ways: something we have committed to memory and often repeated can be spoken while we are thinking of something quite different, as often occurs, for example, when we are singing a hymn; in the second place, by a slip of the tongue certain words may be uttered unintentionally in place of other words; in this case what is heard does not reveal what is in our minds. In fact, liars also are thinking about what they are saying, so that, although we do not know whether they are speaking the truth, we nevertheless know that they have in mind what they are saying; that is, if neither of the two cases I have just mentioned applies to them. If anyone holds that this sort of mistake happens only occasionally and that, when it does happen, it is obvious to everybody, I am in agreement; nevertheless, such mistakes do often pass unnoticed and have frequently misled me when I have been listening to them.

But there is yet another very common sort of difficulty which is the cause of many disagreements and quarrels. In this case the speaker accurately expresses his thought but often only to himself and certain others in his audience. His words do not convey the same sense to all who hear him; for example, let someone say in our hearing that animals are superior to men "in virtue." There and then we raise an objection and stoutly repudiate such a false and harmful opinion. But the speaker may have been using the word "virtue" in the sense of physical strength, and in this way expressing exactly what he was thinking. He is neither lying, making a mistake about the facts nor uttering words which have been memorized while he is thinking of something else; nor is it a slip of the tongue, causing him to say something quite different from what he is thinking. It is merely that he is calling the thing he is thinking about by a name that is different from the name we use. We would immediately be in agreement with him if we could look into his thought, which he has not yet been able to reveal to us by means of the words he has used to that point to reveal his opinion. It is said that definition is the antidote to this kind of mistake, so that in this case, if the speaker were to say what he meant by "virtue," it would be clear that the argument is not about the thing itself, but about the word. But, even if this is conceded, how few people there are who are good at giving definitions! Also, this very science of definition has raised many problems;

but this is not the place to deal with these, and such discussion is not always to my liking.

I pass over the fact that there are many things we do not hear distinctly; thus, we spend time and effort in arguing about what we only think we have heard. For example, not so long ago I had remarked that a certain Punic word meant "pity," and you said that in the usage of those most familiar with the language it meant "gentleness." Whereupon I objected, saying that you must have completely forgotten what you had been told. For I had thought you said not "gentleness" but "faithfulness." This mistake arose in spite of the fact that you were sitting close by me, and the two names could deceive nobody by the similarity of their sounds. Nevertheless, for a long time I was under the impression that you did not understand what had been said to you, when in fact I was mistaken about what you said. For, if I had heard you clearly, I would not have thought it absurd that in the Punic language "gentleness" and "pity" should be called by the same word.

These misunderstandings occur very frequently. But, as I said, let us pass over them in case I seem to be unjustly casting aspersions on words because of the carelessness of listeners or even human deafness. The cases I mentioned previously are more troublesome, that is, ones in which words belonging to our mother tongue, Latin, are heard with great clarity; nevertheless, we are unable to understand the thoughts of the speakers.

But I leave all that and agree that, when someone hears words that are well known to him, he can know that the speaker has thought the things which the words signify. But does he also learn whether these things are true or false? This is the point at issue.

Surely teachers do not claim that their own thoughts are perceived and grasped by their pupils; rather they say that their pupils grasp the subject matter which teachers imagine they are communicating by their talk. Who is so foolishly inquisitive as to send his child to school to learn what the teacher thinks? Think of all the subjects which teachers declare they are teaching, including the disciplines of virtue and wisdom; teachers talk about them, and then those who are called "learners" take thought within themselves to see if what has been said is true. They do this by gazing steadfastly upon the inner truth, to which we have been referring, and this is what causes them to learn. After inwardly discovering that what teachers have spoken is true, their pupils express their approval, being unaware that what they are praising is the teacher's own learning rather than his teaching skill; this, of course, assumes that teachers themselves really know what they are talking about.* We go astray when we refer to 'teachers,' since there are really no teachers at all. The reason that we speak in this way is that frequently there is no time lapse between the moment of speaking and the moment of learning. Because pupils are quick to learn within themselves in

* That is, the precondition of successful teaching is that the teacher should "know" his subject; he must have consulted the teacher within him. Otherwise, he will be merely repeating words which he has learned by heart; then, however polished his teaching techniques, his efforts will be of little help to his pupils.

consequence of the teacher's instruction, they think that in fact they have learned externally, from the person who has instructed them.

At another time, if God permits it, we shall inquire into the whole question of the usefulness of words; this is not a simple problem if it is given thoughtful attention. At the present time I have advised you not to attribute more significance to words than they ought to have. Thus, we should not only believe, but also begin now to understand, how truly it has been written on divine authority that calling anyone on earth a "teacher" is to be avoided because "there is One in heaven who is the teacher of all" *(Matt.* 23: 8-10). We shall be taught the meaning of "in heaven" by Him who, through the agency of man and by signs coming to us externally, urges us to turn toward Him inwardly, so to be instructed. To love and to know Him constitutes the happy life, which all men declare they are seeking; nevertheless, there are few who can rejoice in the actual possession of it.

But now I want you to tell me what you feel about this whole exposition I have given. If you have come to know that all the things I have said are true, then you would have admitted that you understood them, even if you had been questioned about each of the successive steps in the argument one by one.* Therefore, you will understand who has taught you all this. It was certainly not I, to whom you would

* The last part of the dialogue has consisted of a continuous lecture by Augustine, who now points out that Adeodatus would have understood the points at issue, even if Augustine had maintained the method of question and answer instead of finishing with a continuous exposition. Thus, the fact is established that it is not the exposition of the teacher which has caused Adeodatus to learn; the cause has been Adeodatus' inner mental activity.

have given the answers if I had employed the method of questioning. On the other hand, if you have not come to recognize that it is all true, you have been taught neither by Him (i.e., the inner teacher) nor by me; I have not taught you, the reason being that I have no power to teach; nor did He teach you because you are still unable to understand.

ADEODATUS: The fact is that as a result of your verbal instruction I have learned that words simply stimulate a man to learn. I also know that, although a good deal of a speaker's thought appears to be communicated through his words, very little of it is actually expressed. In addition, I have learned that it is God alone who teaches me whether truth is being spoken; He is the one who, when He spoke to us externally,* told us that He dwells within us. With His favor I shall now love Him more keenly as I advance further in learning. But I extend my thanks to you for your talk, which you delivered without interruption. It has anticipated and dissolved every argument I was prepared to advance against you. You did not leave out anything that perplexed me, and in everything the oracle hidden within me gave answers which corresponded with the statements made in your words.

(The end of the dialogue)

[15] The person who becomes preoccupied with, or reveres, a a mere sign, without knowing what it means, is the slave of a sign. On the other hand, if he concentrates on, or reveres, a

*i.e., in the Incarnation.

[15] *Christian Education,* iii, 13.

useful and divinely appointed sign, whose power and significance he understands, he is not honoring something which is seen and then passes away. Instead, he is honoring that to which all such signs ought to be referred.

[16]AUGUSTINE: Do you think that, in the words we employ, sound and meaning are two different things?

EVODIUS: I think there is no difference.

AUGUSTINE: Then tell me this: where does the sound come from when you speak?

EVODIUS: Without doubt from myself.

AUGUSTINE: When you name the sun, does the sun therefore come from your mouth?

EVODIUS: You were asking me about the sound and not the thing itself.

AUGUSTINE: Therefore, the sound is one thing and the meaning another. Nevertheless, you said there was no difference.

EVODIUS: Well then, I agree that a significant sound and the thing signified by it are different things.

AUGUSTINE: Then tell me whether, on the assumption that you know the Latin language, you could possibly give a name to the sun when you speak if you did not know the meaning of the word before you learned the sound.

[16] *The Greatness of the Soul,* 65-66.

EVODIUS: I could not.

AUGUSTINE: So, let us suppose that, at the moment when you intend to pronounce the name, you hold it back for a moment in silence before it comes out of your mouth. In such a situation, what someone else was on the point of hearing from your voice remains shut up in your thought, does it not?

EVODIUS: Of course it does.

AUGUSTINE: Well then, although the sun itself is so very big, surely the idea you have of it, which you are retaining in your thought before giving it utterance, cannot be thought of as long, broad or anything of the sort.

EVODIUS: Certainly not.

AUGUSTINE: Suppose then that the name comes from your mouth, and, on hearing it, I think of the sun. You were thinking of this before you spoke the word and also while you were in the act of speaking it; now we are both thinking of it. Don't you feel that the name itself may be said to have received from you the meaning which it brought to me through the medium of my ears?

EVODIUS: Yes.

AUGUSTINE: Therefore, because a name consists of sound and meaning, sound being connected with the ears and meaning with the mind, would you not agree that in a name, as in a living being, there is both a body and a soul? In the case of a name, the sound is the body and the meaning is, so to speak, the soul of the sound.

EVODIUS: The correspondence is very close.

AUGUSTINE: Then can the sound of a name be divided into letters, while its soul, i.e., its meaning, cannot be so divided? If this is so, you were referring to the meaning a short time ago when you mentioned something that was neither broad nor long.

EVODIUS: I entirely agree.

AUGUSTINE: Therefore, do you think the sound keeps its meaning when the sound is divided into separate letters?

EVODIUS: Separate letters cannot signify what the name, which is made up of the letters, signifies.

AUGUSTINE: Thus, when the meaning is lost and the sound broken up into letters, would you agree that there is a resemblance to the soul departing from a torn body. Could we say that the word has "died"?

EVODIUS: I am quick to agree.

External Words: Internal Logos

The passages from *The Teacher* deal with communication largely from the standpoint of the learner. The following selections deal with the earlier stages in verbal communication, as they take place in the teacher's mind. There are two stages involved: 1) An item of knowledge embedded in the memory gives rise to a thought, i.e., an inner "word" or "logos"; both the knowledge and the inner word are immaterial and general , i. e., they are not framed in the terminology of any particular language. 2) The inner "word" is externally expressed through physical signs; this physical expression of the inner, immaterial thought in a particular linguistic idiom is what is popularly known as a "word" (*verbum*); it would more appropriately be referred to as a "voice" (*vox*), i.e., a physical sound. This external sound merely symbolizes meaning or thought; the inner "word" is the thought itself.

The function of the external word, as explained in *The Teacher,* is to stimulate the recipient of the communication to search within his own mind for verification of what the teacher has said. He does this by deriving from his own inner inquiry a "word" (i.e., a thought), which becomes the criterion against which he tests the external words of the teacher.

[17]In that eternal truth, from which all temporal things have been made, we see with our mental vision the form according to which we exist and with reference to which we act with right reason within ourselves or in our dealings with material objects. The true knowledge of things, derived from this source, is stored up within us like a word (*verbum*), and in speaking we give birth to this word within us. But, although the word is born, it does not depart from us. For, when we speak to other people, we apply the service of our voice to the word, which nevertheless continues to exist within us; or we use some physical sign so that, by a sort of token displayed to the senses, a similar thing may also be brought into being in the mind of the listener; by this I mean a thing which

[17] *The Trinity,* ix, 12.

would be similar to the thing which does not depart from the speaker's mind. Therefore, neither by actions nor by words do we do anything through any of our physical parts to approve or blame the behavior of other people, unless we begin by uttering a word within ourselves. For nobody willingly does anything which he has not first spoken in his heart.

[18]When we speak what is true, i.e., what we really know, the knowledge we have in our memory gives birth to a word absolutely identical with the knowledge from which it originates. Indeed, the thought formed from what we know is the word we speak in our hearts, and this inner word is neither Greek nor Latin nor any other language. But, when it is necessary to carry this piece of knowledge over into the minds of people to whom we are speaking, we use a sign by which the knowledge may be represented. Usually a sound, or sometimes even a nod, is presented either to the ears or the eyes in order that, by means of physical signs, the word we carry within our minds may also become known to the physical senses. For what is the purpose of nodding if not to utter what we may call visible speech? . . . . These physical signs and others of the same kind are presented by us either to the ears or eyes of people around us, to whom we are speaking. In addition, letters have been invented through which we can talk to those who are absent from us. These letters are signs of words, while the words themselves are spoken signs of the things we are thinking about.

Thus, the word which sounds externally is the sign of a word which shines within us, and this inner word better deserves the title of "word." What is uttered with the mouth is merely the sound of a word; it is called a "word" by analogy with the inner word, which has made use of the sound so that it [i.e., the inner word] can be expressed ex-

[18] *The Trinity*, xv, 19–20.

ternally. Thus, our inner word is somehow or other translated into a physical sound by employing that particular sound by which the inner word may be exhibited to the human senses. This is exactly how the Word of God was made flesh—by taking upon itself that flesh in which it might be made manifest to the senses of men. Just as our inner word becomes a sound but is not changed into a sound, so the Word of God became flesh, although it would be wrong to say He was changed into flesh. Our inner word becomes a sound, not by destroying itself in order to be changed into flesh, but rather by putting on a physical form, in the same way as that other Word became flesh. . . . The words of all spoken languages can be thought of even in silence, and the mind can run over songs while the physical mouth is silent. Not only the rhythms of syllables, but also the tunes of songs are present to those who think of them and turn them over silently in their minds. Nevertheless, rhythms and tunes are physical things connected with the physical sense called "hearing."

CHAPTER SIX

The Christian Teacher and His Task

The selections in this chapter deal with the task of the Christian teacher in the secular society. To carry out his responsible duty of instructing those who come to him in search of knowledge of the Christian faith, he must be filled with the love of God and his fellow man. Inasmuch as he loves God, he is in love with truth and is therefore a good man. Understanding is an absolutely good thing; thus, if an evil man attempts to teach, the only possible result is the miseducation of his pupils, for an evil man must necessarily lead them away from truth to a distorted and untenable view of reality.

The practical task of the Christian teacher is the interpretation of the words of the Scriptures, which must form the central core of the Christian curriculum. In *Christian Education (De Doctrina Christiana)* Augustine lays down the principles governing the interpretation of signs, and so reinforces his important distinction between words and symbols. The former are merely the means to the understanding of realities which have no natural connection with their signs. Ends and means must also be distinguished with regard to the various objects of knowledge, of which there are two kinds: things to be utilized for some end beyond themselves, and things to be enjoyed for their own sake. Of the latter the supreme object of knowledge is God, and it is the overriding duty of the Christian teacher to lead his pupils progressively toward a true assessment of means and ends and so to an understanding of the divine nature.

In the elucidation of scriptural meaning the teacher must draw on useful information and significant insights, wherever they are to be found. Thus, Augustine advocates a broad curriculum in which the traditional liberal arts and the best of classical learning would play a prominent part. For example, rhetoric and dialectic can be used to promote either truth or falsehood; therefore, in the hands of the Christian teacher they are indispensable weapons against the skillful arguments of the educated agnostic. Without their aid the Christian teacher must be at a severe disadvantage in the perpetual warfare against the enemies of the truth which he serves.

The Training and Character of the Christian Teacher

[1]EVODIUS: I do not know whether anyone sins without first having learned to sin. If sin is taught, then I want to know who has taught us to do evil.

AUGUSTINE: Is it your view that education is a good thing?

EVODIUS: Surely nobody would be so bold as to say that it is bad.

AUGUSTINE: Could it be neither good nor bad?

EVODIUS: I see it as a good thing.

AUGUSTINE: You are right indeed, if by education knowl-

[1] *Free Will,* i, 2–3.

edge is given and stirred up within us, and if no one learns anything except through education. Or do you think otherwise?

EVODIUS: I think that only what is good is learned through education.

AUGUSTINE: But evil may also be learned, for education *(disciplina)* is derived from the verb "to learn" *(discere)*.

EVODIUS: How could crimes be committed by a man if they were not learned?

AUGUSTINE: Perhaps he turns himself away and separates himself from education, that is, from learning. But whether this is the explanation or not, surely it is clear that, since education is a good thing, and since education means learning, evil simply cannot be learned. If evil is learned, it comes within the scope of education, and so education would not necessarily be a good thing. But you declare that it is a good thing; therefore, evil is not learned, and you would search in vain for someone who can teach us to do wrong. If evil is learned, then we are learning what we ought to avoid rather than what we ought to do. We conclude that evil-doing is merely turning aside from education.

EVODIUS: I am convinced that there are two sorts of education, one through which we learn to do good and another through which we learn to do evil. When you asked whether education was a good thing, my love of the good quickly led me to think of the education which is concerned with doing good. That is why I answered that education is a good thing. But now I am persuaded that there is another sort of education, which, as I see it, is evil beyond any doubt. I am asking who gives this sort of education.

AUGUSTINE: At any rate do you think that understanding is anything other than a good thing?

EVODIUS: Certainly, I think understanding is such a good thing that I do not see what can be more excellent in a man. I could not admit that understanding can possibly be evil.

AUGUSTINE: Therefore, if all understanding is good, and if no one can learn without understanding, everyone who learns is doing a good thing. For everyone who learns understands, and everyone who understands is doing good. Thus, whenever anyone of us seeks out a counselor, through whom we learn something, we are actually seeking a counselor through whom we are doing something good. So give up your desire to find an evil teacher. If a man is evil, he is not a teacher; if he is a teacher, he is not evil.

[2]No matter how impressive the style of a speaker, his life has the greater influence in ensuring that his audience is receptive to his words. For the man who speaks wisely and eloquently but who leads a wicked life, may indeed teach many who are eager to learn, although as it is written, "He is unprofitable to his own soul" *(Eccl.* 37:21).

Therefore, such men do benefit many people by declaring what they do not themselves perform, but they would benefit

[2] *Christian Education,* iv, 59–62.

many more by practicing what they preach. For there is no shortage of those who base a defense of their own wicked lives on the behavior of those who are set over them and who are their teachers. Such people say in their hearts, or even go further and say with their lips, "Why do you not yourself practice what you teach?" Consequently they are not receptive to the teacher's words, because he does not listen to them himself, and, as they despise the teacher, they also despise what is taught, that is, the word of God. This was why the Apostle, writing to Timothy, said, "Let no man despise thy youth," and then added the following advice on the way to avoid contempt: "But be thou an example in word, in conversation, in charity, in spirit, in purity" (*I Tim.* 4:12).

Because his life is beyond reproach, such a teacher makes his audience receptive to his words by speaking without shame, whether he is speaking in the subdued, the moderate, or the grand style. For he lives the good life in such a way that he is also always careful of his reputation, "providing for things honest not only in the sight of the Lord but also in the sight of men" (*II Cor.* 8:21). He does this to the best of his ability, fearing God and attending to the interests of men. Such a teacher would also prefer to please by the content of what he says rather than by his style. He would regard a thing as well spoken if it were spoken with truth. As a teacher he would be the master and not the slave of his words. . . .

To concentrate on words is to neglect the means whereby falsehood may be overcome by truth and to be concerned only that your own style of speech should be preferred to that of someone else. Furthermore, the man who does not concentrate his attention on words, uses words with the sole intention of clarifying truth and making it pleasing and stimulating. This is his aim, whether he is speaking in the subdued, the moderate, or the grand style. For not even love itself, which is "the end of the commandment" and "the fulfilling of the law" (*I Tim.* 1:5; *Rom.* 13:10), can function properly unless what is loved is true and not false. A man with a comely body but a deformed mind is more pitiful than he would be if his body were also deformed. Thus, men who give eloquent expression to falsehood are more to be pitied than those who give it deformed expression. Therefore, to speak eloquently and also wisely is merely to bring words to bear on truths which ought to be listened to. In the subdued style these words are sufficient for the purpose; in the moderate style they are brightly polished; in the grand style they are marked by fervor. But the man who cannot speak both eloquently and wisely should speak wisely rather than eloquently instead of eloquently but foolishly.

However, if a man cannot even do this, let his life be such that he not only obtains a reward for himself but gives an example to others. Let his manner of living be in itself, so to speak, an eloquent flow of words.

Certainly there are some men who can speak well but who cannot think out what they are to say. If they take something which has been wisely and eloquently written by other people, commit it to memory and speak it out publicly, they are not acting dishonestly, that is, if they do not conceal the part they are playing. For this is the way many people become preachers of truth, and it is a good thing that it should be so. Yet not many really become teachers when all are delivering what one real teacher has composed and when there are no divisions among them. However, such people are not to be deterred by the words of Jeremiah, the prophet, through whom God censures those who "steal His words, every one from his neighbor" (*Jer.* 23:30). For people who steal are taking what belongs to someone else, but the word of God is the property of all who obey it. It is the man who speaks well but lives badly who really speaks the words which are another's property. The reason is that the good things he speaks seem to be the product of his own thinking, whereas in fact they contradict his manner of life. So God has said that those who are evil but wish to appear good by speaking God's words are stealing His words. This is because what they do is their own (i.e., not God's). If you consider the question carefully, you see that such people are not actually saying the good things they say. For how can they say in words what they deny by their deeds? It is with good reason that the Apostle says of such men, "They profess that they know God, but in works they deny him" (*Titus* 1:16). Therefore, in a sense such people do say these things, while in another sense they do not. Both these proposition have their source in Him who is the Truth and are therefore true. Thus when Christ speaks about such people, He says: "Whatsoever they bid you observe, that observe and do; but do not ye after their works" (*Matt.* 23:3). This means that you must do what you hear from their mouths but refrain from doing what you see in their lives, "for they say and do not." So such people go on speaking, although they do not practice what they say. But in another place, Christ is censuring such men and says, "O hypocrites, how can ye, being evil, speak good things?" (*Matt.* 12:34). This is to say that when such people appear to be saying what is good, it is not they themselves who say it, for in will and in deed they are denying what they say. So it happens that an eloquent but wicked man may compose a speech in which truth is to be set forth and which is to be spoken by a good man who is not eloquent. When this happens, the composer draws from himself what really belongs to somebody else, while the speaker receives from somebody else what really belongs to himself. Thus, when people who are good believers perform this service for other believers, both parties speak what is their own; for God is theirs, and it is to Him that everything they say belongs. Even those who could not compose what they say make it their own by living lives in agreement with it.

Approach to the Interpretation of the Scriptures

[3]All teaching is either about things or signs, but things are learned by signs. I understand the term "things" in the proper sense, that is, with reference to what is never used as a sign

[3] *Christian Education,* i, 2–5.

of something else, for example, wood, stone, cattle and so on. However, we should not include the wood which we read that Moses threw into the bitter waters to take away their bitterness, or the stone which Jacob used as a pillow for his head, or the animal which Abraham sacrificed in place of his son; for, although these are things, they are also signs of other things. But there are some signs which are used for signifying and for no other purpose, for example, words. No one uses words except as signs of something else; by "signs" I mean things which are used to point to something else. Accordingly, every sign is also a thing, for what is not a thing is nothing at all; but every thing is not also a sign. And so when we talk of things we shall talk in such a way that even if some of them can also be used as signs of other things, it will not interfere with the division of our subject, whereby we shall first discuss things and after that signs. But let us keep in mind that what we have now to consider about things is what they are in themselves, and not the other things beyond themselves of which they are signs.

So there are some things which are to be enjoyed, others which are to be used and others which we enjoy and use. The things which are to be enjoyed make us happy; those which are to be used help and, as it were, support us as we reach out toward happiness, so that we can come to the things which make us happy and cling to them. But we, who enjoy and use all these things, are placed between the first two classes of things. Hence, if we conceive the desire to enjoy the things which ought merely to be used, we are checked in our course, and sometimes even deflected from it. Since we are obstructed by the love of lower things, the result is that we are retarded or even called back from the pursuit of the things which ought to be enjoyed.

To enjoy a thing is to cleave to it for what it is in itself. On the other hand, to use is to employ whatever means are available in the pursuit of what you love, provided only that it is something which ought to be loved. For an unlawful use of a thing should rather be called an "abuse" or "misuse." Suppose, then, that we were strangers in a foreign land and could not live happily away from our homeland. Because we were miserable in our exile and wished to put an end to our wretchedness, we would want to return home, but we would find that we had to use some means of transportation to carry us over land and water to our native country, which is the proper object of our enjoyment. But the attractions of the journey and the very movement of the conveyances give us such delight that we convert the things which ought merely to be used as a means to some other end into objects of enjoyment, and are unwilling to put a speedy end to our journey. And because we are involved in a perverse enjoyment, we are diverted from our country, whose sweetness would make us really happy. So in this mortal life we wander far from God. If we want to return to our homeland, where we can be happy, this world is merely to be used and not enjoyed so that the invisible things of God may be seen and understood through the things which have been created, so that starting from what is material and temporal we may seize upon what is eternal and spiritual.

Therefore, the proper objects of enjoyment are the Father, Son and Holy Spirit, who are one being and supreme, the common possession of all who enjoy Him. . . .

[4]When I was writing about "things,"* I prefaced my remarks with a warning not to consider anything about them, other than what they are in themselves, even when they are signs of something else beyond themselves. So now that I am about to talk about signs, I advise you not to attend to what they are in themselves, but to their being signs, that is, to what they signify. For a sign, quite apart from the actual

[4] *Christian Education,* ii, 1-6.

* "Things" (*res*) or "the things themselves" (*res ipsae*) are contrasted with "signs" (*signa*) or "the signs of things" (*signa rerum*).

impression which it makes on the senses, is a thing which causes something else with which it is associated to come into the mind. Thus, when we see a footprint, we decide that an animal has passed that way. When we see smoke, we know there is a fire underneath. On hearing the voice of a living being, we think of the feeling in his mind. When a trumpet sounds, soldiers know they must advance or retreat, or do whatever else the military situation requires.

Now some signs are natural, others conventional. The former are those which, without any deliberate intention or desire that they should be used as signs, cause something else associated with them to be known, as, for example, smoke indicating fire: the smoke has no express purpose of signifying anything. By attending to and noting the content of our experience we come to know that there is a fire even if we see only smoke. The footprint of a passing animal also belongs to this class of signs, and in the same way the expression of a person who is angry or sad points to the way he feels even if he does not intend to reveal it. Similarly, every other emotion is betrayed by the revealing expression of the face, even when we do not intend to make the emotion known. However, this whole class of signs is one which I propose not to discuss at the moment, but, since it falls into this division of our subject, it could not be completely passed over. At this point it will be enough to have mentioned it.

On the other hand, conventional signs are those which living beings interchange with one another for making as plain as possible the movements of their minds, their perceptions or their thoughts, whatever they may be. There is only one reason for giving a sign: we wish to bring out and convey to someone else what is in our mind. It is this class of signs, with all its implications for men, that we have decided to discuss, because even the signs which God has given us and which are contained in the Holy Scriptures, were made known to us through men, that is, through the writers of the Scriptures. Animals also use certain signs by which they make known what they desire. For example, when a rooster has found some food, he makes a vocal signal to the hen that she should come running to him. The dove summons his mate by cooing, and she in turn calls him in the same way. Many such signs are matters of common observation. But whether these signs, like the facial expression or the cry of a person in grief, follow the movement of the mind, without there being any deliberate intention of giving signs, or whether they are really used with the purpose of signifying something is another question, irrelevant to the present matter. Therefore, we exclude this from our discussion as unnecessary.

Thus, some of the signs by which men communicate their perceptions to one another are visually perceived while a good many of them are heard and a very few are perceived by other senses. When we nod, we are simply giving a sign to the eyes of the person to whom we wish to communicate our will by a sign. Some people communicate a good deal by the motion of their hands. By moving all their limbs actors give signs to those who understand them; they speak to the eyes, as it were. Military standards and flags visually convey the will of generals. All these signs are, so to speak, visible words. But signs, which are addressed to the ears, are, as I have said, more numerous and mainly consist of words. For, although the trumpet, the flute and the lyre very often produce a sound which is both sweet and significant, there are very few of these signs when we compare their number with that of words. Words are by far the chief means of indicating our thoughts when we want to reveal them. Certainly our Lord gave a sign through the scent of the ointment with which His feet were anointed, and by the sacrament of His body and blood He signified his will through the sense of taste. The woman who was made whole by touching the hem of His garment performed an act which had its own significance. Nevertheless, the vast majority of signs by which men express their thoughts consist of words. In fact, I have been able to express in words the meaning of all those various classes of signs which I have briefly touched upon. But it would be utterly impossible to express the meaning of words by means of those same signs.

Words pass away as soon as they strike the air and last no longer than their sound. Therefore, men have used letters to make words into signs so that the sounds of the voice can be displayed to the eyes, not, of course, as sounds but as certain signs which represent them. It is impossible to make those signs common to all nations because of the sin of human discord which arises when every man tries to seize the chief place for himself. The well-known tower built to reach up to heaven was an indication of this pride of spirit.* The ungodly men involved deserved to have their minds and tongues thrown into a state of discord.

Even the Holy Scriptures, which help man to overcome such serious diseases of the human will, were first set out in one language by which they could be disseminated throughout the whole world when the time was ripe. But then they were translated into various languages and spread far and wide, thus becoming known to the nations for their salvation. Man's purpose in reading the Scriptures is merely to find out the thoughts and intentions of those who wrote them and thereby to discover the will of God, in accordance with which we believe those writers to have spoken.

[5]There are two reasons which prevent what has been written from being understood: the meaning may be obscured by unknown or by ambiguous signs. Signs are either literal or figurative. They are called literal when they are used to indicate exactly those objects which they were designed to indicate: we say *bos* (ox), when we mean a certain kind of

* The reference is to the building of the tower of Babel (*Gen.* 2:1-9).

[5] *Christian Education,* ii, 15–17.

beast, because everyone who shares the Latin language calls it by this name. Signs are figurative when the actual things which we indicate by using their literal names are used to signify something else. For example, we say *bos* and understand by that syllable the animal usually called by that name; but we can go further and understand by the word a preacher of the gospel as we find it used in the Scriptures, where according to the Apostle's interpretation we read, "Thou shalt not muzzle the mouth of the ox that treadeth out the corn" (*I Cor.* 9:9).

A knowledge of languages is the great remedy against ignorance of literal signs. People who speak Latin—the people whom we have undertaken to instruct—require two other languages for an understanding of the Holy Scriptures, Hebrew and Greek, which enable them to turn to the original texts, if the endless diversity of Latin translators confuses them. Yet we often find Hebrew words in the Scriptures, as, for example, *Amen, Halleluia, Racha, Hosanna* and others of the same kind. Although some of these could have been translated, for instance, Amen and Halleluia, they have been kept in their original form because they carry the more sacred authority. But it is said that others cannot be translated, for example, *Racha* and *Hosanna;* for in certain languages there are words which cannot be expressed in the idiom of another language. This is particularly true of interjections, which are words expressing an emotion rather than any part of a thought we have conceived. The two just mentioned are said to be of this kind: "*Racha*" is the exclamation of an angry man and "*Hosanna*" of a man rejoicing. But it is not merely because of a few words like these, which it is very easy to note and ask about, that a knowledge of languages is necessary. It is also because of the differences among translators, as has already been said. Those who have translated the Scriptures from Hebrew into Greek can be counted, but the Latin translators are innumerable. The reason is that in the early days of the faith every man who happened to get his hands on a Greek manuscript and thought he had even the smallest ability in the two languages had the courage to translate it. This would have helped rather than hindered the understanding of the Scriptures if only those who read had not been careless, for the examination of a number of texts often clarifies some rather obscure expressions.

[6]When many translators are striving to express a thought, each according to his own skill and judgment, it is not clear what the actual thought is, unless it is studied in the original language. And if the translator is not a very learned man, he often goes astray from the meaning of the author. Therefore, we must either seek a knowledge of those languages from which the Scriptures have come into Latin, or we must use the translations which are closest to the original words. These translations are not sufficient, but starting from them we may expose the truth or mistakes of others who in their translations have preferred to follow the sense as much as the actual words. For not only single words but whole phrases, which could not be translated at all into Latin by anyone who wanted to observe the classical usage of the language, are often translated. Although such words and phrases do not always hinder our understanding of the passage, they offend those who more fully appreciate things whose signs also maintain their own purity. For what is called a "solecism" is simply combining words differently from the way those of our predecessors who spoke with some authority combined them. For example, whether we say *inter hominibus* (among men) or *inter homines* is of no importance to a man who is merely concerned with understanding the facts. Similarly, a barbarism is merely pronouncing a word in a different way from the usual pronunciation of former times. Whether the word *ignoscere* (to pardon) should be pronounced with the third syllable long or short is not of much

[6] *Christian Education,* ii, 19–20.

concern to a person who is begging God to "pardon" his sins. Purity of speech consists simply in the linguistic usage established by the authority of those who spoke the language in the past.

The weaker a person is, the more likely he is to be offended by lapses from linguistic purity; and people are weaker in proportion to their desire to appear well schooled, not so much in a knowledge of those realities by which we are truly instructed as in a knowledge of signs. It is very hard for a person whose knowledge is limited to signs not to be puffed up with pride.

[7]We must now deal with the ambiguities of metaphorical words, and these require no ordinary care and watchfulness. In the first place, you must be careful not to take a metaphorical expression literally. Something which the Apostle Paul says is of relevance here too: "The letter killeth, but the spirit giveth life" (*II Cor.* 3:6). When a statement, meant to be taken in a metaphorical sense, is taken literally it is understood in a physical sense. Nothing is more appropriately called the death of the soul than when that part of the soul which raises us above the animals is put in subjection to the flesh by following the letter. The man who follows the letter takes metaphorical words as if they were literal and does not refer the term to another meaning. For example, if he hears of the "Sabbath," he understands nothing but that one day of the seven which recurs in constant succession. And when he hears the term "sacrifice," his thoughts do not pass beyond the customery offerings of animals and fruits of the earth. It is surely a wretched slavery of the soul to take signs for realities and to be unable to lift the eye of the mind above physical creation to drink in eternal light.

[7] *Christian Education,* iii, 9.

However, in the case of the Jewish people this slavery was very different from what it was in the other nations. For the Jews were in subjection to temporal things in such a way that through all of these things the one God was kept before their minds. They concentrated on the signs of spiritual things in place of the things themselves, and did not know to what they should relate the signs. However, in the minds of the Jews the idea was implanted that it was through this slavery that they pleased the one God of all men, that is, the God whom they could not see. The Apostle writes that this confinement was like boys under a schoolmaster.* It was for this reason that those who persisted in clinging to such signs could not tolerate our Lord's contempt of them, when the time of their revelation had come. Hence, their leaders brought it as a charge against Him that he cured people on the Sabbath. The people, clinging to these signs as if they were realities, would not believe that one who refused to observe them in the same way as the Jews did was God, or that He had come from God. But those who did believe, that is, the people who made up the first church at Jerusalem, showed clearly what a great advantage it was to be so supervised by a schoolmaster that signs, which for a period of time were imposed on those who served, concentrated the thoughts of those who observed them on the worship of the one God who has made Heaven and earth.

The Christian Curriculum: Principles of Content Selection

[8]We (Christians) should not abandon music because of the superstition of the pagans if there is anything we can take

* *Gal.* 3:24-25: "Wherefore the law was our schoolmaster to bring us unto Christ, that we might be justified by faith. But after that faith is come, we are no longer under a schoolmaster."

[8] *Christian Education,* ii, 28–32.

from it that might help us understand the Holy Scriptures. However, because we engage in a discussion about harps and other instruments in the course of our efforts to understand spiritual things, it does not follow that we must involve ourselves in all their theatrical nonsense. Nor is there any reason we should refuse to study literature because it is said that Mercury discovered it. That the pagans have dedicated temples to Justice and Virtue and prefer to worship in the form of stones things which ought to be carried in the heart is no reason we should abandon justice and virtue. On the contrary, let everyone who is a good and true Christian understand that truth belongs to his Master, wherever it is found. And while he recognizes and acknowledges truth, even in the pagans' religious literature, let him reject their superstitious imaginings at the same time. Let him grieve over and look out for men who, "When they knew God, glorified Him not as God, neither were thankful; but became vain in their imaginations, and their foolish heart was darkened. Professing themselves to be wise they became fools and changed the glory of the uncorruptible God into an image made like to corruptible man and to birds and four-footed beasts and creeping things." (*Romans* 1:21-23)

This is a matter which must be discussed, and I shall explain it more carefully. There are two sorts of teachings which are common in the practices of the nations: the first concerns a knowledge of the things which have been instituted by men; the second deals with what men have noted either as having been transacted in the past or brought into being by God. The first deals with human institutions and is partly superstitious and partly not.

All human institutions relating to the manufacture and worship of idols and the worship of created things, or of some part of them, as if they were God should be included among superstitions. We should also include all consultations with oracles and arrangements of signs and leagues with devils, such as the great efforts put into the arts of magic, which poets are usually concerned to recall to mind rather than to teach. The books of the soothsayers and augurs, which are characterized by an even more outrageous deception belong to this class. We should also include all amulets and remedies, condemned by medicine, whether they consist of incantations, certain marks called "characters," hanging or binding certain objects on oneself or even of a kind of dancing. These do not refer to the condition of the body, but to certain meanings, which may be either secret or openly displayed. Rather than calling these remedies "superstitious," people controversially call them "physics," so that they may seem to be taking advantage of the powers of nature rather than engaging in superstition. Examples of these are the earrings on the top of each ear, the rings of ostrich bone on the fingers or the advice to hold your left thumb in your right hand when you hiccup.

We can add to all this the thousands of useless formalities to be observed if a part of the body should twitch, or if a stone, a dog or a boy should come between friends walking arm-in-arm. The habit of kicking a stone as if it were a divider of friends does less harm than giving an innocent boy a blow with the fists, if he happens to run between people who are walking together . . . We may also include the following practices: treading on the threshold when you pass in front of your house; going back to bed if anyone sneezes when you are putting on your shoes; getting back home if you stumble when you are going off somewhere; being more worried at the prospect of some future misfortune than grieved by your present loss when your clothes are eaten by mice. This was the reason for the witty saying of Cato, who gave the following reply to a man who came for advice when his boots had been eaten by mice: "This is no evil omen. It would really have been worth worrying about if the mice had been eaten by the boots."

We ought not to exclude from this kind of destructive superstition those who were called "*genethliaci*" because of the attention they gave to birthdays, but who are now commonly called "mathematici."* These too may follow the actual position of the stars at the time of a person's birth and may sometimes succeed in discovering it; nevertheless, they make a serious mistake when they try to predict from this our actions or the outcomes of our actions. In so doing, they are selling ignorant men into a wretched slavery.

[9]All arts of this sort are parts of a useless and harmful superstition arising from a disastrous association of men and devils. Such arts are to be utterly repudiated and shunned by the Christian as arrangements set up on the basis of a false and treacherous friendship. . . .

[10]When all these superstitions have been cut away and rooted out of the Christian's mind, we must scrutinize those human institutions which are not superstitious. These are the institutions which are set up by men in association with one another and not with devils. All of those arrangements which are in force among men because men have decided that they should be in force, are human institutions. Some of these are superfluous and extravagant, while others are convenient and necessary. If the signs which actors make when they are dancing were meaningful by nature rather than by the arrangement and agreement of men, then in earlier times the public herald would not have announced to the people of Carthage what a dancer was intending to express while he was dancing. This is a custom which old men still remember and which I have often heard from them. We ought to believe

* *Genethliaci,* means literally "people concerned with birthdays." *Mathematici* –"mathematicians" and later, quite commonly, "astrologers."

[9] *Christian Education,* ii, 36.

[10] *Christian Education,* ii, 38–42.

it, because even now, when someone who is inexperienced in such follies goes into a theatre, he will give close attention to the performance and yet fail to understand its meaning unless someone tells him what it means. Nevertheless, all men aim at a certain degree of similarity in their choice of signs, so that, as far as possible, the signs may be like the things they signify. But, because there are many different respects in which one thing may look like another, signs do not have the same meaning to everyone, except when there has been mutual agreement about them.

But in the case of pictures and statues and other such works, which are intended to form likenesses of things, nobody fails to identify what is portrayed as soon as he sees the likenesses, especially if the works are produced by skilled artists. All things of this kind are to be included among the superfluous devices of men, except when it becomes a matter of concern to know why one of them was made or where, when and by whose authority it came into being. Finally, the thousands of tales and fictions whose falsehoods give pleasure to men are human devices. And none of the things which men derive from themselves are to be considered more uniquely their own than the things which are false and deceptive. Among the convenient and necessary arrangements established among men are to be reckoned all the distinctions they have elaborated regarding dress and ornament for the body for the purpose of distinguishing sex or position. There are also the countless varieties of signs without which human association either could not be maintained at all or would be carried on with more difficulty. Then there are all the arrangements about weights and measures, the stamping and weighing of coins which are peculiar to each state and nation, and all other things of the same kind. Now, if these were not devices established by men, they would not vary between peoples at the will of their leaders.

However, the Christian should certainly not reject this whole class of human arrangements which help along the necessary intercourse of life. On the contrary, he should pay sufficient attention to them and keep them in his memory, for some human institutions are in a sense representations and likenesses of natural institutions. As I have said, those human institutions which involve an association with devils must be completely rejected and looked upon with abhorrence. On the other hand, those which bind men together are to be adopted to the extent that they are not associated with luxury and excess. Among these we should especially include the letters of the alphabet, without which we cannot read, and a sufficient number of the various languages, all of which I have discussed above. To this class also belong short-hand characters *(notae),* the people who have learned them being now properly known as "short-hand writers" *(notarii).* All these are useful, and there is nothing unlawful in learning them. They do not involve us in superstition or enervate us by luxury, that is, if they do not occupy us to the exclusion of the more important objectives to the attainment of which they should be instrumental.

However, those aspects of our heritage which were not originated by man but which have emerged from research into the events of history and the arrangements established by God, should not be regarded as human institutions, wherever they may be learned. Some of these are open to the physical senses, others to the rational intelligence. Of the former, some are believed because we are told about them, others are noticed because someone points them out to us, while others are inferred from experience.

Thus, whatever we gather about the course of past events from what is called history gives us considerable help in understanding the Scriptures, even if we learn it outside the Church by instruction in childhood. For we often seek information about a number of different matters by the use of Olympiads and by the names of the consuls. Ignorance of the consulship in which our Lord was born and of that in which He suffered, has led some people into the mistake of thinking that He was forty-six years of age when He suffered. According to the Jews, this was the number of years occupied in building the "temple," which was taken to symbolize our Lord's body.* Now we know on the authority of the Gospel that He was about thirty years of age when He was baptized. As to the length of His life thereafter, we can discover this by piecing together His activities from the text. However, so that no shadow of doubt may arise from some other source, we can establish the facts with greater clarity and certainty by comparing pagan history with the Gospel.

[11]History itself is not to be reckoned among human institutions, although it describes the former institutions of men. This is because what is past and cannot be undone is to be considered as belonging to the course of time, of which God is the author and governor. Telling the story of past events and showing what ought to be done are quite different activities. History performs a faithful and useful function in giving a narrative of past events. But the books of soothsayers and all similar writings aim at teaching what ought to be done, and they do this with the boldness of one who gives advice rather than with the fidelity of a narrator.

There is also a kind of narrative resembling description, in which existing conditions rather than past conditions are pointed out to people who do not know them. In this class we should include all that has been written about the location of places, the nature of animals, trees, herbs, stones and other bodies. I have discussed all this class of things above and have shown that knowledge of this kind has its value in solving the difficult problems found in the Scriptures. These

* *John* 2: 19-21: "Jesus answered and said unto them, 'Destroy this temple and in three days I will raise it up.' Then said the Jews, 'Forty and six years was this temple in the building and wilt thou rear it up in three days?' But He spake of the temple of His body."

[11] Christian Education, ii, 44–45.

objects are not to be used as signs, for example, as remedies or as the instruments of some superstition; for we have already distinguished between that kind of knowledge and the other lawful and free kind. It is one thing to say, "If you shred down this herb and drink it, you will have relief from stomach pain," and another thing to say, "If you hang this herb round your neck, you will have relief." In the former case we approve the wholesome mixture, while in the latter we condemn the superstitious significance. Yet, in cases where incantations and invocations are not employed, it is often doubtful whether an object, which is tied to the body or joined to it in some way or other for the purpose of curing it, succeeds by virtue of some natural property or depends on a symbolic meaning. In the former case the object may be freely used, whereas in the latter case the Christian must exercise greater care in avoiding it in proportion to its apparent efficacy. When the reason for the potency of an object is not clear, what matters is the intention with which it is used, at least in regard to the healing or regulating of bodies, whether in medicine or in agriculture.

[12]Of the other arts some are concerned with the making of something, that is, when a thing is created by a workman and remains after his work is done. Other arts render a kind of assistance to the operations of God, for example, medicine, agriculture and navigation. There are also arts which issue in an action such as dancing, racing and wrestling. In all these arts experience enables us to infer the future from the past. For nobody who is skilled in any of these arts carries out the physical movements necessary for his work without connecting the memory of the past with the expectations of the future. But we need only a superficial and cursory knowledge

[12] *Christian Education,* ii, 47–50.

of these arts. The purpose of this knowledge is not that we should practice the arts, that is, unless we have an obligation to do so, a matter I shall not discuss at the moment; rather it is to enable us to make judgments about the arts. so that we may not be entirely ignorant of what the Scriptures mean to suggest when they employ metaphorical language derived from the arts.

We are left with subjects related to the soul's intellectual part and not to the senses of the body. Of these the chief disciplines are those of reasoning and number. The former is of great help in inquiring into and unravelling all the various questions found in the Holy Scriptures, but in using it we must guard against the love of wrangling and the childish vanity of deceiving an opponent. For there are many examples of what are known as "sophisms," that is, false inferences in reasoning which so closely resemble the truth that they deceive not only dull people but also clever people when they are taken off their guard. For example, a person makes the following statement to someone: "What I am, you are not." The other agrees, either because the proposition is partly true or because he is simple while the first person is cunning. Then the first person adds: "I am a man." The other also accepts this, whereupon the first draws the conclusion: "Then you are not a man." Now, as I see it, Scripture expresses its detestation of this sort of wrong conclusion when it is said: "There is one that sheweth wisdom in words and is hated" (*Ecclesiastes* 37:23). Nevertheless, talk which aims at verbal ornamentation to a degree inconsistent with a proper seriousness, but which has no intention of deceiving, is also called sophistical.

There are also true processes of reasoning which lead to wrong conclusions because we logically follow up a mistake of the person with whom we are having a discussion. These conclusions are sometimes drawn by a good and learned man, his aim being to produce a sense of shame in the person whose mistake led to the conclusion, and so to lead him to renounce his error. If the person wishes to hold to his old opinion, he is forced to adopt other views which he condemns. For example, when the Apostle said, "Then is Christ not risen," and again "Then is our preaching vain,"* he was not drawing true conclusions. And later he drew other conclusions which are completely wrong. The fact is that Christ has risen, and neither the preaching of those who declared this nor the faith of those who believed it was vain. But all these false conclusions were properly derived from the opinions of those who declared that "there is no resurrection of the dead." When the false conclusions are rejected, it follows that there is a resurrection of the dead because, if the dead do not rise, the conclusions would be true. Hence, because valid reasoning processes are equally applicable to true and false propositions, the principles of reasoning can easily be learned in schools outside the Church. But the truth of proposition must be looked for in the Church's sacred books.

Now the truth of logical connections is not something which has been arranged by men; it has merely been observed and noted by them, so that they can learn or teach it. Logical truth exists eternally in the rational order of things and has been arranged by God. The man who describes the events of history does not create those events. The person who describes the situations of places, the nature of animals, roots or rocks, is not describing things instituted by men. When a man points out the stars and their movements, he is not pointing to anything which he himself or any other man has set up. In the same way, a man is speaking the truth when he says, "When the conclusion is false, the antecedent must necessarily be false." Nevertheless, he did not make this truth; he is merely pointing out that it is so. The statements I have just quoted from the Apostle depend on this rule. In this case the antecedent is that there is no resurrection of the dead, which was the statement made by those whose error

* I *Corinthians,* 15:13-14: "But if there be no resurrection of the dead, then is Christ not risen. And if Christ be not risen, then is our preaching vain and your faith is also vain."

the Apostle wanted to overthrow. Following from the statement that there is no resurrection of the dead, the necessary conclusion is, "Then Christ is not risen." But this conclusion is false because Christ has risen, and thus the antecedent is also false, namely, that there is no resurrection of the dead. Therefore, we conclude that there is a resurrection of the dead. All this may be briefly summed up as follows: If there is no resurrection of the dead, then Christ is not risen; but Christ has risen; therefore, there is a resurrection of the dead. Thus, the rule which states that, when a conclusion is demolished, the antecedent must also necessarily be demolished, is not of human origin but merely something which men have pointed out. The rule is concerned with the validity of logical connections and not with the truth of propositions.

[13]There are also certain principles which relate to a richer kind of discussion which is now called "eloquence." The truth of these principles is not affected by the fact that they can be employed for the purpose of teaching falsehood. Because they can also be used in the service of truth, we should not blame the practice of eloquence but the perversity of those who put it to a bad use. The fact that an expression of affection wins over an audience does not come about because men have arranged it that way. It is the same with the principle that a narrative effectively conveys its message when it is short and clear and that variety holds the attention of people without boring them. There are other similar rules which are true whether the causes they are used to support are true or false. The rules are true in so far as they bring about knowledge or belief, or succeed in influencing men's minds to seek out or reject one thing or another. Those rules were found to be so; they were not made that way by men.

[13] *Christian Education,* ii, 54.

[14]Turning now to the discipline of number, even the dullest person can see clearly that this was not instituted by men but rather tracked down and discovered by them. Vergil could make the first syllable of "Italia" long if he pleased, in spite of the fact that in former times people pronounced it short.* Nevertheless, it is not in the power of any man to decide that three threes are not nine. . . . Therefore, whether numbers are considered in themselves or as applied to the principles of shapes, sounds or other motions, they have unchangeable laws which were not devised by men but discovered by the keen intelligence of able men.

However, some men are so entranced by all this knowledge that they want to show off among uneducated people rather than inquire into the grounds for the truth of things which they have perceived to be true. Such people fail to ask themselves why some things, which they have seen to be unchangeable, are not only true but also unchangeable. If they did this, they would pass from physical phenomena to the mind and would find that it also is changeable in that it is sometimes knowledgeable and sometimes ignorant, although the mind occupies a middle place between the unchangeable truth above it and the changeable things beneath it. Thus, they would turn all their knowledge to the praise and love of the one God, from whom they would see that everything derives its existence. Those who do not pursue this course of inquiry may appear to be learned, but are in no sense wise.

Accordingly it seems right to me to warn studious and able young men, who fear God and are seeking the happy life, not to be so bold as to enter heedlessly upon these studies which are popular outside the Church of Christ, as if they could

* The reference is to the second line of the 1st book of Vergil's *Aeneid,* where Vergil makes the first vowel of "Italia" long instead of short:

Arma virumque cano, Troiae qui primus ab oris
Italiam fato profugus Laviniaque venit
litora. . . .

[14] *Christian Education,* ii, 56-61.

bring them the happiness in life which they seek. Rather they should make sensible and careful distinctions among such studies. When studies devised by man appear to show variations owing to the varying intentions of their originators and to be marked by ignorance because of the misleading ideas they express, they should be utterly rejected and abhorred, especially if they also involve entering into an association with devils by means of what may be called leagues and covenants based on signs. Also, young men should pay no attention to those human institutions which are unnecessary and luxurious. But for the sake of the essential business of this life, they should not reject those which enable us to enter into association with those around us. However, I think there is nothing useful in the other branches of learning, which are to be found among the pagans, except their accounts of things which relate to the physical senses, whether these things belong to the past or the present, and also their studies of logic and arithmetic. In the first category I include the experiments and conclusions of the useful mechanical arts. In regard to all this we must remember the advice, "Nothing in excess,"* especially with reference to those arts which relate to the senses of the body and which are therefore involved in relations of space and of time.

Now some men have separately translated all the Hebrew, Syriac and Egyptian terms found in the Holy Scriptures and left untranslated there. Eusebius has performed a similar task with regard to the history of past times with a view to resolving scriptural questions which require a knowledge of history for their solution. Through their labors these men have made it unnecessary for the Christian to work hard on many subjects for the sake of some small items of knowledge. I think that the same might be done in regard to other matters, if some able man cared to carry out what would indeed be a labor of love for the benefit of his fellow men. He could classify unknown parts of the earth, animals, plants and trees,

* "Ne quid nimis." Quoted from Terence, *Andria,* Act 1, Scene 1, line 34.

stones and metals and other classes of things mentioned in the Scriptures. He could give an account of these and commit it to writing. This could also be done with numbers, so that the theory of only those numbers which are mentioned in Scriptures might be explained and written down. Some or all of these things may have been done already. Indeed, we have found that many things have been worked out and committed to writing by good and learned Christians, although we had no idea that this was so. These documents are lying hidden away, either because so many people are careless or because envious people suppress them. I am not certain whether the same sort of thing can be done with reference to the theory of reasoning; but I am inclined to think it impossible, because reasoning permeates the whole tissue of the Scriptures like a system of nerves. On this account, reasoning is of greater assistance to the reader in resolving and explaining ambiguous expressions, of which we shall be speaking later, than in understanding unknown signs, which is the topic we are now discussing.

Now if those who are called philosophers, especially the Platonists, have said anything which is true and in harmony with our faith, we should not shrink away from it but appropriate it for our own use, as though we were taking it from people who were in unlawful possession of it. Think of the Egyptians who possessed not only the idols and heavy burdens which the people of Israel hated and fled from, but also vessels and ornaments of gold and silver and garments, which the Israelites secretly appropriated to themselves when they went out of Egypt, putting them, as it were, to a better use. The Israelites did this, not on their own authority, but by the command of God, and the Egyptians themselves unwittingly provided them with things which they themselves were not putting to good use.* In the same way all the subjects of

* *Exodus* 12:35-36: "And the children of Israel did according to the word of Moses; and they borrowed of the Egyptians jewels of silver and jewels of gold and raiment. And the Lord gave the people favor in the sight of the Egyptians so that they sent unto them such things as they required. And they spoiled the Egyptians."

pagan learning have false and superstitious fancies and heavy burdens of unnecessary labor, which every one of us ought to detest and avoid when we go forth under the leadership of Christ. But pagan learning also includes the liberal arts, which are better suited to the service of truth, some very useful moral instruction, and even some truths relating to the worship of the One God. Now we may say that these elements are the pagans' gold and silver, which they did not create for themselves, but dug out of the mines of God's providence, which is everywhere diffused. They are perversely and unlawfully abusing this gold and silver for the worship of devils. Therefore, when the Christian separates himself in spirit from the wretched fellowship of such men, it is proper that he should take all this away from them and turn it to its proper use in declaring the gospel. It will also be right to receive and possess their garments, that is, those institutions which are of human origin but adapted to the association of man with man, which in this life we cannot do without. All this we must take and turn to a Christian use.

This is precisely what many of our good and faithful people have done. Surely we can see with what a large quantity of gold and silver and garments Cyprian, that most persuasive teacher and blessed martyr, was burdened when he came out of Egypt. So it was with Lactantius, Victorinus, Optatus and Hilary, not to mention men who are still alive. Countless others have done the same and, before them all, Moses, of whom it has been written that he was "learned in all the wisdom of the Egyptians" (*Acts* 7:22). All these men would have been denied access to those subjects of study which they held to be useful if the pagans, with their superstitious habits, had suspected that this knowledge would be directed to the worship of the one true God and to the destruction of the vain worship of idols. This was especially true in those times when the pagans were kicking against the yoke of Christ and persecuting the Christians. But the pagans gave their gold, silver and garments to the people of God as they were going out of Egypt, not knowing how the things they were giving would come into the service of Christ.

The Psychology of Christian Instruction

[15]I do not want you to be disturbed by the feeling you have often experienced that you were delivering a poor and wearisome talk; for it may be that it did not appear in that light to the person you were instructing. The reason may have been that you wished to say something even better, and so you thought that what you were saying was not fit to be heard by others. I too am almost always dissatisfied with my talk, being greedy for something better, which I am often enjoying within myself before I begin to express it in spoken words. Then, when my performance falls short of my inner thought, I am sad that my tongue cannot respond to my heart. My desire is for my hearer to understand all that I understand; at the same time I feel that I am not talking in such a way as to bring this about. The principal cause of this is that the understanding permeates the mind with a sudden flash as it were, while talk is slow and prolonged and very different from thought. While talk moves on, the thought retreats into its secret recesses. However, in a marvellous way it stamps certain impressions on the memory, and these remain for the time taken to pronounce the syllables. From these same impressions we form spoken signs which are called "language," whether Latin or Greek or Hebrew or any other. These signs are either conceived in thought or are also uttered by the voice, whereas the impressions themselves are neither Latin nor Greek nor Hebrew nor any other language. They are formed in the mind as facial expressions are formed in the body. For example, anger is called by different words in Latin, Greek and the many other languages; but the expression of any angry man is neither Latin nor Greek. Therefore, not everyone can understand the words *Iratus sum,* but only Latins. On the other hand when we burn with anger and our mental emotion appears on the face and affects the expression, everyone looking on us knows the reason. Again, it is not possible for us to bring out those impressions which

[15] *The Instruction of the Uninstructed,* 3–4.

understanding imprints upon the memory, and as it were to lay them before the senses of our audience by means of the sound of our voice, in any way corresponding to the open and clear expression of our countenance. For impressions are inside the mind while our countenance is outside on the body. So we have to guess how much the sound of our mouth differs from the flash of the understanding since this sound does not correspond even with the impression made in the memory. We then, who are often eagerly anxious for the welfare of our pupils, desire to express ourselves in harmony with what we understand at the time, but because of the very effort we are making we are unable to express ouselves in speech. Then, because we fail, we are vexed and overcome by weariness, as a result of which our talk becomes still more heavy and dull than it was at the time when it first induced weariness.

However, there are many times when my hearers' attention shows that my talk is not as frigid as it appears to me. I gather from their pleasure that they are finding something useful in it. Therefore, I put a good deal of effort into it to see that I do not fail in the performance of this service, in which I see them appreciating what is set before them. So you also should note that people are often brought to you for instruction in the faith, which should prove that your talk is not as displeasing to others as it is to yourself. You should not think yourself barren simply because you do not set out what you understand exactly as you want to; for it is possible that you do not even have the capacity to understand exactly as you would wish to. In this life who sees except "through a glass darkly"? *(I Corinthians* 13:12). Even love itself is not strong enough to draw asunder the darkness of the flesh and penetrate into that eternal calm from which even transient things derive the light by which they shine. But, as day follows day, the good make a steady advance to the point where they look upon that day in which there is no turning of the heavens nor any encroachment of night—that day which "eye hath not seen nor ear heard nor hath it entered into the heart of man"

(*I Corinthians* 2:9). Thus, the most common reason why the teaching we give to the uninstructed becomes worthless in our eyes is that it is a pleasure for us to have insights that are extraordinary but wearisome to be indulging in ordinary talk. In truth we are listened to with much greater pleasure when we take pleasure in our work. For the thread of our talk is affected by the very joy we feel, and so it comes out with less effort and greater acceptance. Thus, in the matter of things which are put forward as articles of faith, it is not difficult to lay down instructions as to how to begin and end your talk or how to give variety to your exposition so that it sometimes lasts a shorter and sometimes a longer time and yet is always full and complete. It is not hard to show what occasions call for a shorter or a longer talk. However, it is of the greatest importance to consider how we can bring it about that the person who teaches does so in a spirit of joy. For the more a teacher achieves this, the more attractive will he be.

[16]With this love (the love of God for man) set before you as a criterion by which you should measure everything you say, go on to teach all your lessons in such a way that the person who listens to you may believe in consequence of listening to you and by believing may hope and by hoping love.

It is from that severity of God by which the hearts of mortal men are agitated with a most wholesome terror that love must be raised up so that men may be glad that they are loved by Him whom they fear and so may be emboldened to love Him in return. Thus, they become afraid to offend God's love, even if they can do so without punishment. Certainly it very seldom if ever happens that a man approaches us with the desire to become a Christian if he has not first been smitten by a fear of God. For if a man wants to become a Christian because he expects to get some advantage from

[16] *The Instruction of the Uninstructed,* 8-9.

people whom he imagines he can please in no other way, or with the idea of avoiding some unfavorable reaction from people whose displeasure or hostility he fears, then he wants to make a pretense of Christianity rather than to accept it. For faith is concerned with the believing mind and not with the body going through the motions of obedience. Nevertheless, it is clear that God's mercy often comes through the service of a teacher who influences someone by his talk so that the person decides to accept what he had merely intended to make a pretense of. As soon as our pupil begins to have this desire, we can decide that he has really made an approach to us. It is certainly true that the exact moment when a man who is clearly with us in the body makes a real approach to us with his mind, is something hidden from us. In spite of that, we should deal with him in such a way that this desire may rise up within him, even though it is not actually present at the time. For nothing can be lost by this since, if there is any desire at all, it is surely strengthened by our action, although we may not know the time or the exact hour when the desire came into being. If it is possible, it is certainly useful to get from those who know the man some previous impression of his state of mind or the causes which have induced him to want to take up religion. But if there is nobody else available from whom we may learn this, the man himself should be questioned so that our talk may take its start from what he says to us in reply. Now, if he has come with a deceitful heart and merely with the desire for some human profit or in the hope of avoiding some human inconvenience, he will certainly speak what is untrue. In spite of that, the very lie he utters should be our starting point, although your aim should not be to refute his lie on the assumption that you take it for granted. If he declares that he has come with a really praiseworthy intention, whether it is the truth or not, we should nevertheless commend and praise the motive which he has attributed to himself in his reply to us. In this way we aim at making him feel how pleasant it would be to be the man he wants to appear. On the other hand, if his statement indicates that he has in mind what should not be in the mind of one who needs instruction in the Christian faith, we should reprove him with more than usual kindness and gentleness as a person uninstructed and ignorant, pointing out and commending briefly and in a serious spirit the real goal of Christian education. By doing all this in such a way that you neither encroach on the time alloted for the ensuing exposition nor try to impose it on a mind not yet prepared for it, you may bring him to desire what, up to that point, either through ignorance or pretense he has not desired.

The Place of Rhetoric in Christian Teaching

[17]In this preface I want first to curb the expectations of my readers, who may be thinking that I am going to set down the rules of rhetoric, which I have both learned and taught in the secular schools, and to warn them that they need expect nothing like that from me. I do not think rules are useless but, if they have a use, that use is to be learned somewhere else. If any good man has the time to learn them, he is not to seek them from me, either in this book or anywhere else.

Now, since the art of rhetoric is employed to support either truth or falsehood, who would venture to say that truth as represented by its defenders should take its stand unarmed against falsehood? Surely the result would be that those who attempt to support what is false would know how to introduce their subject in such a way as to put the hearer into a friendly, attentive or receptive frame of mind, while the defenders of truth would not know how to do this. The former would expound their falsehoods briefly, clearly and plausibly, while the latter would expound truth in such a manner that it is boring for their audience to listen to, difficult to understand and, in a word, hard to believe. The former would use mis-

[17] *Christian Education,* iv, 2–11.

leading arguments to oppose the truth and to declare what is false, while the latter would lack the power either to defend truth or to refute falsehood. By their speech the former would stir up the minds of their audience and direct them to wrong opinions, making them fearful, sad or elated, and passionately exhorting them; but the defenders of truth would be slow, frigid and sluggish. Who would be so foolish as to call this wisdom? Therefore, since the power of eloquence is open to both sides and is of very great value in advocating either what is wrong or what is right, why do good men not strive to bring it into the field in the cause of truth, when bad men press it into the service of wickedness and error for the purpose of supporting perverse and empty causes?

When you add to the theories and rules on this subject the thoroughly practiced skill and habit of a tongue well versed in the use of a variety of words and ornaments of speech, you have what is called fluency or eloquence. Its theories and rules should be learned by those who can quickly master them, but they must set aside a suitable period of time at an appropriate age and look for the instruction elsewhere than in my writings. The masters of Roman eloquence themselves did not hesitate to say that, "Unless a man can learn this art quickly, he can never thoroughly learn it at all."* Why should we pause to ask whether this is true or not? For even if this art can occasionally be mastered in the end by men of slower understanding, I do not think it of such importance that I would want men of mature or advanced years to spend time in learning it. It is enough that young men should study the art, and not even all of those we want to educate for the service of the Church need rhetoric. It is necessary only for those not engaged in a more urgent and necessary occupation, which should certainly take precedence; for with keen wits and an enthusiastic temperament eloquence comes more easily to a man who reads and listens to eloquent speakers than to one who follows the rules of eloquence. Even if we look

*Quoted from Cicero, *De Oratore,* iii, 31, 123.

beyond the Canon, which for us has the great advantage of being well supported by authority, there is no lack of ecclesiastical writings by reading which a person of ability will be tinged with the eloquence they display. This will be so even when he is not specifically aiming at such eloquence, but is simply concentrating on the content of what is written, and especially if he also practices writing, dictating and finally expressing in speech the views he holds in accordance with the rule of piety and faith. However, when ability of this kind is lacking, the rules of rhetoric are either not understood, or they come to be only slightly understood after being forced in with a great expenditure of toil, in which case they prove to be of no help. Even those who have mastered the rules and speak with fluency and elegance cannot always think of the rules when they are speaking, so that they can direct their talk in accordance with them; that is, unless they are actually discussing the rules themselves. Indeed, I think there is scarcely anyone who can simultaneously speak well and think of the rules for speaking while they are speaking. We must be careful that the content of our speech does not slip out of our minds while we are concentrating on the techniques of expression which we are employing. Nevertheless, in the speeches and statements of eloquent men we find rules of rhetoric being put into practice, although the speakers did not deliberately plan to use them for the purpose of improving their eloquence. They were not even thinking of the rules at the time they were speaking and would speak as they do whether they had learned the rules or had never even heard of them. Indeed, such men demonstrate the rules because they are eloquent; they do not employ the rules in order to be eloquent.

Therefore, since young children cannot learn to speak except by learning the words of people speaking to them, why cannot men become eloquent without being instructed in the art of speech, simply by reading and learning the speeches of eloquent men and by doing their best to imitate them? And what do we find about this when we look at actual examples?

We know very many men who, without having any knowledge of the rules of rhetoric, are more eloquent than very many who have learned them. But we know nobody who is eloquent without having read and listened to the debates and speeches of eloquent men. Even the art of grammar, by which correct speech is taught, need not be learned by boys if they have the opportunity of growing up and living among men who speak correctly. For, although children are not familiar with the names of any of the faults of style, their exposure to correct speech will lead them to seize upon and avoid whatever is faulty in the speech of anyone they are listening to. In the same way men who have been reared in the city, even when they are illiterate, seize upon the faults of country people.

Thus, it is the duty of the interpreter and teacher of the Holy Scriptures, that is, the person who defends the true faith and who subdues error, to teach what is good and to refute what is evil. In the performance of this task he should win over the hostile, stir up the careless and inform the ignorant, both about the present condition of things and about their expectations for the future. When he finds his audience friendly, attentive and ready to learn or has made them so himself, the rest of his task should be carried out in whatever way the circumstances require. If those who are listening to him need teaching, then he must employ the method of narrative. On the other hand, if doubtful points are to be cleared up, he must bring forward proofs and employ reasoning. However, if his hearers need to be aroused rather than instructed so that they may be rigorous in putting into practice what they already know and give their approval to facts whose truth they already admit, more forceful forms of speech are required. In this case entreaties, reproaches, exhortations, pressures and every other means of arousing men's minds are necessary.

All the principles I have mentioned are continually employed by almost everyone on the occasions when they use speech to accomplish their purposes. But some men use the principles in a dull manner, with no elegance or warmth, while others use them with penetration, elegance and zest. Therefore, the work I am speaking of should be taken up by someone who can debate and speak with wisdom, if not with eloquence, and with some profit to his audience, even if that profit is smaller than it would be if he could speak with eloquence as well. We must beware of the man who overflows with eloquent foolishness, particularly if his audience takes pleasure in listening to him talking about things not worth listening to and imagines that, because a man is speaking eloquently, he must necessarily be speaking the truth as well. This conclusion is supported even by those who have thought that the art of rhetoric should be taught. For they have declared that "although wisdom without eloquence is of little service to states, yet eloquence without wisdom is very often harmful and never of service."* Therefore, those who have taught the principles of eloquence have been compelled by the promptings of truth to make this declaration in those books in which they deal with the subject of eloquence. Nevertheless, they had no knowledge of the true wisdom, that is, the heavenly wisdom which comes down from the Father of Lights. How much more then should we be of this opinion, who are the sons and the servants of this higher wisdom! Now the wisdom which a man expresses in speech varies in accordance with the progress he has made in his knowledge of the Scriptures. I do not mean that he should have spent much time in reading them and committing them to memory, but that he should have understood them correctly and have tracked down their meaning. For there are those who read the Scriptures and nevertheless neglect them. They read them in order to lay hold on the words but are careless when it comes to understanding what they mean. We should certainly much prefer those people who hold less to the words but who, with the eyes of the heart, look into the heart of the Scriptures. However, better than both of these is

* Cicero, *De Inventione*, i, 1.

the man who can recite the Scriptures when he wants to do so and yet at the same time properly understands their meaning.

Now, it is particularly necessary for the man whose duty it is to speak wisely, even if he cannot speak eloquently, to hold on to the words of the Scriptures. For the more he realizes the relative poverty of his own words, the more he should realize the wealth to be found in the words of the Scriptures. In this way he would win approval for what he expresses in his own words by quoting the words of Scripture, and, although he may be puny in his own words, he could, as it were, grow in strength through the testimony of great men. For he gives pleasure by reason of the proofs he establishes when he cannot please by his own manner of speech. But, if a man wants to speak not only with wisdom but also with eloquence, and he will certainly be of greater service if he can do both, I would be more willing to advise him to read, listen to and imitate eloquent men than to spend time with teachers of the art of rhetoric. This is especially true if the men he reads and listens to deserve the praise they are given and are properly regarded as not only eloquent but also wise speakers. For eloquent speakers are listened to with pleasure, while wise speakers are listened to with profit. This is why the Scriptures refer to "the multitude of the wise" rather than to "the multitude of the eloquent," when they declare that "the multitude of the wise is the health of the world."* As there are many occasions when we must consume things which are bitter but at the same time good for us, so we must always avoid what is agreeable but bad for us. Best of all are the things which are both agreeable and good for us, or which are good for us and also agreeable. In that case, the more we seek after what is agreeable, the more easily can we turn to our advantage what is good for us. There are writers of the Church who have dealt with the divine eloquence, not only with wisdom but also with eloquence. Students and those

* From the apocryphal *Book of Wisdom* 6, 26: *Multitudo autem sapientium sanitas est orbis terrarum.*

who have leisure to read them never have enough time to exhaust their resources.

At this point perhaps someone may ask whether our writers, whose divinely inspired writings constitute our canon and carry with them the most wholesome authority, are to be regarded as showing wisdom alone or wisdom supplemented by eloquence. Certainly this is a question which, in my view and in the view of those who agree with me, is very easily settled. For where I understand these writers, it seems to me that nothing else could exceed them in wisdom and also in eloquence. I venture to say that all who properly understand what these writers are saying, understand at the same time that what they say should not have been said in any other way. There is a kind of eloquence more appropriate to youth and one better suited to old age; nothing can be properly called eloquence unless it is in harmony with the personality of the speaker. Thus, there is an eloquence which is right for men who have most fully deserved the highest authority and are obviously divinely inspired. This was the eloquence our writers employed; no other eloquence is right for them any more than their sort of eloquence is right for any other people. It is an eloquence which suits them, and the more our eloquence seems to fall below the eloquence of others, the more it actually rises above them when we take account of solid substance rather than of sound and fury. However, in places where I do not understand these writers, their eloquence is certainly less apparent to me. But I am always sure that it is of the same sort as it is when I understand what they are saying. The very obscurity of these divine and wholesome words had necessarily to be mingled with eloquence of a kind which would serve to develop our intellects, not only by the discovery of truth, but also by the opportunity given to exercise our powers.

As for the people who prefer their own sort of language to the language of our Christian authors because their own language is turgid and pompous rather than dignified, if time were available I could show them that all those qualities and ornaments of eloquence about which they boast are to be found in the sacred writings which divine providence has provided for our instruction and guidance from this wicked age to the age of blessedness to come. The qualities which please me more than I can tell in the eloquence of our authors are not those they share with pagan orators and poets. What amazes me is that our authors use another sort of eloquence, which is distinctively their own, in such a way that it is present in their writings without being very conspicuous. It was not their duty either to condemn eloquence or to make a display of it. If they rejected it, they would be doing the former; on the other hand, if it could be easily recognized, it might be thought that they were doing the latter. In those passages where learned men are perhaps aware of the presence of eloquence, the subject matter being talked about is such that the words employed appear not so much to be searched out by the speaker as to be spontaneously linked, so to speak, to the subject matter itself. It would seem that wisdom is emerging from its home, that is, from the heart of the wise man, and that eloquence is following after it without being summoned, like an inseparable attendant.

For everyone can see what the Apostle meant to say and how wisely he said it when he declared: "We glory in tribulations also; knowing that tribulation worketh patience; and patience, experience; and experience, hope; and hope maketh not ashamed; because the love of God is shed abroad in our hearts by the Holy Ghost which is given unto us" *(Romans* 5:3-5). Now if a man were, as we might say, so learnedly unlearned as to argue that in this passage the Apostle had followed the rules of rhetoric, would he not be laughed at by all Christians, whether educated or not? Nevertheless, here we find demonstrated the figure of speech which in Greek is called "climax" (ladder) because the words or the ideas are connected together, one following another. Some people have called it *gradatio* (gradation) in Latin because they have not wanted to call it *scala* (ladder). Thus, in the example given, "patience" is connected to "tribulation," "experience" to "patience" and "hope" to "experience." But there is still another embellishment which can be identified in this passage. Certain statements which our people call "clauses" and "sections" *(membra et caesa),* but which the Greeks call *cola* and *commata,* are uttered in one tone of voice. Then there follows a rounded sentence which we call an "ambit" *(ambitus)* or a "circuit" *(circuitus),* but which the Greeks call a "period." The clauses of this are held in suspense by the voice of the speaker until the whole sentence is brought to a close by the last clause. In the statements which come before the period, the first clause is "knowing that tribulations worketh patience"; the second is "and patience experience"; and third "and experience hope." Then the period subordinated to this is completed in three clauses; the first is "and hope maketh not ashamed"; the second is "because the love of God is shed abroad in our hearts"; and the third is "by the Holy Ghost which is given unto us." Now these and other techniques are taught in the art of elocution. Therefore, whereas on the one hand we do not claim that the Apostle was following the rules of eloquence, on the other hand we do not deny the fact that eloquence issued from his wisdom.

[18]There are some parts of the Scriptures whose proper meaning is not understood or understood only with difficulty, no matter at what length or how clearly and eloquently they may be expounded by the speaker who discusses them. These passages should never be brought to the attention of the people at all, or only on rare occasions when there is some urgent necessity. However, we must not abandon the duty of bringing to the understanding of other people the truths we ourselves have already grasped, no matter how difficult they may be to understand or how much effort we may have to put into the task of arguing them. We must do this in books written in such a way that, when they are understood, they hold the reader's attention as it were and that, when they are

[18] *Christian Education,* iv, 23–29.

not understood, they cause no trouble to those who do not want to read them. We must also do this in conversations with people. However, it is necessary that the person listening to us or talking with us have the desire to learn and that he should have the mental capacity to receive our lessons in whatever form they may be communicated. As for the teacher, he should be concerned, not so much with the eloquence he brings to bear on his teaching, as with its clarity.

A persistent desire to achieve such clarity can sometimes lead to a neglect of the more polished forms of speech and to attention being focussed on the clear expression and communication of the intended meaning at the expense of appeal to the ear. For this reason, in the course of a discussion of this sort of speech, someone has remarked that we have here "a kind of studied negligence."* Yet, while this form of speech removes stylistic ornaments, it does not admit slang. However, good teachers give, or ought to give, such careful thought to teaching so that they sometimes employ a word according to the usage of uneducated rather than educated people. This is the kind of word which cannot be rendered in pure Latin without being obscure or ambiguous, but which avoids ambiguity or obscurity when it is used according to the popular idiom. For example, our Christian translators were not ashamed to say, "I shall not assemble their meetings for blood offerings," because they regarded it as important for the sense to use a word in the plural which in Latin is used only in the singular.** Why then should a teacher of religious truth who is addressing uneducated people hesitate to use *ossum* instead of *os* when there is the possibility that the latter might be understood (not as the singular of *ossa* (bones) but as the singular of *ora* (mouths), seeing that the ears of Africans are not alive to the distinction between short and

* The quotation is from Cicero, *Orator*, 23, 78: *Quaedam neglegentia diligens.*

** Psalm 15:4: "*non congregabo conventicula eorum de sanguinibus.* "*Sanguis*" (blood) is here used in the plural form in the sense of "blood offerings."

long vowels?* What advantage is there in purity of speech when it is not meaningful to the person listening to us? There is absolutely no reason for speaking if we are not understood by the very persons for whose sake we are speaking. Therefore, the teacher will avoid all words which do not teach. If he can substitute words which are both pure and intelligible, he will give preference to those. But if this is not possible, either because there are no such words or because they do not occur to him at the moment of speaking, he will use words of lesser purity, provided that the subject matter of his lesson is taught and learned in its purity.

This is indeed the principle we must emphasize if we are to be understood, whether we are conversing with one person or many, but much more when we are speaking in public. In conversations it is open to anyone to ask a question; but when everyone falls silent so that one person may be heard and all faces are turned attentively upon him, then it is neither customary nor proper for someone to ask a question about something he does not understand. For this reason the speaker should take care to give the greatest assistance to his hearers, since they are not in a position to ask for it. However, a crowd anxious for instruction generally shows by its movements whether it understands what is being said. Until some such indication is given, the subject under discussion should be turned over and over and expressed in a variety of different ways, a thing which is impossible when the speaker is repeating words prepared in advance and memorized verbatim. However, as soon as it is clear to him that what he is saying is understood, he should either bring his talk to a close or pass on to other topics. A man gives pleasure when he is throwing light on matters on which people need to be informed. But equally, when he dwells at length upon things which are already known, he becomes boring, at least to

* *Ossa* (bones) and *ora* (mouths) both have the singular form *os*, the meaning being normally distinguishable by the difference in the length of the vowel.

those whose attention is concentrated on resolving difficult problems which are being opened up. On the other hand, even things which are well known can be told for the purpose of giving pleasure. But in this case the attention is directed, not to the subject matter, but to the style in which it is presented. Furthermore, when the style itself is already well known and is pleasing to the audience, the question of whether a person speaking is actually a speaker or merely a reader is a matter of little or no concern. For what is gracefully written is often read with pleasure by people making their first acquaintance with it, but it also gives pleasure on a second reading to those who are already familiar with it and have not yet forgotten it. There is also pleasure to be got from hearing such passages read by someone else. However, at the moment I am not concerned with the method of giving pleasure but with the way in which people who desire to learn should be taught. And the best method is the one which causes the listener to hear the truth and to understand what he hears. When this point has been reached, no further labor needs to be spent on the truth itself, as if the truth needed more prolonged teaching, although perhaps something may be done to fix it firmly in the heart. If it seems right to do this, then it should be done with such restraint that boredom is avoided.

Certainly as far as teaching is concerned, the function of eloquence is not to make people like what they dislike or to make them do what they do not want to do but to make clear what is obscure. However, if this is done with no regard to elegance of style, the benefit comes only to a few very enthusiastic students who are anxious to get to know anything that is to be learned, no matter how rough and unpolished the style in which it is expounded. When they have achived this objective, they take pleasure in the nourishment they derive from the unvarnished truth. Furthermore, it is a distinctive mark of good abilities to love truth and not mere words. Of what service is a golden key if it cannot open the door we want to open? Or what disadvantage is there in a wooden key if it can do this, seeing that our sole aim is to open up what is locked? Eating and learning have this in common: that even the food which is essential to the maintenance of life must be flavored to meet the fastidious tastes of the majority of people.

Thus, a great orator has rightly said that an eloquent man must speak so as to teach, give pleasure and persuade. Then he adds, "To teach is a necessity, to give pleasure is agreeable, to persuade is a triumph."* Now of these three, teaching, which is a matter of necessity, is concerned with what we say, whereas the other two are concerned with the way we say it. Therefore, the man who speaks when he wants to teach should not think that he has said what he has to say as long as he is not understood. For even when he has said what he himself understands, we should not conclude that he has really said it at all, when his pupil does not understand what he is saying. On the other hand, if the teacher is understood, then he has said what he wants to say irrespective of his manner of saying it. But if he also wants to give pleasure to the person to whom he is speaking or to persuade him, he will not achieve this by speaking in any manner; for this purpose his style of speaking is a matter of importance. Just as the hearer must experience pleasure if his attention is to be held, so he must be persuaded if he is to be moved to action. And as he is gratified if you speak in a pleasant manner, so he is persuaded if he comes to desire the rewards you promise, stand in awe of the threats you present to him, hate what you condemn, embrace what you commend and grieve when you pile up objects of sorrow. He is also persuaded if he rejoices when you point out to him a cause for rejoicing, pities people whom you present to him as objects of pity, and shuns those whom you hold out as people to be avoided and feared. These and other results can be achieved under the influence of a

* Cicero, *Orator,* 21. Augustine misquotes Cicero, who actually says, "That man will be eloquent who speaks in such a way that he makes his point, gives pleasure and also persuades." (*Erit igitur eloquens qui ita dicet ut probet, ut delectet, ut flectat.*)

powerful eloquence so as to move the minds of people who listen, not in the way of telling them what they ought to do, but rather stimulating them to do what they already know ought to be done.

However, if they do not yet know this, they must certainly be instructed first and moved afterwards. And perhaps when they have received the instruction, there will be no need for them to be moved with a more powerful eloquence. Nevertheless, when this is necessary, it must be used; and it is necessary when people fail to do what they know they ought to do. On this account teaching is a "necessity," for men can choose either to do or to refrain from doing what they know. But who would claim that it is their duty to do what they do not know? On the same grounds, to persuade is not a "necessity," for it is not always needed, as for example, when a listener gives his assent to someone who simply teaches or who also gives pleasure. Also for this reason, to persuade is "a triumph," because it is possible for a man to be taught and pleased and yet not give his assent. What advantage will be gained from the first two if the third is lacking? Nor is it a necessity to give pleasure because, when truth is being pointed out in a speech, which is the function of teaching, the end is not achieved by eloquence; nor is it the intention that either the truth itself or the eloquence should give pleasure. But what is being declared gives pleasure in its own right, just because it is the truth. Hence, even falsehoods frequently give pleasure when they are brought out and refuted, although the pleasure they give does not arise from their falsity. It is true that they are false, and the pleasure is caused by the demonstration of this truth in a speech.

Now, for the sake of those who, being of a fastidious disposition, do not care for truth unless it is expounded in such a way that the talk of the speaker also provides pleasure, the study of eloquence has given considerable attention to the art of pleasing. But, even when pleasure is added, it is not enough for those stubborn people who derive no profit either from having understood what a teacher is saying or from the pleasure it has given them. For what advantage is it for a man to agree with a truth and to express approval of the speaker's eloquence if he does not actually accept the truth, seeing that it is for this very reason that a speaker gives careful thought to what he is saying when he is urging some course of action? If the truths that are being taught are such that it is sufficient to believe or to know them, then to accept them is simply to agree that they are true. But, when something is taught which must be put into practice and when teaching is given with the sole intention that something should be done, then there is no point in merely being persuaded that what is said is true. Nor is it enough to derive pleasure from the manner in which something is said if it is not learned in such a way that it issues in action. Therefore, when an eloquent churchman is recommending that something be done, he must not only teach so as to provide instruction and to give pleasure with the aim of holding the attention of his audience, but must also move his listeners so as to convince them. For when the truth is demonstrated to a man right up to the point where he agrees with it and yet it does not have the effect of moving him, even when it is presented in a pleasing style, there remains the duty of winning him over to acceptance of it by the force of eloquence.

[19]The speaker who aims at persuading people to accept what is good should not despise any of these three aims, that is, to teach, to give pleasure and to move. As we have said above, he should direct his prayer and his work to the end that he should be heard with understanding, with pleasure, and with ready acceptance. When he does this in an appropriate and fitting style, he can deservedly be called eloquent, even though he does not carry with him the assent of his audience. The great founder of Roman eloquence seems to

[19] *Christian Education,* iv, 34–35.

have been referring to these three aims when he said in the same vein: "That man will be eloquent who can say little things in the subdued style, moderate things in the moderate style, and great things in the grand style."* It is as if he were adding together the three aims mentioned above and summing them all up in one sentence in some such way as this: "That man will be eloquent who can say little things in the subdued style for the purpose of teaching, moderate things in the moderate style for the purpose of giving pleasure, and great things in the grand style for the purpose of moving his audience."

Now this author could have demonstrated these three points, as set down by himself, with reference to legal issues, but he could not have done this with reference to issues concerning the Church. And these are the only issues with which we are concerned in the sort of speech we wish to shape. In legal questions, small issues are those in which judgment is to be passed on financial matters; great issues are those relating to a man's safety or life; issues which are not concerned with either of these, and where the intention is not to prevail upon the listener to act or pass judgment on anything but merely to give him pleasure, occupy as it were a middle place between the first two. On that account they are called "ordinary" or "moderate" issues. The term "moderate" is connected with *modus* (measure), and it is an abuse and not a proper use of the term "moderate" to make it synonymous with "little." But in issues of the sort we deal with, where everything, especially what is addressed to the people from a place of authority, ought to be concerned with man's salvation, everything we speak of is a great issue. And by salvation we should mean not temporal but eternal salvation. Similarly where eternal ruin is to be guarded against, everything we say is important. So much so that, even when

* Cicero, *Orator,* 29, 101. The last phrase, which Augustine renders *granditer dicere* (to speak in the grand style) corresponds to *graviter dicere* (to speak in the serious or weighty style) in Cicero's text.

the preacher talks about financial matters, whether he is referring to acquiring or losing money and whether a large or a small amount is at stake, what he says should not seem unimportant. For justice is never a small matter and certainly should be upheld, even with reference to small sums of money. Of this our Lord says, "He that is faithful in that which is least is faithful also in much" (*Luke* 16:10). What is "least" is certainly a small matter; yet it is a great matter to be "faithful in that which is least." For as the principle of a circle, namely, that all lines drawn from the center to the circumference are equal, is the same whether we are referring to a great disc or a tiny coin, so the greatness of justice is not at all diminished when small matters are being justly transacted.

[20]Certainly if we were giving men advice as to how they should conduct secular business before church courts, it would be proper for us to advise them to conduct their business in the subdued style since it involves matters of small importance. But we are dealing with the style of speech of the person whom we want to be a teacher of those truths by which we are delivered from eternal evil and brought to eternal good. Wherever these truths are spoken of, whether in public or private, to one person or many, before friends or enemies, in a continuous speech or conversation, in treatises, books, or letters which may be either long or short, they are great themes. We could of course argue that, because a cup of cold water is a very small and ordinary thing, our Lord said a small and ordinary thing when He declared that the person who gives such a cup to one of his disciples "shall in no wise lose his reward" (*Matthew* 10:42); or that, when a preacher bases his sermon on this text, he should regard his subject as a petty one and therefore imagine that he must not treat it either in the moderate or in the grand style but in the subdued

[20] *Christian Education,* iv, 37–38.

style. When we have come to speak to the people on this text and when God has been present with us so that what we say is well matched to the subject, has not a tongue of fire sprung up out of that cold water to kindle even the cold hearts of men to carry out works of mercy?*

Yet, although the teacher we refer to ought to be speaking of great matters, he should not aways speak of them in the grand style. He should use the subdued style when he is giving some instruction and the moderate style when he is blaming or praising something. But when something is to be done and we are speaking to those who ought to do it but have no inclination to do it, then great matters must be spoken of in the grand style and in a manner calculated to move the mind. Moreover, there are times when the same important matter is dealt with in all these different styles. The subdued style is employed when instruction is being given in it, the moderate style when it is being publicly proclaimed, and the grand style when we are urging a mind which is turned away from the matter to concentrate on it. Is there anything greater than God Himself? Is this a reason why He should not be studied? Should a person who is teaching the Trinity discuss the matter in anything other than the subdued style so that a subject like this, which is difficult to analyze, should be as clearly understood as possible? In such a case are ornaments of style rather than proofs required? Is the listener to be persuaded to do something? Or isn't he rather to be instructed so that he learns something? But when God is being praised, whether in Himself or His works, what an opportunity for fine and glowing language is offered to the man who can exert himself to his fullest capacity in praising Him whom no man can adequately praise, although there is nobody who does not praise Him in some way or other! If He

* II *Maccabees* i: 31-32: "Nehemiah ordered the remaining water to be poured over the larger stones. When this was done, a flame was kindled from them. But the flame was consumed by the light which shone from the altar."

is not being worshipped, or if idols are being worshipped in preference to Him, whether they are demons or any created beings whatsoever, then certainly we have the duty of speaking out in the grand style about the enormity of this evil and of urging men to turn themselves away from it.

[21] If a speaker is applauded more frequently and enthusiastically than usual, we are not to take this as implying that he is speaking in the grand style. For this result is often produced by the subtleties of the subdued style as well as by the ornaments of the moderate style. On the other hand the grand style frequently subdues the listeners by its weight but draws out their tears. For example, there was the occasion when I was at Caesarea in Mauritania and was advising the people to abandon the fights which used to take place among their citizens. I refer to the *Caterva* (Rabble), a civil war or something even worse, which took place regularly at a fixed time of the year and continued for several days, during which everyone killed anyone they laid hands on. The participants were not merely fellow citizens but also relatives, brothers and, worst of all, fathers and sons, who divided themselves into two factions and fought each other with stones. I treated this subject in the grand style and to the best of my ability, intending by means of speech to uproot and banish from their hearts and customs an evil so cruel and so hallowed by time. But it was not when I heard their applause but rather when I saw their tears that I felt I had really accomplished something. For their applause showed they were being instructed and delighted, but their tears were evidence that they had been persuaded. Thus, when I observed their tears, I was sure, even before it was proved by the event, that this monstrous custom was overthrown, a custom which had been

[21] *Christian Education,* iv, 53–55.

handed down to them from their fathers and grandfathers and from generations long past and which, like an enemy, was laying siege to their hearts, or rather was in possession of them. Immediately on the conclusion of my sermon I turned their hearts and voices to giving thanks to God. And wonderful to tell, with the favor of Christ, it is now eight years or more since anything of the kind was attempted there. Many other examples have taught us that men show the effect produced on them by the grandeur of a wise man's speech, not so much by clamorous applause, as by groaning, sometimes even by tears, and finally by a change of life.

Many a man has been changed by the subdued style as well. But then it was used to inform people of something they did not know or to bring them to a belief in something which had seemed incredible to them, and not for the purpose of making them do what they already knew to be their duty but were unwilling to do. To break down this kind of obstinacy, the grand style needs to be employed. But when praise and censure are eloquently expressed, even in the moderate style, they produce such an effect on some people that they are not merely pleased with the eloquence in which the praises and censures are couched but are filled with the desire to live praiseworthy lives and reject what is blameworthy. However, we cannot say that everyone who derives pleasure from listening changes his life accordingly, as everyone who is moved by the grand style is driven to action or everyone who is taught by the subdued style comes to know or believe that what he was ignorant of is true.

We may infer from this that the aims of the two last mentioned styles are those which it is most necessary for people who want to speak with wisdom and eloquence to set before themselves. But the aim of the moderate style, which is to give pleasure by virtue of mere eloquence, is not a worthy end in itself. However, when we have to say something useful and honorable and our listeners are acquainted with it and well disposed to it so that it is unnecessary to employ a form of speech which either instructs or moves them, then their acceptance of it may be gained a little more quickly or they may hold on more tenaciously to what they have learned because of the enjoyment they have had from the eloquence. For, as the universal function of all eloquence, in whatever style it may be cast, is to speak in a manner which results in persuasion, and as the aim is through the medium of speech to persuade people to accept what you have in mind, an eloquent man speaks persuasively whatever style he uses. But unless he is successful in persuading, his eloquence fails in its objective. In the subdued style he persuades his listeners that what he says is true; in the grand style he persuades them to do what they are aware that they ought to do but are not doing; in the moderate style he persuades them that his speech has beauty and eloquence. But what profit is there in our reaching this last objective? Those people may value it who glory in their tongues and who talk boastfully in panegyrics and speeches of that kind, where their aim is not to instruct the listener or move him to a course of action but merely to give him pleasure. As for ourselves, we should relate this objective to another, namely, that we should achieve the same purpose when we use the moderate style as we do when we employ the grand style. This purpose is to promote a love of good habits and a detestation of evil habits, and we can achieve this by the moderate style of speech, provided that our listeners are not so far removed from such behavior that they seem to need the stimulus of the grand style. Also, in cases where people are already disposed this way, we may induce them to act more enthusiastically and to persevere in their course of action with greater constancy. Thus, even in the moderate style we should use beauty of expression, not for show, but for prudent ends. We should not be satisfied merely with seeing to it that the listener experiences pleasure, but, by the use of this style we should rather aim at helping him toward that good thing which we want to persuade him to accept.

Dialectic in the Service of Truth

The following passage is addressed to Cresconius, a teacher of grammar and an adherent of the sect of the Donatists, who had broken away from the African church. As Bishop of Hippo, St. Augustine had denounced the sect as heretical, and Cresconius in turn had circulated among his fellow members of the Donatist church a "Letter to Augustine," in which he had defended the views of a Donatist bishop, Petilian. In reply Augustine wrote the four books, *Against Cresconius the Donatist Grammarian,* from which this extract is taken. Among other things, Cresconius had accused Augustine of indulging in dialectic, which he stigmatized as mere logical quibbling. In return, Augustine argues for the respectability of dialectic and shows that the Christian teacher, following the example of Christ and of the Apostle Paul, must use dialectic as a means of winning over the opponents of Christianity. The work was written in 405-406 AD in the 10th year after St. Augustine's consecration as bishop.

[22] You know how much dialectic flourished among the Stoics. Yet even the Epicureans, who were not only unashamed of their ignorance of the liberal arts but even rejoiced in it, boasted that they possessed and taught a body of rules for argument by the use of which a man might be less exposed to deception. For what is dialectic other than skill in argument? I have thought it right to explain this, because you have been inclined to cast dialectic up at me as if it contradicted Christian truth. On this account your teachers have marked me down as a dialectician to be avoided and shunned rather than refuted and defeated in argument. However, they have not succeeded in persuading you of this, for you have

[22] *Against Cresconius the Donatist,* i, 16-17.

been very active in your arguments with us even in writing. But now you have launched an accusation of dialectic against me, whereby you hope to deceive ignorant people and ingratiate yourself with those who have been unwilling to join in argument with me. But are you not clearly employing dialectic when you attack us in writing? Surely you run a great danger of being drawn into argument when you do not know how to argue. Or, if you do know, why do you fling a charge of dialectic in my face? Are you either so rash that you do not hold in check the ignorance by which you will be defeated or alternatively so ungrateful that you attack the subject by which you are supported? I examine the speech which you have sent me in writing and observe that you expound certain matters in a style which is well rounded and pleasing. This is to say that you speak eloquently. You discuss other things with subtlety and penetration, that is, in a dialectical (logical) manner. Yet you find fault with eloquence and dialectic. If they are harmful, why do you indulge in them? If they are not harmful, why do you censure them? But let us not be tangled up in argument about a word. Since the thing itself is understood, we must not worry too much over the name which men have chosen to give it. If we grant that the man who speaks, not only in a rich and elegant style but also truthfully, is properly to be called eloquent and that the one who speaks with subtlety and also with truth is rightly referred to as a "dialectician," then you are neither eloquent nor a dialectician. This is not because your style of speech is spiritless and disorderly, nor because your argument lacks force and is dull, but rather because you abuse your eloquence and skill in the defense of falsehood. If it is correct to talk of "eloquence" or "dialectic" not only in the context of truth but also when an evil cause is being argued and vigorously advanced, then you are both eloquent and a dialectician on the grounds that you are uttering empty sentiments with eloquence and are skillfully discussing falsehood. But enough of yourself.

The Stoics were certainly the most consummate dialecticians. Why then did the Apostle Paul not carefully avoid them in case they entered into argument with him? You praise your bishops because they do not want to talk with us as being dialecticians. If Paul was a dialectician and was willing to confer with the Stoics because he could argue, not only with skill, as they did, but also with truth, as they did not, then because you agree that the Apostle used it, you must beware of imputing dialectic as a crime to anyone. But when you cast it up to me, I do not think that you are being led astray by inexperience. Rather I think that you are deceiving me by your adroitness. "Dialectic" is a Greek term which, if usage allowed, might be called in Latin *disputatoria*, just as the most learned men in both languages have called grammar *litteratura* (literature) in Latin. As grammar is so called from the Greek word for "letters," so dialectic has received its name from "argument" (*disputatio*), the Greek word for which is "dialogue." As the teacher of grammar (*grammaticus*) has become known in Latin as the "teacher of letters" (*litterator*), so what is known in Greek as "dialectician" is now more commonly and appropriately known in Latin as "disputer" (*disputator*). I think you would not deny the title of "disputer" to the Apostle Paul, even though you deny him that of dialectician. If so, you are being compelled to attack him with a Greek word for what you approve of under its Latin name. On the other hand, if you deny the title of "disputer" to the Apostle, who debated so continuously and so skillfully, then you know neither Greek nor Latin; but it is easier to assume that with a Greek word you are misleading those who do not know Greek and doing exactly the same with a Latin word to those who do not know Latin. What greater evidence of ignorance, or alternatively of the desire to mislead, could we have than that you hear or read so many of the Apostle's sermons which declare truth and refute falsehood, and yet you deny that he indulges in argumentation, although without it he could not possibly accomplish what he does? . . .

[23]The person who enters into controversy is making distinctions between truth and falsehood. Those who cannot do this and still wish to appear dialecticians win over gullible people by means of cunning questioning designed to trap them. They hope their answers may lead to conclusions which will cause these people to be caught in a blatant falsehood and be exposed to ridicule. Or on the other hand these "dialecticians" hope to deceive the people they argue with and so lead them to accept some hidden fallacy, which they themselves generally accept as truth. The man who is truly devoted to discussion, that is, who is really concerned to sift the true from the false, in the first place argues with himself to see that he himself is not deceived. This he cannot do without divine help. Then, when he brings his own experience to bear on teaching others, he first looks to see what they already know for certain, so that he may lead them on from this to what they did not know or were unwilling to believe. He shows that this is a consequence of what they already accepted either by knowledge or by faith. The result is that, through those truths about which people agree, they are drawn to approve other truths which they had previously denied. In this way a truth previously considered false is distinguished from falsehood when it is found to be in agreement with a truth which has already been understood and accepted . . . .

[24]When someone is defeated in argument by his own answers to questions and if these answers are inadequate, he cannot blame the questioner but only himself. On the other hand, if he gives good answers, he capitulates to himself and not to his questioner. Thus, when our Lord was repeatedly engaged in argument with the Jews, who were trapped by

[23] *Against Cresconius the Donatist,* i, 19.
[24] *Against Cresconius the Donatist,*i, 21-23.

their own answers and convicted of error, they had not listened to you (the Donatists) nor had they learned from you what to taunt Him with. For perhaps they would have been better pleased to give Him the more individious title of "dialectician" rather than "Samaritan." In what way do you think they were twisted and confused, when, in their desire to condemn him out of his own mouth, they first asked him whether it was lawful to render tribute to Caesar? Were they not plotting to catch Him in a dilemma so that He would be caught whatever he answered? If He said it was lawful, He would be accused by God's people. On the other hand, if He declared that it was not lawful, He would be punished as an enemy of Caesar. When He asked them to show Him a penny and asked whose image and inscription it carried, they replied "Caesar's," an answer forced on them by an obvious truth. Immediately our Lord drew them along, securely fastened in the bonds of their own answer, saying, "Render to Caesar what is Caesar's and to God what is God's." I ask you then, "Were these people dialecticians who strove to deceive and to overcome our Lord by trapping Him in a net of questions? Or rather was He the dialectician who, taking his start from their question, elicited a true reply by the use of a prudent question? By doing this He forced them to admit a truth which they considered He would utter at His peril.

If you say that these Jews who sought to trap our Lord by cunning and malicious questions were dialecticians, which is the image you want to create of us, why did our Lord reply to them? Why did He lead them to give a full reckoning and declare the truth? Why did He say to them, "Why do you tempt me, O hypocrites?" (*Matthew* 22:18) without adding "dialecticians"? Why did He ask for a coin to be produced so that he might wrest the truth from the mouths of deceivers? Why did He not rather say, "Depart. I must not talk with you who propose captious questions and wish to engage in dialectic with me"? He said nothing of the sort. This was not the example He gave us of how to deal with carping questioners and cunning twisters of our words. Instead, He was showing us that by alert questioning and unconquerable reason we must compel those enemies of the truth to give their own testimony to the truth. Let your people treat us similarly if we are evil-minded dialecticians. But are they perhaps betraying their fear that we might use dialectic on them? If you declare Christ to be a dialectician, you praise dialectic, which is exactly what you had imputed as a crime to me.

To avoid this, I imagine you will perhaps say that neither the Jews nor He employed dialectic in that discussion. But if people who speak cunningly and deceitfully so as to lead astray those they enter into discussion with, or those who cause others to convict themselves of error by the answers they give, are not employing dialectic, then tell us what dialectic really is. Tell us what evil there is in it, what harm it does, and why it must be avoided. You hold the name "dialectic" contemptuously before the ignorant, but we ask you to tell us what is the charge you level against it. You do not want to admit that the person who skillfully and honestly questions men who are turned away from truth and leads them to truth by means of the replies they give to his questions, is using dialectic. This is because you do not wish to admit that Christ employed dialectic against the Jews. At the same time you refuse to admit that dialectic is being used by people who, by crafty and misleading questions, aim at deceiving the person questioned, in case it is proved to you that this is what the Jews did with Christ. But Christ did not turn away from them in silence; He overcame them with speech. So you fear you may be forced to agree that your bishops, who in your opinion are learned and wise, are wrong in refusing to enter into discussion with dialecticians for the purpose of teaching irrefutable truth. As I see it, you are suffering great embarrassment over your definition of a dialectician. He must not be called a skilled controversialist; otherwise, you would be forced to praise what you have hitherto blamed. Nor must he be a deceitful manipulator of words, lest it be said to you, "As Christ entered into discussion with such people, so also should the Christian."

Therefore, if you (Cresconius) want to be free of this dilemma, define a dialectician as one with whom your Donatist lawyers do not wish to enter into conversation. What other definition could be supplied by you, a person who hurls a charge of dialectic against us and thereby proclaims that his bishops are unwilling to have discussion with us? . . .

[25]This art known as dialectic, which teaches only the logical consequences of premises, whether we are concerned with true conclusions following from true premises or false conclusions from false premises, must never be feared by Christian teachers. The Apostle Paul did not fear it in the Stoics, whom he did not turn away when they sought to enter into discussion with him. (*Acts* 17:16-31). Dialectic asserts the truth, namely, that no one is driven to a false conclusion in argument unless he first consents to what is false, in virtue of which he must reach the same conclusion whether he wants it or not. Wherefore the man who is concerned lest false conclusions, which he does not desire, should follow from his words, must beware of false premises. For if he holds fast to true premises, then he is instructed and accepts whatever consequences follow, even when they contradict his former beliefs and doubts. This will be so if he is a lover of undisturbed truth rather than of contentious vanity. . . .

[26]Listen, Cresconius, while I say briefly that throughout your whole letter you have disproved nothing that I said in my letter. Nevertheless, you may have taught me one lesson, namely, how to derive or decline nouns. You have taught me to say "Donatians" and not "Donatists. . . . When I wrote

[25] *Against Cresconius the Donatist*, i, 25.
[26] *Against Cresconius the Donatist*,ii, 2–3.

"Donatists," I was simply repeating what other people have said, and I did not care to change it because it seemed to me that the term I was using sufficiently pointed the distinction I wanted to make. The very famous orator Demosthenes had a great a concern for words as our authors have for facts; but, when Aeschines had objected to some unusual expression employed by Demosthenes, the latter declared that the fortunes of Greece did not depend on his using this or that word or on his stretching out his arm in this direction or that. How much less should we fuss over the rules for the derivation of words when what we say is understood without ambiguity whatever expression we use! For our important concern is with the demonstration of truth rather than with the decoration of our speech. . . . So, in regard to this question, which in no way affects the strength of our case, I show myself compliant. When I enter into discussion with you, I shall say "Donatians"; but with others I shall follow the usual custom, which rightly dictates the forms of words. Only remember that I, to whom you have attributed such great eloquence, do not yet know how to decline nouns. Therefore, you can give a comforting message to your people that they are not to fear someone in the guise of a dialectician who in your opinion has yet to become proficient in grammar. The discipline of argument, whether you choose to call it "dialectic" or anything else, sensibly instructs us that we must not worry too much over the words we use to describe something when there is agreement about the thing itself. Whether or not this discipline should be called "dialectic" does not worry me; nevertheless, I am very much concerned to develop skill and ability in argument, that is, to use speech to distinguish between truth and falsehood. The reason is that, unless I am concerned about this, I shall fall into very dangerous errors. Thus, I do not care whether it is a mark of greater knowledge or learning to call you "Donatists" or "Donatians"; nor do I care whether, for the sake of clarifying the distinction, the term we use should be derived from Donatus, who was the first to institute sacrifices outside the Church, or from Marjorinus, who gave the greatest strength to the movement of dissent and was the first to be set up as a bishop of your party in opposition to Caecilian.* On the other hand, if I am not concerned to show that you are heretics and, therefore, to be carefully avoided in case you deceive others, I shall come under a heavy charge of negligence in proportion to the great responsibility of my official position.

* The reference is to an incident, which occurred in Carthage about the year 311 AD, when some of the Numidian bishops, who had arrived there too late to play their part in the election of Caecilian as bishop of Carthage, ignored the election of Caecilian and set up Marjorinus as a rival bishop, thus splitting the church into two parts. The group supporting Marjorinus included a bishop Donatus, while another Donatus, whom Augustine sees as the true founder of the Donatist movement, succeeded Marjorinus as bishop of Carthage.

Bibliography

For those interested in further general reading on St. Augustine's life and thought, the following are a few suggestions:

Battenhouse, R. W., *A Companion to the Study of St. Augustine* (Oxford University Press, 1955).

Bourke, V. J., *Augustine's Quest for Wisdom: Life and Philosophy of the Bishop of Hippo* (Milwaukee: Bruce, 1945).

Gilson, E., *Introduction a l'Etude de St. Augustin* (Paris: J. Vrin, 3rd. ed., 1949).

Howie, G., *Educational Theory and Practice in St. Augustine* (London: Routledge and Kegan Paul, 1969).

Marrou, H. I., *St. Augustin et la Fin de la Culture Antique* (Paris: de Boccard, 4th ed., 1958).

O'Meara, J. J., *The Young Augustine: The Growth of St. Augustine's Mind up to his Conversion* (London: Longmans, Green, 1954).

Paolucci, H. (ed.), *The Political Writings of St. Augustine* (Chicago: Henry Regnery Co., 1962).

West, Rebecca, *St. Augustine* (New York: Nelson, 1938).

A Monument to St. Augustine: Essays on Some Aspects of his Thought written in Commemoration of his 15th Centenary (London: Sheed and Ward, 1930). Includes essays by E. Gilson, J. Maritain, E. Przywara and other notable Augustinian scholars.

Published translations of the writings of St. Augustine most relevant to his educational theory are as follows:

Library of Christian Classics (London: S. C. M. Press, 1953-1955); vol. 6 (J. H. S. Burleigh, ed.) includes *Soliloquies, The Teacher, The Free Will, True Religion;* vol. 7 (A. C. Coulter, ed.) includes *The Confessions;* Vol. 8 (J. Burnaby, ed.) includes *The Trinity* (books 8, 9, 10 and 14).

The Authentic Writings of the Fathers of the Church, R. D. Deferrari, ed. (Washington: Catholic University of America Press); vol. ii includes *Christian Education;* vol. iv includes *The Greatness of the Soul* and *On Music*; vol. v includes *The Happy Life, Against the Academics, Soliloquies, The Principle of Order;* vols. viii, xiv, xxiv, *The City of God;* vols., xii, xviii, xx, xxx, xxxii, *Letters*; vol. xvi, *The Eight Questions of Dulcitius*; vol. xxi, *The Confessions*; vol. xlv, *The Trinity*; vol. lvi, *The Practices of the Catholic Church.*

The Works of Aurelius Augustine, Marcus Dods, ed. (Edinburgh: Clark, 1872-1883); vols. i and ii, *The City of God*; vols. vi and xiii, *Letters* (selected); vol. vii, *The Trinity*; vol. ix, *Christian Education, The Instruction of the Uninstructed.*

Christopher, J. P., *St. Augustine, The First Catechetical Instruction* (Westminister, Maryland: Newman Press, 1946).

Colleran, J. M., *The Greatness of the Soul* and *The Teacher* (Westminster, Maryland: Newman Press, 1950).

Jolivet, R.; Labriolle, P de; Thonnard, E. J.; *Dialogues Philosophiques,* with preface by E. Gilson (Paris: Desclée de Brouwer, 1955) contains a French translation of all the dialogues including *Against the Academics, The Happy Life, The Principle of Order, The Soliloquies, The Greatness of the Soul, The Teacher, The Free Will, On Music* (book 6).

Oates, W., *Basic Writings of St. Augustine,* 2 vols. (New York: Random House, 1948); vol. i includes *The Confessions, Soliloquies, The Practices of the Catholic Church, The Teacher*; vol. ii, *The City of God, The Trinity* (abridged).

Robertson, D. M., *St. Augustine: On Christian Doctrine* (New York: Liberal Arts Press, 1958). A translation with introduction of *Christian Education.*

Sheed, F. J., *The Confessions* (London: Sheed and Ward, 1945).

Index of Selections Used

When a work is divided into books, the Roman numeral indicates the book from which a selection is taken. The Arabic numerals indicate the section or chapter. The figures in brackets indicate the pages of this volume on which the passages occur.

Index of Topics